1,000,000 Books

are available to read at

Read online
Download PDF
Purchase in print

ISBN 978-1-397-83721-9
PIBN 10516929

This book is a reproduction of an important historical work. Forgotten Books uses
state-of-the-art technology to digitally reconstruct the work, preserving the original format
whilst repairing imperfections present in the aged copy. In rare cases, an imperfection in
the original, such as a blemish or missing page, may be replicated in our edition. We do,
however, repair the vast majority of imperfections successfully; any imperfections that
remain are intentionally left to preserve the state of such historical works.

English
Français
Deutsche
Italiano
Español
Português

www.forgottenbooks.com

Mythology Photography **Fiction**
Fishing Christianity **Art** Cooking
Essays Buddhism Freemasonry
Medicine **Biology** Music **Ancient
Egypt** Evolution Carpentry Physics
Dance Geology **Mathematics** Fitness
Shakespeare **Folklore** Yoga Marketing
Confidence Immortality Biographies
Poetry **Psychology** Witchcraft
Electronics Chemistry History **Law**
Accounting **Philosophy** Anthropology
Alchemy Drama Quantum Mechanics
Atheism Sexual Health **Ancient History**
Entrepreneurship Languages Sport
Paleontology Needlework Islam
Metaphysics Investment Archaeology
Parenting Statistics Criminology
Motivational

DOCUMENTARY

History of Rhinebeck,

IN DUTCHESS COUNTY, N. Y.,

EMBRACING

Biographical Sketches and Genealogical Records of Our First Families

and First Settlers,

WITH

A HISTORY OF ITS CHURCHES AND OTHER PUBLIC

INSTITUTIONS.

BY

EDWARD M. SMITH.

RHINEBECK, DUTCHESS COUNTY, N. Y.

1881.

INDEX. .

INTRODUCTORY.

The map on the preceding page includes the patents to Maj. Peter Schuyler and Gerrit Artsen & Co., in 1688, and that to Henry Beekman in 1697, and shows the territory which constituted the town of Rhinebeck from 1788 to 1812. The precinct of Rhinebeck, organized in 1734, contained, in addition to this territory, "Pawling's purchase" on the south, becoming in part the property of Dr. Samuel Staats, of New York, in 1701, and known thereafter as Staatsburgh. (See Appendix.) The town of Red Hook covers all of the Schuyler, and we think a part of the Beekman patent, while the town of Rhinebeck contains the Beekman patent, and also the patent to Artsen, Roosa, Elton, and the two Kips, known as Kipsbergen in our early history. The town of Rhinebeck contains 21,353 acres, about 2,200 of which were included in the Artsen patent, and the town of Red Hook 22,225 acres. Rhinebeck creek is so-called because it has its main springs in the part of the town laid out for the "High Dutchers," and called Rein Beek. It runs through level meadow land from beginning to end ; has no falls, and has, therefore, never turned a mill. Landsman's creek was so-called, either because all its water-falls, capable of turning a mill, were reserved by the "Landsman," or landlord, in his sales to the settlers ; or, because it was discovered or first settled upon by Casper Landsman, whose name is found in our old church records. These two streams join in Fritz's mill-pond. At this point the Rhinebeck creek terminates, and from thence to the river it is Landsman's creek, and was Beekman's property. A short distance below the junction, it falls over a rocky precipice sixty feet high, and when it is full forms a beautiful cascade in a deep and picturesque dell, in full view from the highway, called by a Rhinebeck poet the "Buco Bush" (Beechwood) Falls. This creek at one time turned a grist and saw-mill at the river ; a grist-mill and woolen factory in Fox Hollow ; a paper mill at the falls ; a saw-mill, an oil mill, and a woollen factory at the junction ; a grist-mill west of the post-road, built by General Richard Montgomery ; a grist mill and woollen factory east of the post-road ; a grist-mill east of the village, known as Isaac Davis' mill ; a saw-mill and Schuyler's woollen factory further east ; and Rutsen's grist and saw-mill at Mrs. Miller's place. Of these mills, the Fox Hollow mill burned many years ago, the paper mill at the falls later, Ludekke's mill at the junction, and the two mills at the post-road a few years ago. A grist and saw-mill at the junction are all that are left to the town. The Sawkill in Red Hook was so named, because the first use made of it was to turn saw-mills. It at one time turned Judge Livingstone's mill at the river ; General Armstrong's mill at Cedar Hill ; Van Benthuysen's mill, and a woollen factory in the same place ; the Chancellor's mill, now Hendrick's mill, in the interior ; and Robert G. Livingston's mill on the Rock City branch. Gen. Armstrong's and the Chancellor's mills, we believe, are maintaining a feeble existence. The White Clay creek is so-called because it runs through, or from a layer of white clay somewhere. This creek at one time had Jannetje Bradt's mill at the mouth, Park's mill at Myersville, Cook's factory, and Zachariah Hoffman's mill. It is doing very little, if anything, in the milling line now. These creeks have thus all lost their value to the towns, which have become simple agricultural communities, with sumptuous country seats on the banks of the Hudson; well-stocked retail dry-goods and grocery stores; skillful mechanics of all kinds; learned and eloquent ministers of the Gospel of different orthodox denominations; and a full supply of lawyers and doctors, in all the post villages and hamlets.

Before the invention of steamboats, when all the work on the river, in the conveyance of freight and passengers, was done by the sloops, the post-road carried a lively opposition to the river; and after the invention of the steamboat, when the Winter closed the river, the post-road carried the mail and all the freight and passengers between New York and Albany, and the growing cities North and West; and the villages along the line knew something of life and business. But now all is changed. The railroad knows no Winter or Summer; it maintains an unceasing draft on the life-blood of the small towns for the benefit of the larger; and hence there is a dark future for all the country villages that have not the facilities and advantages of location for the conduct of profitable manufacturing enterprises.

Of the Hudson River Railroad, eight miles and fourteen one-hundredths are in Rhinebeck; of the Rhinebeck and Connecticut, five miles and five-sixteenths. The assessed value of the real estate in the town is $3,152,348; of the personal estate, $450,460. The number of people in the town is 3,905; of taxable people, 716. The aggregate State tax against all the taxable property in the town, in this year of our Lord one thousand eight hundred and eighty, is $23,045.00.

HISTORY OF RHINEBECK,

DUTCHESS COUNTY, N. Y.

CHAPTER I.

INDIAN DEEDS FOR LANDS IN RHINEBECK.

THE following, in English, in a hand very hard to read, is a record found in book A A, opened in 1685, in the office of the Ulster County Clerk, in Kingston. It is the first Indian deed for lands in Rhinebeck :

" *Translated.*—It is acknowledged by these presents that upon the 8th day of June, 1686, in the presence of the magistrates, have Aran Kee, Kreme Much, and Korra Kee, young Indians, appeared, the which do acknowledge to have sold to Gerrit Artsen, Arie Rosa and Jan Elton a certain parcell of land, lying upon the east shore, right over against the mouth of the Redout Creek, bounded between a small creek and the river, the which said creek is sold to the purchasers. The bounds of the said land beginneth at the parting of the lands of Henry Kip, and by a small creek called, in the Indian speech, Quanelos ; and then runs right through to a great oak tree, marked and scored by the Indians ; then runs south to where the upper-most creek comes into the same ; and then by the said creek to the river ; for which the purchasers promise to pay to the aboriginal sellers, or cause to be paid, as follows: Six buffaloes, four blankets, five kettels, four guns, five horns, five axes, ten kans of powder, eight shirts, eight pairs of stockings, forty fathoms of wampum, or sewant, two drawing knives, two adzes, ten knives, half anker rum, one frying pan ; which payment shall and must be made on the 1st of November next ensuing ;

and with the payment the Indians are bound to give a free transport and license unto them, the which both parties promise to adhere to.   The day and year as above said.

GERRIT ARTSEN,

ARIE ROÓSA,

JAN ELTON.

His
ARAN ◎ KEE,
mark.

His
KREME ◯ MUCH,
mark.

His
KORRA ▬ KEE.
mark.

In the presence of us Magistrates :

BENJAMIN PROVOOST,
His
JAN ✗ JORKEN,
mark.
His
HENRY ✗ ELISON.
mark.

" Upon ditto the sale of the land the same Indians acknowledge to have given unto Gerrit Artsen, Arie Rosa and Jan Elton a valley situate eastward from the land bought by them, named Mansakenning,* and a path to the same, upon approbation of his honor, on the 8th day of June, 1686, Kingston.

His
ARAN ◎ KEE,
mark.

His
KREME ◯ MUCH,
mark.

His
KORRA ▬ KEE.
mark.

In the presence of us Commissioners :

BENJAMIN PROVOOST,
His
JAN ✗ JORKEN,
mark.
His
HENRY ✗ ELISON."
mark.

---

* This meadow, called Mansakenning by the Indians, is now known as Jacomyntie's Fly, probably because this was the name of the wife of Jan Eltinge, who was at one time the owner of the Fly ; conveyed it to Henry Beckman in 1689, who conveyed it back to his heirs in 1705.

The second, and only other Indian deed, is to Hendrick Kip. It is not on record in the Ulster County Clerk's Office. It states no consideration or boundaries. What purports to be the original deed is in the possession of William Bergh Kip, Esq., of this town. It is in English, and, we think, in the same handwriting as the record of the deed to Artsen, Rosa and Elton, in the Kingston book. It is as follows:

"We, the under written Ankony, one of ye Esopus Indians, and Anamaton, and Calycoon, one of the Esopus Sachams, do acknowledge to have received of Henry Kip, of Kingston, full satisfaction for a parcell of land lying over against the Redout kill, on the north side of Arie Rosa, on the river, which is received by me, Ankony, Anamaton and Calycoon, in full satisfaction for the above said lands. In witness whereof, have hereunto set our hands, this 28th day of July, 1686.

The mark of **w** ANKONY,
The mark of (·) ANAMATON.
The mark of **U** CALYCOON.

Testis :
    HENRY PAWLING."

The land conveyed to Artsen, Rosa and Elton by the first deed lies below a line run due east from the river where it is entered by the small creek between the Radcliff and Hutton premises, to the Rhinebeck creek, and includes all that lies between the said creek and river to Vanderburgh's cove. The land conveyed to the Kips by the second deed lies on the north of this tract, including all between the said creek and river to a line run due west to the river from the Hog bridge. The Artsen antedates the Kip deed by forty-eight days; but, one referring to the other, the lands were doubtless purchased from the Indians on the same day, with the understanding that they were to be covered by the same Royal Patent, the full text of which is in the language following:

THE ROYAL PATENT.

" Thomas Dougan, Captain-General and Governor-in-Chiefe in and over the Province of New York and Territoryes depending thereon in America, under his most sacred Majesty, James, the second, by the grace of God King of England, Scotland, France and Ireland, Defender of the faith, &c. To all to whom these presents shall come sendeth greeting. *Whereas*, Gerrit Arsen, Arrian Rose, John Elton, Hendrick Kipp, and Jacob Kipp, by vertue of my lycense, consent and approbation, have purchased of and from the Indians, natural owners and possessors of the same, a certain parcell of land lying on the east side of Hudson's river, in the Dutchess' County, over against the Rondout Kill, beginning at a certain marked tree at the river side ; from thence running up on a direct line eastward two hundred and seventy Rodds to a certain small creek ; thence along the said creek southwesterly seven hundred ninety and four Rodds ; and thence westerly along the said creek to the river, containing twelve hundred acres, or thereabout. And, Whereas, the said Gerrit Arsen, Arrian Rose, John Elton, Hendrick Kipp and Jacob Kipp have made their requests unto me, that I would, on behalf of his Majesty, grant and confirm unto them, the said Gerrit Arsen, Arrian Rose, John Elton, Hendrick Kipp and Jacob Kipp, their heirs and assigns, the before mentioned parcell of land and premises, with the appurtenances : Know ye that by vertue of my commission, and authority from his most sacred Majesty, and power in me being and residing, in consideration of the quitt-rent and chiefe rent herein after reserved, and divers other good and lawful considerations me thereunto moveing, I have given, granted and confirmed, and by these presents do hereby give, grant and confirm unto the said Gerrit Arsen, Arrian Rose, John Elton, Hendrick Kipp and Jacob Kipp, their heirs and assigns forever, all the before recited parcell of land and premises, with all and every the appurtenances, together with all and singular lands, meadows, woods, moors, marshes, waters, hunting, hawking, fishing and fowling, and all other proffitts, advantages, commoditys, emoluments and hereditaments to the said parcel of land and premises belonging, or in anywise appertaining. *To have and to hold* the said parcell of land and premises, with all and singular, the hereditaments and appurtenances, unto the said Gerrit Arsen, Arrian Rose, John Elton, Hendrick Kipp and Jacob Kipp, their heirs and assigns, to the only proper use and

behoof of them, the said Gerrit Arsen, Arrian Rose, John Elton, Hendrick Kipp and Jacob Kipp, their heirs and assigns
forever.   To be holden of his most sacred Majesty, his heirs
and successors, in free and common socage, according to the
tenure of East Greenwich, in the county of Kent, in his Majesty's Kingdome of England, yeelding, rendering and paying
therefor unto his said Majesty, his heirs and successors, forever,
yearly, and every year, the quantity of eight bushels of good,
sweet, merchantable winter wheat, as a quitt rent, to be delivered at the city of New York, unto such officer or officers as
shall from time to time be impowered to receive the same, in
lieue, place and stead of all service due, and demand whatsoever.   In testimony whereof I have signed these presents with
my hand writing, and caused the same to be recorded in the
Secretary's office, and the seal of this his Majesty's province to
be thereunto affixed, this second day of June, in the fourth
year of his Majesty's reign, and in the year of our Lord, One
Thousand Six Hundred Eighty and Eight.

THOMAS DOUGAN."

ENDORSEMENTS.

" May it Pleas yor Exc^y
    " The Attorney General has perused this grant and finds
therein nothing prejudicial to your Majesties interests.
" Ex^{ad} May 31, 1688."   W NICOLLS."   •

    " Att a councill held at ffortt James, July 28, 1688; Pres-
ent, his Excellency, Major Antho: Brockholls, Major Baxter,
Major Phillips, Major Cortlandt, Coll. Bayard, this pattent was
approved of.

GEO. BREWERTON."

    " Recorded in the Secretary's office for the province of
New York, in Lib. No. 2, begun 1686, Page 349 &c

" Exad. by   GEO. BREWERTON."

    The original of this patent fell into the hands of the Rosa
family, and descended from them, through the Van Elten family, to John N. Cramer, from whom it passed into the possession

of the late Hon. William Kelly, whose lands are all within the limits of the territory which it conveyed. It is of parchment, perfectly preserved, and has a seal four inches in diameter, enclosed in a tin box. The lands conveyed by it lie between Landsmans and Rhinebeck creeks and the river, and extend from Vanderburgh's cove north to a line drawn directly west from the Hog bridge to the river.

Holgate, in his genealogy of the Kip family, says: "We find them purchasing from the Indians, on the east side of the Hudson river, where Rhinebeck now stands, a tract of land extending four miles along the river and several miles inland. The original deed, still preserved, is dated July 28, 1686, and signed by three Indian chiefs—Ankony, Anamaton, and Callicoon. Two years after, a royal patent, dated June 2, 1688, was granted by his excellency, Thomas Dougan, governor of New New York, under the name of the Manor of Kipsberg, in confirmation of the Indian title." It is very evident Mr. Holgate had not read the royal patent, and had no knowledge of the Indian deed to Artsen, Rosa and Elton when he penned these lines. The royal patent did not cover the land where Rhinebeck now stands, and was not a manorial grant.

There is no evidence that the lands conveyed by this patent were occupied by the owners before the year 1700. They were divided among the partners on the 26th of May, 1702, by deeds to each from all the others, on record in the office of the Ulster County Clerk, in Kingston. Of the lands purchased from the Indians by the Kips, Hendrick Kip took two-thirds of his share on the south and one-third on the north of the tract, Jacob taking his share in one lot between Hendrick's two parcels. Having set over to the Kips their share, the other three partners divided theirs into six parcels, and assigned two to each. In this assignment, lots one and four became the property of Arie Rosa; two and five of Roeloff, oldest son of John Elton, deceased; and three and six of Gerrit Artsen.

A small stone house was built on Hendrick Kip's south lot, with what are supposed to be two portholes under the eaves, looking toward the river. This house has a lintel on the east side, of stone, with the inscription distinctly cut, "Ao

1700 HK AK." These are evidently the initials of Hendrick Kip and Annatje Kip, his wife; and the house was evidently built by Hendrick in this year. And this is the house between the village of Rhinebeck and the river which Benson J. Lossing says was built by William Beekman, the first settler, and of which Martha J. Lamb, the historian of New York, says: " William Beekman purchased all the region of Rhinebeck from the Indians, and built a small stone house, which is still standing." The house at the Long Dock, now the property of Frederick G. Cotting, is near the south side of the land which fell to Jacob Kip. The stone part of this house has in the front wall a stone, very distinctly inscribed, " 1708.' This was, doubtless, Jacob Kip's house, built in this year.

On the 21st day of April, in the year 1709, Gerrit Artsen, of Kingston, sold to his son, Evert Van Wagenen, of Dutchess County, husbandman, for seventy pounds, "all that certain tract, or parcel of land, situate, lying and being in Dutchess county * * to the south of the land of ye Kips, and to the north of ye land of the heirs of Jan Elting, to the east of ye Hudson river, and to the west of a small creek; it being ye lot number six, counted ye half of ye land belongeth to ye said Gerrit Artsen, to have and to hold the said parcell of land with all and every its appurtenances thereunto belonging, * * * unto the said Evert Van Wagenen, his heirs and assigns forever; * * * the said Evert Van Wagenen to pay yearly, and every year, the tenth part of the quit rent mentioned in ye general patent." Signed, sealed and delivered by Gerrit Artsen, on the 21st day of April, 1709, in presence of Conraat Elmendorp, Jacobus Elmendorp and D. Mayer, in Kingston, Ulster County. Recorded in Ulster County.

This deed was for the land of which the Hutton farm is part. It lay " right over against the mouth of the Redout creek," and thus very convenient to the older Kingston settlement.

On the 10th day of March, 1710–1, Arie Roosa sold to Evert Roosa, for sixty pounds, lot number four; the said Evert Roosa to pay one tenth part of the quit rent. Witnesses present—Laurens Osterhout, Evert Van Wagenen, W. Wattingham.

On the 11th day of March, 1710-1, Arie Roosa sold to
Laurens Osterhout, of Hurly, for sixty pounds, lot number one,
" it being the south end of the patent," he to pay one-tenth of
the annual quit rent.   Witnesses present—Mattys Ten Eyck.
Evert Roosa and W. Wattingham.   Recorded in Ulster County.

On the 1st day of April, 1710, Arie Roosa sold to Henry
Beekman, Jr., six acres of lot number one, for six pounds, the
deed for which reads as follows : " Beginning at a certain
marked tree at the brink of the mill-creek and a stone set in
the ground at the foot of said tree, marked HB on the south
side, and AR on the north side of said stone, at a point about
one hundred yards above the mill-dam, now built, in the possession of his father, Henry Beekman ; and thence westerly to
another marked tree and stone, marked as aforesaid, on the
south side of a hollow gap; and from thence southwesterly
along several marked trees and stones set and marked HB and
AR, to the river ; and from thence along the bank of the
river, easterly and northeasterly, to the mill-creek ; and along
said creek to the place of beginning."

The inference from this language is that the old Tillotson
mill, or one on the same site, was built by the elder Henry
Beekman, as early as 1710, on land purchased from Arie Roosa.
It was located near the river, where grain could be taken to it
and flour away from it by water as well as by land.   It was thus
serviceable to settlements on both sides of the river; and,
whether viewed with relation to its own interests, or those of
the settlements to be served, was well located.   The settlers of
new countries must be preceded by the grist and saw mill, or
take them with them.   This was certainly one of the first mills
—if not quite the first mill—erected in Dutchess County ; and
was erected on the borders of a wilderness whose very few
white settlers were confined to the shores of the river, and, on
the east side, to the patent of Arie Roosa and company.

The partition deeds set forth that if either of the partners
" shall see cause to build a mill or mills, on ye above mentioned
creek, on either of said lots of ground, that then, and in such
case, there shall be and remain two acres of ground in general
to ye proper use and benefit of such mill or mills, wherein all

ye above said five partners, their heirs and assigns, are equally to be concerned." The mills thus provided for were never built.

KIPSBERGEN.

None of the deeds we have considered has named "Kipsbergen" as the residence of either of the parties interested. They have named Dutchess County only. We meet the name for the first time in 1712, in a deed from Laurens Osterhout, the owner of lot number one, the south end of the patent, to Jacobus Van Elten, for a lot of land in Harly, Ulster County, wherein he refers to himself as a resident of "Kipsbergen, in Dutchess County." Jan Elton, of the five partners, had married a widow with four children, by whom he had five. She was thus the mother of nine children at his death. In his will, he left half of his property to his five, and the other half to his wife's nine children. In this way, his lot number two of the patent was divided into five, and his lot. number five into nine shares. In 1714, Gerrit Artsen became the owner by purchase from the heirs of the whole of number two, and five-ninths of number five—the shares which fell to Elton's children. He thus became the owner of nearly two-thirds of the land covered by the Indian deed to Artsen, Rosa and Elton. In 1716 he sold to his son-in-law, Hendricus Hermance, all the land included in number three, and referred to it as part of the land called "Kipsbergen," "bounded northerly by lot number four, easterly by a creek on which Henry Beekman's corn mill stands, southerly by lot number two, and westerly by Hudson's river." This lot is now included in the Ellerslie estate. The record of the marriage of Roeloff Kip to Sarah Dumon, on the 9th of January, 1721, says: "He was from Kipsbergen, she from Kingston." The record of the marriage of Nicholas Van Wagenen to Maria Kip, on the 31st of November, 1731, says they were "both born and living in Kipsbergen." It is thus certain the name was applied to the whole patent from 1712 to 1731, and that at the latter date the name of Rhinebeck had not been applied, where Peter A. Jay says William Beekman settled several poor families from the banks of the Rhine, in the autumn of 1647, "and founded the little village of Rhinebeck." The house which Lossing and Mrs. Lamb say was built by William Beekman, in 1647, became the property of his grandson, Henry, by an exchange of lands with Hendrick Kip, the son of Hendrick, the patentee, in 1726. The conveyance says it is "the place where the said Hendrick now resides, and known by the name of Kipsbergen." We presume this name was given to the tract because the Kips, though the owners of but two-fifths of the land, were the first to settle upon it; and, probably, also, because the name Kip blended more euphoniously with *Bergen* than either of the others. It is very certain there was never a " Manor of Kipsbergen " in the present town of Rhinebeck.

The Hermance House became the Beekman House when it became the property of Henry Beekman, the second, whose daughter—not granddaughter—became the mother of Chancellor Livingston. The farm obtained from Hendrick Kip by Henry Beekman in this purchase and exchange contained less than two hundred acres; and it was not through this purchase that the lands of Rhinebeck passed into the Livingston family, as Mr. Holgate assumed.

CHAPTER II.

THE BEEKMAN PATENT.

THERE is no record of lands purchased from the Indians in 1647, or at any other time, by William Beekman, in what is now the town of Rhinebeck. The "Calendar of Land Papers" tells us that in 1695 Henry Beekman, the son of William, petitioned the Government for a patent for land in Dutchess County, lying opposite Esopus Creek, and known by the name of Sepeskenot. On the 22d of April, 1697, he obtained a patent for these lands, which says it is for lands "lying to the north of Hendrick Kip, and alongst Hudson's river, to the bounds of Major Peter Schuyler, containing in length about four miles, and in breadth into the woods as far as the bounds of the said Major Schuyler." He was to pay therefor yearly and every year forever, next and after the expiration of seven years * * * upon the first day of annunciation (the 25th of March,) at the City of New York, the yearly rent of forty shillings. Dated April 22, 1697.

This patent did not define the boundaries of the lands as fully and accurately as Mr. Beekman desired, and he obtained another in the place of it, on the 25th of June, 1703. This new patent sets forth the boundaries as follows:

" All that tract of land in Dutchess County aforesaid, situate, lying and being on the east side of Hudson's river, beginning at a place called by the Indians, Quaningquious, over against the Klyne Sopus effly, being the north bounds of the lands called Pawling's purchase ; from thence extending northerly by the side of the Hudson's river aforesaid, until it comes to a stone creek, over against the Kallcoon Hoek, which is the southerly bounds of the land of Colonel Peter Schuyler; from thence so far east as to reach a certain pond called by the Indians, Waraughkeemeek ; and from thence extending southerly by a line parallel to Hudson's river aforesaid until a line run from the place where first began easterly into the woods does meet the said parallel line.   Bounded westerly by the Hudson's river, northerly by the lands of the said Peter Schuyler, eastterly by the said parallel line, and southerly by the line drawn from the place where it was first begun, and meeting the said parallel line, which is the northern bounds of the said land before called Pawling's purchase."

Now this patent by its terms carried Henry Beekman's lands north to the point where the Sawkill enters the river— that is, to the creek between the Bard and Barton premises, in Red Hook—and included the lands patented to Arie Roosa & Co., called Kipsbergen; and thus took in more than Beekman was entitled to, or able to hold.   Schuyler pushed him down to the little creek called "Stein Valetie," the point on the river which divides the present towns of Rhinebeck and Red Hook ; and we think the elder Henry Beekman, the patentee, never asserted a claim to the land owned by the Roosa & Co. patentees. But Henry, the son, evidently pretended to have a claim to the whole, or part of the land ; and when he procured the land which fell to the share of Hendrick Kipp, the son, by an exchange of lands therefor in his purchase from Peek De Witt,

in the Schuyler patent, he went through the formality of waiv-
ing his claim in the instrument which follows:

" Know all christian people to whom these present writings
shall or may come, that I, Henry Beekman, of Dutchess county, in
the province of New York, for divers good causes and considerations him thereunto moving, hath remised, released and forever
quit claimed, and by these presents for himself and his heirs doth
fully, clearly and absolutely remise, release and forever quit
claim unto Jacob Kipp, Mathias Sleight, Evert Van Wagenen,
Evert Roosa, Henricus Heermance, Goose Van Wagenen, Barent Van Wagenen and Lawrens Osterhout, all of said Dutchess
county and province of New York, yeomen, in their full and
peaceable possession, and seizen, and to their heirs and assigns
forever, all such right, estate, interest and demand whatsoever,
as he the said Henry Beekman had or ought to have of in or to
all that certain tract or parcel of land in Dutchess county which
tract of land is heretofore granted to captain Arie Roosa, John
Eltinge and others in company, cituating and being over against
the Rondout Kill   *   *   *   containing the quantity of land
as it is comprehending and lays within its boundaries according
to the express words of said pattint grainted as above said, and
in the year of our Lord one thousand six hundred and eighty-
eight (Alway acceptd, and it is hereby forever reserved to the
said Henry Beekman, his heirs, exects, adminsts, or assigns, or
to any of them, all such right title clame and demand or possession which he, the said Henry Beekman, hath and ought to have
in said pattint by vertue of such title and conferences from and
under hand and seal of Hendrick Kip, and all other assurances,
divisions and contracts made over and confirmed to the said
Henry Beekman. which of right did to the said Hendrick Kip
belong as his inheritance from his father, Hendrick Kip, deceased, one of ye partners of ye above resighted patin, all which
right so belonging heretofore to the said Hendrick Kip is hereby excluded by these presents)   *   *   *   Dated: March 19,
1726. Witnessed by Jacob Kip, jr. and William Van Vredenburgh, jr."

We have given the substance of the instrument. It is all in
the handwriting of Henry Beekman, and is doubtless his own

composition. It was never recorded. We have never seen the deed from Hendrick Kip, the son, to Henry Beekman for the Heermance premises, given in 1726. It may be that Henry Beekman claimed all the land held by the partners over and above the twelve hundred acres named in the patent, and that he waived the claim for some consideration named in the conveyance from Kip. But Beekman, and all the old patentees, claimed and held more land than they bargained for. Mrs. Lamb says a boy once asked a farmer if there was any land in the moon. He answered that he did not know, but, if there was, it would be found that Henry Beekman had a patent for it.

But we have no evidence that Henry Beekman, the father, ever disputed the validity of the Artsen patent, or claimed any part of the land covered by it. On the 17th of February, 1711, he issued a deed to William Traphagen, for lands beginning at a plain of said colonel Henry Beekman, on the east side of a certain small run of water, by some people, called Kipskill, "parting it from the lands of Hendrick Kip, Jacob Kip and Gerrit Artsen; bounded on the south by Landsman's Kill, where both the said Kills do meet and join together in one, making a point." Neither Kipsbergen or Rhinebeck is named in this deed, and the Flats are as yet simply "a plain of the said Col. Henry Beekman."

RHINEBECK.

When Colonel Robert Hunter came from England, in 1710, to take the governorship of the province of New York, he brought with him about four thousand Germans from the Palatinate, on the Rhine. An account of these people settled on Hudson's river, rendered to the British government by Governor Hunter, on the 7th of August, 1718, placed thirty-five families, containing one hundred and forty persons, besides the widows and children, in Rhinebeck. In what year these people came on to Beekman's patent, we do not with certainty know; but it is rendered quite certain, it was they who gave the name to the town.

On the 29th of November, 1714, Henry Beekman, the elder, sold to Peter and William Ostrander a tract of one hundred and twenty-four acres of land, "the whole being bounded to the northwest by a hill: to the northeast by the lands of said Beek-

man *laid out for the High Dutchers.*" And this deed further describes these lands as lying "in Dutchess County, at
Ryn Beek." Part of this land is now included in the farm of
Thomas Reed. The other part reached the post-road, is now
the property of William Van Steenburgh, and was owned by
Dr. Ananias Cooper, before the Revolution, who built the brick
and stone house now thereon, at the post-road, still known as
the "Cooper House." On the 28th of February, 1715, Henry
Beekman gave to Jacob Kip, "of Kipsbergen," a deed for eighty-
nine acres of land in Dutchess County, at Ryn Beek. This land
joined that of the Ostranders, and embraced the land about the
Hog Bridge, and doubtless the homesteads of Chas. I. Kramer
and William Van Steenburgh, and a part of the Hoffman farm.
The deed says, "The said Beekman has further bargained and
sold unto ye aforesaid Kip * * * all the high land that lies
between ye said Jacob Kip's east bounds or lyne to ye southern
bounds of Peter and William Ostrander." The survey for these
lands was made by John Beatty, Deputy Surveyor, November
29, 1714; and he says, on his map: "On ye bounds of ye said
Coll. Beekman, called Reinebaik, in Dutchess County."

These "High Dutchers" were the Palatines placed in
Rhinebeck by Governer Hunter's report in 1718, and the lands
laid out for them lay north of the Hog bridge, and principally
about the old German Reformed Church at Pinck's Corner.
The name was confined to these lands for many years by the
early settlers, and we think it was written for the first time in
the deed to Peter and William Ostrander, in 1714. They did
not get their deeds until October 20, 1718, two years after the
death of Henry Beekman, the patentee. We have seen about a
dozen of these deeds, all bearing this date. A census of the
county, taken in 1714, found but sixty-seven heads of families
in the county. We have the names of these, and easily distinguish those located in what are now Rhinebeck and Red Hook.
They are all Holland and Huguenot, and thus tell us that the
Palatine founders of Rhinebeck had not taken possession of
their lands when this census was taken. They probably came
in in 1715.

The name of the Kips was given to the whole of the grant

to Artsen and Co.; and it is possible Beekman intended Rein Beek should apply to the whole of his; but it is certain this did not take place at once. When the German Reformers bought out the interest of the Lutherans in the old Rhinebeck Church in 1729, in the writings from the one to the other, the church was located at " Rhynbeek." When the lands on the Flats were laid out for the "Low Dutchers" or Hollanders, in 1730, they were de. scribed as being " in Dutchess County, in the North ward, situated on the southwesterly side of a large plain near the now grist-mill of the said Henry Beekman." Nothing was said of Rhinebeck. Apparently, the name was confined to the land laid out for the High Dutchers until the organization of the precinct in 1734, which took in all of " Pawling's purchase " on the south, then called Staatsburgh; all of the present town of Red Hook, on the north; and all of the patent of Gerrit Artsen & Co.; which from thenceforth ceased to be Kipsbergen. And to-day the people about the country still distinguish between Rhinebeck and the Flats. The road from Mrs. Mary R. Meller's to Pink's corner is still the road to Rhinebeck. St. Peter's Lutheran Church is the Rhinebeck Church, while the Reformed Dutch is still the church on the Flats. It is thus certain that Peter A. Jay, Benson J. Lossing, and Martha J. Lamb were not only mistaken as to the time when, but also as to the place where, and the person by whom, Rhinebeck was founded.

Henry Beekman, the patentee, died in 1716, apparently without a will; his wife was living in 1724; in 1713, he gave a deed to his son, Henry, for all of his Rhinebeck patent lying south of a line, run from the junction of Landsman's and Rhinebeck creeks in the Saw-mill pond, directly east to the end of the patent, and included the mill at the mouth of Landsman's creek. In 1737, on the 30th of August, the balance of the patent was divided between him and his two sisters. For the first step a middle line was run from the Saw-mill pond to Schuyler's Fly, on the north; from this line as a base the land was divided into six parts, intended to be equal, by lines to follow the angle of the Schuyler patent, those on the west reaching the river, and those on the east extending to the end of the patent. This gave to each of the parties a lot fronting on the river. In this division, Nos. 1 and 6 fell to Henry; 2 and 5 to Catherine, wife, first of John Rutsen, and now of Albert Pawling; 3 and 4 to Cornelia, wife of Gilbert Livingston. No. 1 included the Flats "where Rhinebeck now stands," which thus became the property of Henry Beekman, the second. (*See Map.*)

CHAPTER III.

THE TOWN OF RED HOOK.

HAVING purchased from the Indians the land lying over against Magdalene, now Cruger's Island, Col. Peter Schuyler obtained a patent therefor from Governor Thomas Dongan on the 2d of June, 1688, in which the boundaries are thus defined: "Situate, lying and being on the east side of Hudson's river in Dutchess County, over against Magdalene Island, beginning at a certain creek called Metambesem; thence running easterly to the southmost part of a certain meadow called Tanquashqueick; and from that meadow easterly to a certain small lake or pond called Waraughkameek; from thence northerly so far till upon a due east and west line it reaches over against the Sawyer's creek; from thence due west to the Hudson's river aforesaid; and from thence southerly along the said river to the said creek called Metambesem." This deed, according to the "Calendar of Land Papers recorded in the Secretary of State's office, at Albany," was not recorded until the 25th of June, 1787, one hundred years after it had been obtained. A confirmatory patent obtained on the 7th of November, 1704, the calendar tells us, was at once recorded in Vol. 3 of patents, page 184.

An old map, in the possession of Colonel Henry B. Armstrong, tells us that the creek called Metambesem is now the Sawkill, entering the river between Montgomery Place and the Bard premises; that the meadow, called Tanquashqueick, was Schuyler's, and is now generally known as Radcliff's Fly; and that Waraughkameek is now the "Ferer Cot," which means the Pine Swamp, mainly on the premises of the late Albert Snyder, three miles east of the village of Upper Red Hook. Now, conceding that the Sawkill was the creek named Metambesem by the Indians, the patent erred in making it the southern limit of

Peter Schuyler's lands ; they came down to the " Stein Valetie " (Little Stone Falls), somewhere on the premises of Francis H. Delano, Esq.

In 1689, the year after he had obtained the grant, Peter Schuyler sold one-half of what he estimated to be one-fourth of his patent to Harme Gansevoort, a brewer, of Albany. The fourth of the patent out of which this sale was made lay north of a line run due east from a point on the river opposite the south end of Slipstein Island (the small island north of Cruger's). On the 1st of May, 1704, Harme Gansevoort sold his moiety of this part of the patent to Lawrence, Cornelius, Evert, and Peter Knickerbacker, of Dutchess County; Anthony Bogardus, of the city of Albany, and Janetje, his wife ; Jan Vosburgh, of Dutchess County, and Cornelia, his wife ; sons and daughters of Harme Jans Knickerbacker, late of Dutchess County, deceased, for one hundred and fifty pounds.

In 1722, Peter Schuyler had this upper fourth of his patent carefully surveyed, and divided into thirteen lots. Of these, he set seven over to the above named Knickerbackers, retaining the six in his own possession. What he ultimately did with these we have not learned. The other three-fourths of his patent he sold to Tierk De Witt, of Ulster County, Joachem Staats, of the manor of Rensselaerswick, and Barent Van Ben-thuysen, of Dutchess County. A partition deed and map in the possession of Col. H. B. Armstrong show the disposition ultimately made of his patent by Col. Peter Schuyler. The deed reads as follows :

" Barent Staats, of the manor of Renselaerswick, of the county of Albany, in the province of New York in America, of the first part : Barent Van Benthuysen, of Dutchess County in the said county and province, yeoman, of the second part ; and Henry Beekman, of the said Dutchess County, gentleman, of the third part. Whereas, Coll. Peter Schuyler, late of ye county of Albany, deceased, Tierk De Witt, late of Ulster county, deceased, and Joachem Staats, late of the said manor of Rense-laerswick, deceased, were partners to the purchase of that certain tract or parcell of land, situate, lying and being in the said Dutchess County, beginning at a certain creek called Metambesem, over against Calkoenhoek; thence running easterly to the southmost part of a certain meadow called Tanquashqueak; and from that meadow easterly to a certain small lake or pond, called Warachkameek; and from thence northerly so far till upon a due east and west line it reaches over against the south end of the island in Hudson's river called and known by the name of Slipsteen Island; thence southward along the east side of said river to the creek called Metambesem. * * The said tract of land * * * was by letters patent from Coll. Thomas Dougan, heretofore Lieutenant Governor of the said province, granted unto the said Peter Sehuyler, as by said patent bearing date the second day of June, 1688, and since confirmed by another patent, under the broad seal of the said province, from Edward, Viscount Cornbury, some time governor of the said province, bearing date the 7th day of November, 1704. And whereas the said Tierk De Witt, in his life time, by virtue of a conveyance from the said Peter Schuyler of one-third part of the above recited tract or parcell of land, did make and convey that same third part of the said tract or parcell of land unto his son, Peck De Witt, who by another instrument under his hand and seal hath conveyed the same unto the said Henry Beekman, to have and to hold the said third part of the said tract or parcell of land, to him, the said Beekman, his heirs and assigns forever, except any part in the meadow called Magdalene Islands Vly, that lyeth between the main shore and the said Magdalene Island; which said third part of the said tract or parcell of land is afterwards confirmed and released unto them by indentures with the said Peter Schuyler, bearing date the eleventh day of February, 1718-19. * * And whereas the said Peter Schuyler by other indentures executed between him and the said Barent Staats, son and heir of Joachem Staats, bearing date the eleventh day of February, 1718-19, whereby the said Peter Schuyler granted, released and confirmed unto the said Barent Staats for himself and others, the children of the said Joachem Staats, deceased, another third part of the said above recited tract of land, and of the above mentioned meadow, called Magdalene Islands' Vly, under such quit rent as in the said indenture is specified. * * * The other third part of the said tract or parcell of land the said Peter Schuyler hath sold and delivered to the said Barent Van Benthuysen, his heirs and assigns forever.   Now this indendure witnesseth that the said parties to these presents being now fully minded and agreed that the aforesaid tract or parcell of land shall be divided and layed out in lotts as equall and conveniently as may be, in manner as the same are laid out, delineated, proportioned and ascertained on the surveys, draft or chart thereof, reference whereunto being had may now plainly appear."

Tanquashqueick meadow (Schuyler's Vly) was divided into three parts and disposed of by lot, Barent Staats drawing the south, Barent Van Benthuysen the middle and Henry Beekman the north part.

The Sawkill was found to have three falls of water, and "eight acres of land conveniently located to each fall of water, being in all twenty-four acres, which creek, falls and twenty-four acres are reserved, and undivided, and remain as yet in company between the said parties, each one-third part thereof, for the use of such saw-mill and saw-mills, grist-mill, or grist-mills, as at any time hereafter by the said parties, their heirs and assigns, shall be thereon erected.". For the building of these mills the parties reserved to themselves the right to enter on any of the parties' lands not " infenced and improved, and cut down and have, and carry away timber " for any of the mills mentioned.

In this final partition and disposition of the Schuyler patent, Barent Staats acted for himself, and for his brethren, Abraham, Richard, and Isaac, and sister Elizabeth. The deed was signed, sealed and delivered in 1725, in presence of Harmanis Schuyler, Peter Livingston, and Robert Livingston, Jr.

The reservation of the mill sites, and the right to cut timber therefor on each other's lands, seem to indicate that there were no mills on the Sawkill in 1725 ; and the reservation of the right to pass over each other's lands with teams and wagons, indicates that there were no highways constructed at this date, excepting, perhaps, the post-road.

The deed from Peek DeWitt to Henry Beekman, Jr., bears date the 9th day of August, 1715, and reads as follows:

"To all christian people to whom these presents shall or may come, Peek De Witt, of Dutchess, in the province of New York, in America, sends greeting. Now know yea that the said Peek De Witt by and with the consent and good liking of Maritje, his wife, testified by her signing and sealing of these presents, for divers good causes him thereunto moving, but more especially for and in consideration of an exchange of a certain tract of land lying and being in the county of Ulster, in the corporation, Kingston, on the south side of the Rondout creek, above the great fall, in said Rondout creek, and of ten acres of fly or meadow, lying on the north side of said Rondout creek, between the fly of John Frere and the fly of Coll. Henry Beekman, this day conveyed and assured unto the said Peek De Witt by the said Coll. Henry Beekman, have given, grant-ed, bargained, sold, released, certified and confirmed * * * unto Henry Beekman, jr., of Kingston, in Ulster County, gent. the just third part of all that certain tract or parcell of land, situate, lying, and being in Dutchess County, beginning at the north bounds of the land of the said Coll. Henry Beekman, and so along Hudson's river to a certain small creek or run of water to the north of Magdalene's Island and as far into the woods as the said patent for the said land to Coll. Peter Schuyler extends, with the just third part of the mill, and mill creek, and the appurtenances thereunto belonging, together with all and singular the orchards, buildings, gardens, fencing and improvements on the same, to have and to hold the said just third part of the said tract or parcell of land, mill and mill creek, with all and singular the profits, benefits, advantages, commodities * * * unto him, the said Henry Beekman, jr., his heirs and assigns forever. In witness whereof the said Peek DeWitt, and Maritje, his wife, have hereunto put their hands and affixed their seals, in Kingston, this ninth day of August, in the second year of the reign of our sovereign Lord George, by the grace of God of Great Brittain, France and Ireland, King, Defender of the Faith, &c., Anno Domine, 1715.

"Sealed and delivered in the presence of us,

His
HENRY BEEKMAN, PEEK P. D. W. DEWITT,
mark.

Her
JOHANNES WYNKOOP, MARITIE ✗ DEWITT.
mark.

In presence of me, MATTYS JANSEN.

W. WATTINGHAM, Justice of the Peace."

Recorded in Ulster Co., Liber No. 66, Folio 383, Watting-ham, clerk.

By this purchase from Peek DeWitt, Henry Beekman, jr., obtained five thousand five hundred and forty-one acres of land on the north of and adjoining the patent of his father, Col. Henry Beekman, obtained in 1697, which covered all of the present town of Rhinebeck except the patent of Artsen, Roosa & Co., heretofore described.

A middle line was run through the three quarters of the Schuyler patent falling to these three parties, extending from the Beekman patent to the north quarter assigned to the Knickerbacker heirs and retained by Schuyler. For his third, Henry Beekman took both sides of this line; for his third, Barent Van Benthuysen took the east part of the middle third, and the west part of the north third, obtaining five thousand six hundred and fifty-two acres; Barent Staats took the west part of the middle, and the east part of the north third, and obtained five thousand six hundred and twelve acres. If the north quarter, previously disposed of, contained the same number of acres, the Schuyler patent covered about twenty-two thousand four hundred acres of land.

CHAPTER IV.

THE KIPS AND THEIR LANDS.

HENRY KIP, as we have learned, took two-thirds of his share of the patent south, and one-third north of Jacob. He built the old stone house called the Beekman house on the south lot, in 1700. While he occupied this house, his eldest son, John, built himself a house on the north lot, and occupied it until the year 1716.

John, the eldest son of Hendrick Kip, was baptized at

Kingston, March 31, 1678.   He married Lysbet Van Kleeck, at Kingston, September 28, 1703.   They had children baptized at Kingston, as follows:

Hendricus, September 3, 1704; Baltus, March 17, 1706; Baltus, May 23, 1707; Mathew, October 31, 1708; Tryntje, May 7, 1710; Barent, January 27, 1712; Annatje, January 24, 1714; Baltus, September 4, 1715; Jacob, January 12, 1718.

On the 26th of March, 1716, John Kip sold his land to his uncle Jacob by a deed which describes the premises as follows: "A certain piece or parcell of land lying and being on the east side of Hudson's river, beginning at the north bounds of the said Jacob Kip by said river; then along the river to a market tree, being the northermost bounds of a pattane belonging to said Kip and company; then east, as said pattane mentions, to a certain krick; then along said krick to the bounds of said Jacob Kip; then along his bounds to the first station."

Signed,   ẎAN KEP, L. S.,
LYSBET KIPS, L. S.

In presence of
His
TUNIS Y ELLISE,
mark.
HENDRICK KEP.

JOHN CROOKE, Jur., Justice of peic."

Recorded in Ulster County Clerk's Office, Book 66, pages 432–3.

Catholyntie, daughter of Hendrick Kip, married Mattys Sleight.   They had children baptized as follows:

Mathew, April 29, 1711; Hendricken, November 15, 1713; Anna, October 12, 1712 (Hendrick, the patentee, and his wife, Anna Van Putten, were sponsors at this baptism); Hendrickus, June 9, 1717; Maria, October 16, 1720; John, April 26, 1724; Tryntie, June 15, 1729; Maria, July 24, 1715; Cornelius, April 23, 1727.

Hendrick Kip, the son, married Jacomyntie (Jane or Joan) New Kirk, September 28, 1715.   Their only child on record is Jannetje, baptised September 23, 1716.   We think the Hendrick who married Appolonia Van Vradenburgh, and appears in Rhinebeck records, was his son.

A deed from Hendrick Kip and Jacomyntje, his wife, **to** Mattys Sleight says, it gives, grants and assigns to him and his heirs forever, " The one just half, or deemed to be so, by consent, as divided this day, being the one just half of two-thirds of the land of Hendrick Kip, late of Dutchess County, father of the said Hendrick, which land was conveyed to said Hendrick and Catholyntie, his sister, by their eldest brother, John Kip, eldest son of Hendrick Kip, deceased; and by these presents do fully and absolutely give * * * to Mattys Sleight, jr., * * * Beginning on the banks of Hudson's river, at a stone set in the ground; from thence running south, forty-one degrees east, fourteen chains; thence south, sixty degrees east, nine chains and a half; thence north, forty-four degrees east, seven chains and fifty-seven links, to a marked stone; and from thence east, ten degrees and a half south, to a certain creek, being the creek that goes to Beekman's mill; and thence along the said creek as it runs to a marked stone, being the division line between the said Sleight and Evert Van Wagenen; thence along his bounds west, twelve degrees and a half north, to a marked stone on the banks of the Hudson's river; then along Hudson's river to the first station; to hold the said lands forever, and to pay the quit rent, it being the one-third of six pecks and a half of good, sweet winter wheat.

" Dated, April 16, 1719.

HENDRICK KIP, L. S..

Her
JACOMYNTIE ✖ KIP, L. S.
mark.

Witnesses,
EVERT VAN WAGENEN,
ISAAC KIP,
JNO. CROOKE, JR."

These records show that Hendrick Kip, the patentee, was living in 1712, but dead in 1719; and that his son, Hendrick, was living in the Heermance house, and his son-in-law, Mattys Sleight, on the Radcliff farm.

Holgate says Jacob Kip was twice married, first to Henritta Wessels, widow of Gulian Verplank, and, second, to Rachel Swartwout, daughter of John Swartwout.   Dr. Purple, better authority, in the Geneological Record of April, 1877, says it· was his cousin, Jacobus, who married the widow Verplank; and that *his* only wife was the daughter of Roeloff, not John Swartwout; that both bishop Kip and Mr. Holgate give the date of her birth, April 10, 1669, and that of her death, September 16, 1717; and that she was living, and with her husband, then called Jacob Kip, sen., sponsors at the baptism of Rachel, daughter of their son, Isaac, on the 2d of October, 1726. He made his will in 1731, and died in 1733. He had nine children, as follows:

Isaac, baptised February 9, 1696, married, January 7, 1720, Cornelia Lewis; Roeloff, born October 31, 1697, married, February 9, 1721, Sara Dumon; Jacobus, born November 26, 1699, married, February 17, 1733, Klartjen Van Wagenen, daughter of Evert Van Wagenen; Rachel, twin sister to Jacob, married, February 16, 1720, Gerrardus Lewis; Eva, born April 15, 1707, married, December 9, 1733, Gerrit Van Wagenen; Catalyntie, baptised at Albany, February 18, 1705, married William Van Vradenburgh; Johannes, married Marytjen Van Etten; Maria, born February 18, 1709, married John Van Benthuysen; Abraham, born January 24, 1714, married Elsie Pruyn. His landed estate at his death was divided between these nine children.

The Kips were the first to build and settle in what is now the town of Rhinebeck, and the Rhinebeck genealogist and antiquarian will find an interest in the question: What of them? and what has become of them? As we have seen, Jacob's nine children, five of them sons, all married; and all of them married Vans and Hollanders, save Roeloff, who married a DuMont, and hence a woman of Huguenot extraction; and Rachel, who married a Lewis, and hence a man of Welsh extraction. These sons all had families, and gave a large infusion of Kips to our early population. And yet the name, like that of nearly all the old Holland settlers, has nearly died out. There is but one of the name left on the territory of ancient Kipsbergen; and we think some of his lands have never had any but Kip owners, and have nearly all come to him by right of inheritance from his ancestors.

Isaac Kip's wife, Cornelia Lewis, we are told, was the

daughter of Leonard Lewis and Elizabeth Hardenburgh, his wife, born November 9, 1692. He died July 2, 1762; she, July 10, 1772. Their children were Elizabeth, born April 9, 1721; Leonard, 1725; Rachel, 1726; Elizabeth, 1728; Isaac, 1732; Abraham married Dorothea Remsen; Jacobus married Elizabeth Frazier.

Leonard Kip married Elizabeth Marschalk, April 11, 1763. He died 1804; she, 1818. Their son, Leonard, married Maria Ingraham. He born 1774; she, 1784. Their son, William Ingraham, married Elizabeth Lawrence, and became Bishop of California. Their son, Isaac, married Sarah Smith; Rev. Dr. Francis M. Kip was their son, and Sarah Smith Kip, wife of William C. Miller, of Albany, their daughter. The latter were the parents of William A. Miller, at one time pastor of the Reformed Dutch Church in Rhinebeck.

Roeloff was the second son of Jacob Kip, the patentee, born October 31, 1697. He married Zara, the daughter of John The Baptist DuMont, of Kingston, on the 9th of February, 1721. They had ten children, as follows: Greetjin, baptised December 24, 1721; Jacob, baptised May 19, 1723; John The Baptist, baptised February 28, 1725; Isaac, baptised January 22, 1727; Rachel, baptised September 8, 1728; Neeltje, baptised January 25, 1730; Neeltje, baptised March 25, 1732; Zara, baptised September 16, 1733; Ignatious, baptised October 17, 1736; Abraham, baptised October 17, 1738. Of these ten children we have the line of John The Baptist, as follows:

John The Baptist Kip married Catharina, probably the daughter of Andries Heermanee and Neeltje Van Wagenen, baptised April 14, 1728. Their children were: Roeloff, baptised April 25, 1758; Neeltje, baptised November 12, 1759, married Gerrit, grandson of Evert Van Wagenen, December 18, 1785; Andrew, born 1761, married Sarah, daughter of Jacobus Kip, born 1772; Sarah, baptised November 10, 1765; Gerrit, baptised July 12, 1767, married Clarissa, daughter of Jacobus Kip, baptised May 26, 1776; Clartje, baptised September 1, 1770; John, baptised June 19, 1772.

Of these seven children, Andrew had children as follows: Clarissa, John, James, Catharine, Andrew, Sarah and Jane. Of these there are no descendants. Gerrit had Catharine, Henry James, Clarissa and William. Of these, Henry James, born June 15, 1805, alone had a descendant, as follows: William Bergh Kip, born October 14, 1846.

William Bergh Kip is thus a lineal descendant from Jacob, the patentee, in the sixth generation. He is the possessor of nearly two hundred of the ancestral acres, and an elegant country seat on the Hudson, which he calls Ankony, in honor of the Indian chief from whom the land was originally and justly purchased. He is our town supervisor, an intelligent, public-spirited gentleman; and we know of no one more competent. to represent the town of Rhinebeck at the county seat, and protect the interests of his constituents.

On the 16th of October, 1719, Henry Beekman, then of New York, sold to Jacob Kip, the patentee, three hundred and one and a half acres of land for two hundred and fifty pounds, described as "on the east side of Hudson's river, at a place called 'Kipsberry,' beginning by the river, on the south side of a small creek where John Kip heretofore lived, * * * being the bounds of Jacob Kip and Company." This tract appears on the map north of the patent to Arie Rosa & Co. This, with the lands previously purchased from Beekman, at the Hog bridge, put Jacob Kip in possession of about seven or eight hundred acres of land at his death.

On the 5th of August, 1752, a charter for a ferry was granted to Abraham Kip on the east side, and Moses Contine on the west side of the river. It gave them the exclusive right "to run a ferry across the Hudson between the landing place of said Kip on the east shore of said river, and the landing place of said Contine on the west shore of said river, exclusive of all others within the space of two miles above and two miles below the said landings, and to take tolls." The grant was perpetual on condition that two sufficient ferry-boats were to be kept, one on each side of the river.

The ferry on this side was Kip's down to 1785. In this year our town records tell us Andries Heermanee was road master from the Hog bridge to Beekman's mills, and from the mills to Kip's ferry. After this date the mills are Madame

Livingston's, and we think the ferry is for the last time Kip's. In 1792, the record, made by Henry Lyle as town clerk, says William Radclift is overseer of the highway "from Radclift's landing to the post road, and from the Hog bridge to Mrs. Livingston's mills." In 1802, the record tells us Hans Kiersted is road master from Radcliff's landing to the post road, and from the Hog bridge to Livingston's mills. In this year the river road became the "Ulster and Saulsbury Turnpike," with a toll-gate at Hager's bridge, and ceased to be a town charge, and we hear nothing more of the landing until 1816. In this year we get this record: "Path Master, Henry F. Talmage, on the abolished turnpike from the Long Dock east to the adjoining town." Who was the owner of the landing and the ferry in the meantime, the record does not tell us. From this time on it is simply the "Long Dock." Governor Lewis' dock and mills are named for the first time in 1806, and in 1820 we get this record: "Martin Heermance, path master from the Long Dock easterly to the centre of the post road at the Flats, and from the Slate Dock to Mr. Rider's, including W. Radclift;" and this is the first we hear of the Slate Dock.

CHAPTER V.

THE VAN WAGENENS AND THEIR LANDS.

A VAN WAGENEN Genealogy, published last year in the New York Genealogical and Biographical Record by a descendant of the family, informs us that Gerrit Artsen was the son of Aart Jacobson and Annetje Gerrits, and was probably born in Albany. He married Clara, daughter of Evert Pels and Fannetje Symens, who was baptised in New York, September 10, 1651, and became a member of the Kingston Church in 1666. He had ten children who took Van Wagenen for a family name, after the Dutch custom, because his father came from a place in Holland called Wageninge, in Gilderland, ten miles west of Arnheim. The name in our old churcl. records is always spelled "Wageninge," when written by dominie Vas, of Kingston. His children were thus, as follows.:

Aart Van Wagenen, probably born in Kingston, about 1670, married, October 6, 1695, Altje, daughter of Jan Elting, the patentee; Evert Van Wagenen, baptised April 18, 1675; Barent Van Wagenen, baptised April 18, 1675, and, therefore, probably twin brother to Evert; Goosen Van Wagenen, born in Kingston; Jannetje Van Wagenen, baptised June 25, 1672; Annetje Van Wagenen, baptised September 7, 1684; Jacob Van Wagenen, baptised October 3, 1686; Simon Van Wagenen, baptised April 7, 1689; Neeltje Van Wagenen, baptised April 17, 1692; Rebecka Van Wagenen, baptised November 11, 1697.

Of these ten children, four are known to have become the owners and settled upon the Artsen, and the larger part of the Elting share of the patent.

1. Evert purchased lot number six, and settled upon it in 1709. He had nine children, as follows:

Gerrit, Janneka, Nicholas, Aart, married, May 14, 1731, his cousin Rebecka, daughter of Barent Van Wagenen; Klaartje, married, February 17, 1733, Jacob Kip, Jr.; Jacob, Margaret, Johannes, married, November 30, 1745, his cousin Annatje, daughter of Barent Van Wagenen; Sara, married, October 16, 1736, her cousin Hendrickus Heermans, Jr.

2. Barent Van Wagenen purchased and settled on three-fifths of lot number two, and had eleven children, as follows:

Clara, married, June 18, 1726, Jacob Van Vradenburgh; Maria, married, November 15, 1735, her cousin Johannes Van Benthuysen; Gerrit, married, December 29, 1733, Eva, the daughter of Jacob Kip, Sen.; Johannes, married, July 4, 1747, Gertrude Schot; Rebecka, married her cousin Aart, son of Evert Van Wagenen; Sara; Neeltje, married, November 20, 1742, Mathew, son of Jacobus Van Etten; Annatje, married her cousin Johannes, son of Evert Van Wagenen; Jacob; Catrina; Benjamin, married, December 4, 1756, Margaret Burger, widow of Gerardus Van Buiren.

3. Annatje Van Wagenen married Hendrickus Heermance, who bought and settled on lot number three, the original Ellerslie farm. He had six children, as follows:

Hendrickus, married, October 16, 1736, his cousin Sara, daughter of Evert Van Wagenen; Margaret, married Jacobus Ostrander, September 29, 1739; Phillipus, married Clara Heermance, probably his cousin; Jannetje, married Cornelius

Ostrander; Wilhelmus, married Neeltje Hoghland; Andries, married Rachel, daughter of Jacobus Van Etten.

4. Goosen Van Wagenen, married, June 15, 1715, Gertrude Swart. He purchased and settled upon two-fifths of lot number two, and a home lot of seven acres on lot number three. He had no children.

5. Neeltje Van Wagenen married Andries Heermance, and had thirteen children baptised in Kingston, as follows:

Jan, August 19, 1711; Engeltie, May 9, 1714; Jacob, September 23, 1716; Annatje, January 1, 1718; Janneka, January 8, 1721; Clara, March 22, 1719; Gerrit, November 18, 1722; Petrus, September 16, 1724; Hendricus, May 19, 1726; Catrina, April 14, 1728; Wilhelmus, February 1, 1730; Nicholas, March 5, 1732; Phillippus, March 17, 1734; Abraham, August 7, 1737.

These people probably migrated from Kingston to Rhinebeck, and mostly to that part of the precinct which is now the town of Red Hook. Jacob probably married Catharina Vosburg, and settled in the stone house west of Henry Benner's old place. They were the parents of General Martin Heermance, who married and settled on Rhinebeck Flats, and thus the grandparents of the family who are now the owners and occupants of the old Beekman mansion in Rhinebeck.

Lot number six was in the possession of Evert Van Wagenen's descendants to a period probably as late as 1800. His grandson, Gerrit, who married Neeltje, the daughter of John The Baptist Kip, on the 8th of February, 1785, was road master from Radclift's to Captain Kip's, in 1798; and in 1804 Jacob Kip, a carpenter, and, we think, brother-in-law to the said Gerrit Van Wagenen, sold to Aldert Smedes " the easterly part of a farm released by Arent Van Wagenen and Johannes Van Wagenen to Johannes Van Wagenen." Rhinecliff, the eastern terminus of the Rhinebeck and Kingston ferry, is located on part of the lands conveyed to Evert Van Wagenen by his father, Gerrit Artsen, in 1710.

Lot number three was disposed of by Hendricus Heermance in his will, dated March 23, 1750, as follows: " I give to my dear and loving wife during her widowhood for her use the one-half of my farm whereon I at present am dwelling, with the house, barn and homestead so as at this time I occupy and use them. * * * It is my will and desire that my son, Hendricus Heermance, shall have and enjoy all that whole piece of land or farm whereon we now at present are both residing, with all that depends thereon, so as my father-in-law, Gerrit Artsen, has made the same over to me, on condition that it shall be accounted to him out of my estate for the sum of two hundred and sixty-six pounds, * * * but on condition that my said wife shall wholly possess and use one-half of the land during her widowhood, as above mentioned." This will further says: " I appoint for my heirs my six children—namely, ' Hendricus, Phillipus, Wilhelmus, Andries, Margaret, wife of Jacobus Ostrander ; and Annatje, wife of Cornelius Ostrander.' " To Phillipus, Wilhelmus and Andrie she left about eight hundred acres—two hundred and seventy-five each—on Wapping-er's Kill, which is now in the town of Fishkill, and was then in Rombout precinct.

We can find no evidence that at the date of this will the river road, from Radcliff's through this farm to the school house at Garretson's, was in existence as a public highway. And we are not quite certain that the old Kelly farm-house, though on the farm, was the homestead of Hendricus Heermance. The "home lot" of seven acres, sold to Goosen Van Wagenen by his father, Gerrit Artsen, in 1720, seems to us to have included the ground occupied by this house. And how long Hendricus Heermance, Jr., continued in the possession of the premises after the death of his father, in 1750, we have not learned. We find the property in the possession of Jacobus Kip in 1789; and we find a road district "from Radcliff's to Hans Van Wagenen's," the Garretson place, for the first time in 1791, with Johannes Van Wagenen, Jr., for road master. In 1794 the record is as follows: " Jacobus Kip, from Radclift's to Jacobus Kip's." In 1795, it is as follows: " From Radclift's to Jacobus Kip's, none chosen. Jacobus Kip served last year, but is now dead."

This Jacobus Kip was the grandson of Jacob, the patentee. The Dutch descendants among us give James for the English of Jacobus, and never use Jacob for Jacobus. The only one of the sons who had a Jacobus baptised was Jacob, who married Clartjen, the daughter of Evert Van Wagenen.   He had one thus baptised on the 23d of May, 1742.   We assume, therefore, that he was the Jacobus Kip who succeeded Hendricus Heermance, Jr., in the possession of the Ellerslie farm ; that his wife was Clartjen, the daughter of the said Hendricus Heermance, Jr., baptised on the 27th of October, 1745, and that she was thus his second cousin ; and we assume, farther, that he became the owner of the said farm by virtue of his son-in-lawship to the said Hendricus Heermance, Jr.

Jacobus Kip had two daughters, his only children.   Of these, Sarah, the elder, became the wife of Major Andrew, and Clartjen, the younger, of his brother, Garret Kip.   After the death of his father-in-law, in 1795, Major Andrew Kip became the owner of the Ellerslie farm, and retained it until 1814, when he sold it to Maturin Livingston, the son-in-law of Governor Morgan Lewis, for five thousand dollars.   Maturin Livingston retained the property for two years, and built the present Kelly mansion on a site and plans, we are told, selected by his wife.   Mrs. Livingston was the only child of Governor Lewis, and a short experience of her absence from home sufficed to satisfy them that she was needed there.   The governor's mansion at Staatsburgh, a few miles below, was ample for all, and, yielding to their earnest wishes, she returned to it with her family, and made it her future home.   Accordingly, in 1816, the Ellerslie farm was sold to James Thompson.   He retained it until his death, when it became the property of his son, James, whose wife, we are told, was the daughter of Harry Walter Livingston, of Columbia County.   He retained it until 1837, when he sold it to James Warwick, who retained it for three years, when, becoming pecuniarily embarrassed, he made an assignment to Wm. B. Platt, of Rhinebeck Village.   In 1841 Mr. Platt sold the estate to William Kelly, of New York, for forty-two thousand dollars.   The property at this time, we are told, embraced four hundred acres, Mr. Thompson having added one hundred acres to his original purchase.   Mr. Kelly increased his acres, by additional purchases, to seven or eight hundred.   He must thus have become the owner of lots three and four of the original division.

Mr. Kelly not only multipled his acres, but did what money, taste, intelligence and enterprise could do to adorn them and increase their productiveness. The mansion, though of an ancient type, is stately and capacious, and commands a river and mountain view of great extent and beauty. It stands in the borders of a park of five hundred fenceless acres, embracing wood and meadow land, lakelets and rivulets, and every variety of natural and charming scenery. With its avenues, walks, lawns, flower-plats, fruit-houses, orchards, gardens and conservatories, all artistically planned and arranged, and open to the public on week days under a few indispensable restrictions, there is nothing of which Rhinebeck may so justly take pride to itself, because there is nothing for which it is so widely and favorably known as the presence within its borders of the Ellerslie park and gardens.

The three-fifths of lot number two, and five-ninths of lot number five, which became the property of Barent Van Wagenen in 1721, by conveyance from his father, Gerrit Artsen, were disposed of to all his children by his will dated 1731. Four of his daughters, with their husbands—viz.: Marytje with her husband, Johannes Van Benthuysen; Clara with her husband, Jacobus Van Vradenburg; Rebecka with her husband, Aart Van Wagenen; and Anna with her husband, Johannes Van Wagenen, Jr., all of Rhinebeck precinct, sold to their three living brothers, Johannes, Benjamin and Jacob Van Wagenen, all their right, title and interest in the said real estate.

Goosen Van Wagenen had no children, and willed his two-fifths of lot number two to his two nephews, Johannes and Benjamin Van Wagenen, the children of his brother Barent, his next door neighbors, requiring them to support his widow during life.

Of Barent Van Wagenen's sons, Benjamin is the only one of whose children we have record. In 1795, lot number two, containing one hundred and sixty acres, was owned by his four sons, Jacob, Benjamin, Barent B. and Johannes B. Van Wagenen; and on the fifth day of May in this year, the three former disposed of all their right, title and interest therein to the latter. In the year 1799, Johannes disposed of the same to the Rev. Freeborn Garretson, taking in exchange therefor the lands in the vicinity of Schooterhook, in the interior of the town, which remained the inheritance of his children to a recent date, and at the date of the exchange were in the occupation of the Rev. Freeborn Garretson and his wife, Catherine Livingston, who was a Beekman heir.

The children of Benjamin Van Wagenen and Margaret Burger were as follows: Johannes married his cousin, Margaret Schryver; Jacob married his cousin, Anna Schryver, the sister of Margaret; Leah married her cousin, Martinus Schryver; Maria married her cousin, Alburtus Schryver; Benjamin married Catharine Root; Barent married Eva Van Etten; Catharine married John Welch, Jr.; Sarah married John Baxter.

The best known of the descendants of these sons were those of Jacob and John. Jacob's were as follows: Leah married John W. Cramer; Benjamin; John I. married Sally Addison; Catharine married David Myers; Martin married Elanor Lent. John's were as follows: Benjamin married Clarissa Van Wagenen; Martin; Jacob married Charlott Winship; Mary; Barent married Sally Neher; David; William.

CHAPTER VI.

ARIE ROOSA AND HIS LANDS.

ARIE ROOSA'S wife was Maria Pels, and doubtless the daughter of Evert Pels, of Kingston. He was thus brother-in-law to Gerrit Artsen. His children were: Evert, born October 26, 1679, married Tryntie Van Etten; Engeltie, born September, 1685; Arie, born June 3, 1694, married Gertie Ostrander; Mary, born August 28, 1698. These are all of whom we have record; there were probably others.

Evert Roosa, as we have seen, became the owner of lot number four, in 1710. His children, of whom we have record, were: Catharine, Jacobus, Arie, Marytie, Rachel, Abraham, Isaac, Leah and Aldert.

A deed from Jacobus Schoonmaker and Annatje, his wife, to Jacobus Kip, dated April 8, 1775, says, Annatje was the

daughter of Hendricus Sleight, Jr., deceased; that Matthyes
Sleight and Catholyntie, his wife, in their life time, by a deed
of conveyance, dated August 17, 1742, sold to Hendricus
Sleight, Jr., forever, two-thirds of lot number four, "to be
taken with a straight line from one end to the other, so that
his two-thirds of that lot may lay in one piece together, on
that side of the said lot where Arie Roosa, Jr., was formerly
settled;" that the said Hendricus Sleight, Jr., in his life time,
made his last will and testament on May 4th, 1755, and
devised it to his son Matthyes and three daughters—to wit:
"Catholyntie, the now wife of Jeremiah Van Aken; Annatje,
the now wife of Jacobus Schoonmaker; and Majeke, the now
wife of Daniel Schoonmaker, Jr., all his whole estate real, to
be equally divided between them, share and share alike; that
the said Matthyes, son of the said Hendricus Sleight, Jr., deceased, departed this life before he attained the age of twenty-
one years, and left no lawful issue; so his part did descend to
his three sisters." These parties, with their husbands, divided
the said two-thirds of lot number four by lot, on the 1st of
September, 1774, the south lot falling to Jeremiah Van Aken,
the middle to Jacobus, and the north to Daniel Schoonmaker.
Jacobus sold his share to Jacobus Kip on the 8th day of April,
1775, for three hundred and twenty pounds. What became of
the south third of the lot of Evert and Arie Roosa, Jr., we
have not learned. Daniel Schoonmaker sold his share to William Radclift, brother-in-law to Jacobus Kip, and he in turn
sold to Van Wagenens.

Laurens Osterhout's wife was Rebecka Roosa. Of her
relationship to the patentee we have no knowledge. Their
sons were: Jan, Jacob, Benjamin and Isaac. As we have
seen, Laurens Osterhout became the owner of lot number one
by purchase from Arie Roosa, in 1710. He retained it until
the 3d of November, 1741, when he sold it to Jacobus Van
Etten for three hundred and seventy pounds, the lot at this
time containing about one hundred and sixty acres of land.

Jacobus Van Etten's wife was also Rebecka Roosa. Of
the relationship to the patentee, or the wife of Laurens Osterhout, we have no record. Of the children of Jacobus Van

Etten we have record, as follows: Jan married Rachel West-fall; Annatjen married Gysbert Westfall; Rachel married Andries Heermans; Jacobus married Margrita Kool; Abraham; Benjamin married Helentie Van Vradenburgh; Matthew married Neeltje Van Wagenen; Helegond married Jan Maris; Margrieta married Johannes Kip; Leah; Isaac.

Mathew and Isaac Van Etten were the owners in common of lot number one, in 1790. In this year Isaac sold out his half interest therein to Thomas Tillotson, the land to be divided on a line selected by Mr. Tillotson. In this division eighteen acres above the half of the land fell to the north of the line, and thus to Matthew Van Etten, he accounting for the same to Mr. Tillotson. Mr. Tillotson at once took possession of the property, and built thereon the present brick mansion, which remained his residence until his death, in 1830. His wife, Margaret Livingston, the granddaughter of Henry Beekman, Jr., died several years earlier. After the death of his father, the property passed into the possession of John Tillotson, who sold it to Dr. Federal Vanderburgh, together with the land now owned and occupied by Mrs. Dyar, for nineteen thousand dollars. Doctor Vanderburgh retained the land on the east side of the creek, and built for himself the residence which is now the Dyar mansion, and sold the Tillotson mansion, with the lands on the west side of the creek, to his son-in-law, John B. James. John B. James sold it to his brother, Augustus James, and the latter in turn sold it to Alfred Wild. For beauty of location and scenery it is one of the finest country seats on the banks of the Hudson. With a view to reconstruction and improvements, Mr. Wild had commenced the work of demolition, when his fortune was lost in the enterprise of the Portage Canal, and the property passed out of his hands into those of a mortgagee. It has been without an occupant for a number of years, is going to decay, and beginning to wear a wild and dreary aspect. With men of taste and wealth everywhere looking for residences on the banks of the Hudson, it is a wonder this estate did not find an occupant when it found an owner.

Mathew Van Etten died on the 28th of May, 1808, aged

eighty-six years.   His wife, Elenor Van Wagenen, died on the 17th of August, 1798, aged eighty-two years.   She thus had birth six years before her husband.   They were both buried in the "Kerk Hof," near the Hutton gate.   At the death of Mathew Van Etten his son, Barent, became the owner of the homestead.   His wife was Sarah Froeliegh, and their children were: Elenor, who married Jacob, the son of Johon Nickolas Cramer; Mathew, who married Rebecca Schryver; Margaret, who married Asa Sherman; and Peter, who married Elizabeth McCavy.

Barent Van Etten died on the 12th of February, 1833, aged seventy-two years.   His wife died on the 16th of August, 1845, aged seventy-nine years.   At the death of his father-in-law Jacob Cramer bought out the other heirs, and became the owner and occupant of the Van Etten Homestead.   Jacob Cramer and his wife both died in the same year and month— he on the 20th, and she on the 24th of August, 1850—he in the seventy-second year of his age, and she in the sixty-seventh of her age.   Soon after the death of their parents the Cramer heirs disposed of the estate, comprising about eighty acres of land, to Miss Elizabeth Jones, for eighteen thousand dollars. The ground was at once occupied by Miss Jones and her brother, Edward, and his family; and the Jones' mansion, the most complete and the most costly in the town, erected.   Edward Jones died December 8, 1869, and his sister Elizabeth, May 29, 1875; and the estate is now, by inheritance, in the possession of Edward, the only son of Edward Jones, deceased.

The Camp-meeting woods were purchased by the Rev. Freeborn Garretson of Maj. Andrew Kip, May 1, 1801, for $787. The land on the west side of the creek, occupied by Governor Lewis' mills, and Governor Lewis' dock on the river, are on the Van Wagenen lands, and must have been purchased from the Garretsons by Governor Lewis some time before 1806.   Our old town records tell us that in 1806 Jacob Ackert was road master "from George Marquart's to Lewis' Landing."   The Camp-meeting woods and Governor Lewis' Landing are now included in the Kelly estate.   Our people remember well when Governor Lewis' mills and landing did a thriving business.   A gentleman at our elbow says the governor's mill-dam sometimes took the water from Tillotson's mill, a short distance below; and sometimes Tillotson's dam raised the water so high at the Governor's as to obstruct the action of his great over-shot wheel, when there was " trouble in the camp;" and the opera-tives threatened " to cut down Tillotson's dam."

William Schell was the occupant of the Tillotson mills during the last war with England, and, we are told, found them very profitable.   There was a saw-mill and a whiskey distillery included in the premises, and all were in the use and occupa-tion of Mr. Schell, as lessee.

. A map of the farm purchased by Major Andrew Kip when he sold the Ellerslie farm to Maturin Livingston, in 1814, made in 1795, shows an " Oil Mill" on the site of the present grist mill, and gives a quantity of land on the west side of the creek to Henry B. Livingston.   This is now the only grist mill left on the creek, and the only one in the town of Rhinebeck.

CHAPTER VII.

JAN ELTON AND HIS LANDS.

JAN ELTON's wife was Jacomyntje Sleight, and a widow, with four children, when he married her.   Her children were: Jannitje Newkirk, Hilletje Wynkoop, Jacomyntje Pawling and Tryntje DuBois.   Jan Elton's children were: Roeloff, Corne-lius, William, Gertje and Altje.   In his will he left half of his property to his five, and the other half to his wife's nine children.   Lot number two in this patent fell to his own five children.   And this explains why lot number two was divided into five, and lot number five into nine shares.   In 1713–14 Gerrit Artsen became the owner, by purchase from these heirs, of the whole of number two, and five-ninths of number five. Of Jacomyntie's Fly, sold to the heirs of John Elting by Henry Beekman, in 1705, the northern half fell to his five, and the southern half to his wife's nine children.   And in the same manner the whole of the northern half, and five-ninths of the southern half of this Fly became the property of Gerrit Artsen. He was thus the owner of nearly two-thirds of all the land cov-ered by the Artsen, Roosa and Elting purchase from the Indians.

On the 19th of February, 1719, Hendricus Heermance deeded back to Gerrit Artsen, in fulfillment of a promise made when he purchased, "all that certain home lot" lying within the bounds of number three, and on the north of "Jan Elting's Kill," containing seven acres of land.

.On the 22d of July, 1720, Gerrit Artsen deeded to his son, Goosen Van Wagenen, of Dutchess County, for sixty-two pounds, two-fifths of number two, two-ninths of number five, and two-fifths in the northern, and two-ninths in the southern half of Jacomyntie's Fly and the "home lot," conveyed back to him by Hendricus Heermance.

We learn from Barent Van Wagenen's will, dated April 28, 1731, that he owned three-fifths of lot number two, "bounded southerly by Laurens Osterhout, northerly by Goosen Van Wagenen, easterly by the Kill, and westerly by the river;" also five-ninths of lot number five, bounded southerly by lot number four, of Evert Roosa; northerly, by Solomon DuBois; easterly, by the Kill; and westerly, by the river; and also five-ninths in the southern half, and three-fifths in the northern half of Jacomyntie's Fly. In reference to this property, Barent Van Wagenen says in his will, that it came to him by "transpoort van myn vader, Gerrit Artsen, or Gerrit Van Wagenen." This "transpoort" or deed is not on record, and the date cannot be precisely determined. Gerrit Artsen's will was proved on the 9th of March, 1722. It makes no reference to property in Dutchess County, all of which must, therefore, have been previously deeded.

Excepting Solomon DuBois, we can find no person who owned and occupied land on the grant by virtue of his relationship to John Elting.

Each of the five partners to this patent was required to pay one-fifth of the annual quit rent. The lands assigned to each were, therefore, intended to be the same in acres or the same in value. We gather from the tax-book, now in the hands of the collector of the town of Rhinebeck, that the patent, intended to cover about twelve hundred, really included about twenty-two hundred acres; and that of this amount about fifteen hundred acres fell to the share of Artsen, Roosa and Elting, leaving about seven hundred to the Kips.

CHAPTER VIII.

THE NORTH WARD.

DUTCHESS COUNTY was organized in 1683, and was attached to Ulster for a number of years. Its bounds were the county of Westchester on the south of the Highlands; on the east, twenty miles from the river, it extended to Roelof Jansen's Kill on the north, and followed the said Kill to the river. In 1717, the portion of Livingston's manor lying south of Roelof Jansen's Kill was attached to Albany County, and remained thus attached until April 4, 1786, when Columbia County was formed. Dutchess County, including this territory, was separated into three divisions, called wards, before 1722; the South Ward extending from Westchester to Wappinger's Creek; the Middle Ward from the said creek to the south line of Pawling's purchase; the North Ward from the said line to the north end of the county.

These wards elected supervisors, assessors, overseers of the fences, overseers of the King's highway, a constable and collector, every two years; and the taxes were levied on an assessment made bi-annually by three county assessors.

The first election in the North Ward on record was held in April, 1722, and the officers chosen were as follows:

Constable, William Schot; Supervisor, Hendricus Beekman; Assessors, Barent Van Benthuysen, Hendricus Heermanse; Collector, Roelof Kip; Overseers of the King's Highway, Hendricus Buys, Hendrick Kip, Gerardus Lewis; Surveyors of the Fences, Dierk De Duytser, Tunis Pier.

TAX ASSESSMENT, 1723.

The inhabitants, residents, sojourners and freeholders of Dutchess County are rated and assessed by the assessors chosen for the said county, as follows:

	£	s.	d.		£	s.	d.
Widow Harmon Knicker-backer		5	5	Hans Jacob Dencks	12	0	12
Widow Adam Van Elstyn		5	5	Aarent Feinhout	6	0	6
Laurens Knickerbacker	18	1	0	Nicolas Row	18	0	18
Barent Van Benthuysen	10		0	Fallentyne Bender	8	0	8
Johan Jacobus Melus	7		7	Philip Feller	5	0	5
Jacob Hooghtyling	12		12	Johannes Risdorph	8	0	8
Jan Vasburgh	11	8	11	Barent Noll	8	0	8
				Jurrie Soefelt	17	0	17

	£	s.	d.		£	s.	d
Lawrence Hendrick	10	0	10	Hendrick Buys	8	0	8
Annaniaas Teel, Waganer..	10	0	10	Jacob Van Kempen	10	0	10
Frederick Mayer	10	0	10	Nicolas Bonesteel	7	0	7
Karl Neher	14	0	14	Areyen Hendrick, Van Pine	12	0	12
Philips, cooper	12	0	12	Isaac Borhans	10	0	10
Herry Teder	12	0	12	Evert Knickerbacker	7	0	7
Hans Jerry Prigell	8	0	12	Johannes Row	6	0	6
Hans Adam Frederick	8	0	8	Simon Westfall	14	0	14
Henrick Sheerman	unable			John Windfield	5	0	5
Henrick Beem	7	0	7	Jacobus Van Etten	5	0	5
Johannes Backus	9	0	9	Martten Boock	6	0	6
Andries Countreman	6	0	7	Peter Dob	12	0	12
Jurryan Saltman	6	0	6	Johannes Dob	6	0	6
Hans Felten Woleven	9	0	9	Cornelius Knickerbacker..	11	0	11
Peter Woleven	14	0	14	Vallentine Shaver	5	0	5
Frans Kelder	12	0	12	Peter Wolleven, Jr	5	0	5
Joseph Reykert	15	0	15	Bastian Traver	7	0	7
Hendrick Shever	16	0	16	Deirk De Duytser	13	0	13
Peter Van Ostrander	14	0	14	Barent Van Wagenen	21	1	1
Estate Marytie Ostrander..	5	0	5	Abraham Freer, Jr	8	0	8
William Traphagen	28	1	8	Gerardus Lewis	8	0	8
Jacob Kip	55	2	15	Jurrie Westfall	8	0	8
Hendrick Kip	15	0	15	Johannes Berenger, seve-			
Mathys Sleight	32	1	12	maker	8	0	8
Abraham Freer	5	0	5	Wendel Polefer	8	0	8
Evert Van Wagenen	29	1	9	Arie Roosa	8	0	8
Hendricus Heermanse	12	0	12	Peter Van Etten	8	0	8
Goose Van Wagenen	12	0	12	Roelif Kip	9	0	9
Laurense Osterhout	21	1	1	William Simon	5	0	5
Hendricus Beekman	63	3	0	Martin Burger	5	0	5
Jacob Ploegh	5	0	5	Adam Dinks	10	0	10
Tunis Pier	14	0	14	Henrick Swetselar	8	0	8
Larense Teder	8	0	8	William Vredenburgh	8	0	8
Peter Tybell	15	0	15	William Schot	5	0	5
Alburtus Schryver	5	0	5	John Jurie Aere	5	0	5
Nicolas Eemeigh	10	0	10	Christian Berg	5	0	5
Henrick Ohle	10	0	10	Lazuroz Dome	5	0	5
Carel Ohle	unable			Simon Coal	5	0	5
Adam Eykert	18	0	18	Aerya Rosa, Jr	5	0	5
Hans Lambert	19	0	19	Jurie Shever	5	0	5
Stephen Froelick	8	0	8	Philip Saloman	5	0	5
Martten Wheitman	6	0	6				

North Ward, 97 people, assessed................................£1088 15 7
Tax, at 1s. on a pound.......... ....£54 8 0
Middle Ward, 48 people, assessed........ ....   812 0 0
Tax, at 1s. on a pound........................... 40 12 0
South Ward, 48 people assessed..................   543 0 0
Tax, at 1s. on a pound........................... 27 3 0

                                                £122 3 0   £2443 15 7

It will thus be seen that in 1722 the North Ward, which
comprised the present towns of Red Hook and Rhinebeck, contained more taxable people than both the others, paid very
nearly twice as much tax as the South, which contained the
town of Fishkill, and was assessed £276 15s. more than the

Middle Ward, which contained the town of Poughkeepsie. Of course, the North Ward contained the thirty-five families of Gov. Hunter's Palatines, found there in 1718; and, as our list of names will show, quite a number besides.

The elections in the North Ward were held in Kipsbergen "at the usual place." On the 7th of April, 1724, the officers following were chosen:

Constable, William Schot; Supervisor, Barent Van Wagenen; Assessors, William Traphagen, Jacob Ploegh, Matyas Sleight; Surveyors of Fences, Tunis Pier, Roelof Kip, Jacob Ploegh; Collector, Arie Hendricks; Poundman, Tunis Pier.

In 1732, the last ward election held in Kipsbergen, at the usual place and time, the following were the officers chosen:

Constable, Laurense Tiel; Supervisor, Barent Van Benthuysen; Assessors, William Schot, Jan Vosburgh; Collector, Isaac Kip; Surveyors of the King's Highway, Hendrick Shever, Wendel Polver, Goosen Van Wagenen; Pounder, formerly for cattle and horses, Johannes Kip; Surveyors of the Fences, Mathys Sleight, Laurens Osterhout, Evert Van Wagenen.

The book in which we found these records contained premiums awarded to different persons for wolves and bears captured in the county.

CHAPTER IX.

ORGANIZATION OF THE PRECINCT.

RHINEBECK was organized as a precinct on the 16th of December, 1734. We are not told who were its first officers. The precinct extended from the Columbia County line on the north, below Mulford's place on the south, and from the river to the Nine Partners' line on the east. Of course, when the name Rhinebeck was thus legally applied to this territory, there was an end of Kipsbergen, the "High Dutchers" having overwhelmed the "Low Dutchers" by the strength of the tide with which they came into the country.

We have a census of the county taken in 1740. It is of the county as a whole, not by precincts. We think the following list embraces all the freeholders in the precinct of Rhinebeck at this date:

Henry Beekman,
L. Knickerbacker,
Nicholas Hoffman,
Martinus Hoffman,
B. Van Benthuysen,
Philip Louden,
Hendrick Kip,
Nicholas Row,
Jury Soefelt,
Zacharias Haber,
Frederick Sipperly,
Johannes Spaller,
Jury Felder,
William Cole,
Hans Hayner,
Johannes P. Snyder,
Michael Sipperly,
David Richart,
Jacob Moul,
Mathys Eernst,
Adam Ostrander,
Simon Kool,
Gotfried Hendrick,
Wendel Yager,
Jacob Drom,
Martinus Shoe,
Jury Adam Soefeldt,
Philip Foelandt,
Andries Widerwax,

Frans Nicher,
Christovel Snyder,
Marten Tiel,
Arnout Velie,
Lawrence Tiel,
Jacob Cool,
Philip More,
Jan Van Benthuy-
sen,
Zacharias Smith,
Josias Ross,
Gysbert Westfall,
Alburtus Schryver,
Lawrance   Oster-
hout,
Roeloff Kip,
Mathys Sleight,
Tunis Pier,
Jury Ackert,
Evert Knickerback-
er,
Nicholas Bonesteel,
Jacobus Van Etten,
Jr.,
Basteaan Trever,
Conradt Berringer,
Wendel Polver,
Peter Van Etten,
William Simon,

Abraham Kip,
Hendricus   Heer-
mance,
Evert Van Wagenen,
Johannes Backus,
Hans V. Wolleven,
Hans Lambert,
Joseph Rykert,
Hendrick Sheffer,
Peter Ostrander,
B. Van Steenburgh,
Hans Velte Shaffer,
William Freer,
William Schot,
Peter Tippel,
Stephen Frelick, ——
Andries Heermance,
Michael Polver,
Johannes Weaver,
Wm. Van Vreden-
burgh, Jr.,
Johannes Kip,
Arie Hendricks,
Wm. Van Vreden-
burgh,
Isaac Kip,
Jacob Kip,
Goese Van Wagenen,
Arent Ostrander.

It will be noticed that there are no Livingstons or Rutsens in the precinct of Rhinebeck at this date. And it is worthy of note that Zacharias is the only freeholder of the name of Smith.

Our town records commence in 1748. In this year eight justices of the peace, of whom one was Arnout Velie, held a Court of General Sessions at Poughkeepsie, and " ordered that all and every precinct clerk in this county, to be chosen yearly on every first Tuesday in April, do, within ten days thereafter, make due return of the election of their respective precincts of the officers chosen, on the said first Tuesday in April, unto the clerk of the peace, under the penalty of thirty shillings to be paid by every such precinct or town clerk omitting, the same to be recovered by the clerk of the peace, who is hereby empowered to sue for and recover the same."

Dutchess County, ss. After a true copy signed,

pr. HENRY LIVINGSTON, Clerk.

pr. JOHANNES A. OSTRANDER, Precinct Clerk.

The first election in the precinct of Rhinebeck, under this act, was thus recorded:

Dutchess County, ss.: Att the election held in Rynbeek precinct on the first thursday in Aprill, and in the year Anno Dom. 1749, PURSUANT by an act of General Assembly Made in the third year of the reign of the late Majesties, King Wil_liam and Queen Mary, to the freeholders of said county and precinckt, on behalf of themselves and others, for electing of officers for said precinckt of Rynbeek, the following officers of this present year New Elected, viz.:

"Supervisor, Jan Van Deuse; Assessors, Gerret Van Wagenen, Philip Feller; Constables, Johannes Seever, Jacob Oostrander, Frederick Haaver; Masters of the Poor, Frederick Strydt, Roelof Kip; Pound Master, Johannes Kip; Fence Viewers, Jacob Sickenaer, Joeannes herkenburg, Gerret Van Wagenen; Surveyors of the Highways, Isaac Kip, Peter tiepel, Joseph Craford, Michael Siperlie, Godtvret Hendrick, John Maris, Lawrens Rysdorp, Petrus Velie, Johannes Van Wagenen, Christian Dederick. pr. Johannes Ostrander, Clerk."

It will thus be seen that the precinct of Rynbeek in 1749, covering the towns of Rhinebeck, Red Hook, and part of Hyde Park, had ten road districts. In the next year the record has eleven, as follows: 1. Isaac Kip, from the mill to Beekman's— that is, from the mill south of the church to the Heermance house. Isaac Kip lived at the Flat rock, and the road from thence north had no existence at this date; it was laid out in 1764. 2. Nicholas Bonesteel, from Cole's bridge to the Hog bridge; 3. Jacobus Van Etten, from the mill to Staatsburg; 4. Peters Van Aaken, to Leija Van Wagenen's; 5. Jan Van Etten, to Mathew Van Etten's; 6. Wendel Jager, from Albany line to Cole's bridge; 7. Jacob Jager, for Waragkameek—that is, from the post road in upper Red Hook east to the Milan line; 8. Peter Pitcher, to Hofman's; 9. Peter Schot, to Rutsen's.　There are thus Rutsens in the precinct in 1750, of whom we shall have more to say further on.　The district to which Peter Schot was assigned was from the church on the Flatts east, to Mrs. Miller's.　10. Johannes Feller, to the Hooke; 11. Peter Schryver, from Staatsburg to the end of precinct.

In a census of slaves in the county of Dutchess, taken in 1755, their numbers and owners in the precinct of Rhinebeck were as follows:

Captain Zachariah Hoffman's List.—Col. Martin Hoffman owned ten; Captain Zachariah Hoffman, four; Vullared Widbeck, two; Harmon Knickerbacker, two; John Van Benthuysen, four; Barent Van Benthuysen, eight; Anthony Hoffman, one; Adam Pitzer, one; John Vosburgh, three; Captain Evert Knickerbacker, one; Rier Schermerhorn, one; Peter Heermance, one; Garret Heermance, one—altogether thirty-eight.

Captain Evert Knickerbacker's List.—Jacob Siemon, one; Margaret Benner, one; Symon Kool, two; Nicolas Stickel, one; Johannes Feller, one; Petrus Ten Broeck, five; Mrs. Catharine Pawling, two; Andries Heermance, two—altogether fifteen.

Captain Frans Neher's List.—Mrs. Alida Rutsen, six; Mrs. Rachel Van Steenburgh, two; Lawrense Tiel, one; Philip Veller, two; Johannes Lambert, one; Jack Keip, four; Roelof Keip, two; Abraham Keip, three; Gerrit Van Benthuysen, three; George Soefeldt, one; George Adam Soefeldt, one; Susan Agnes Sheever, one; Cornelius Ostrander, one; Mrs. Cathlyntie Van Vredenburgh, one—altogether twenty-nine.

Captain Hendricus Heermance's List.—Hendricus Heermance, three; Gerrit Van Wagenen, two; Aart Van Wagenen, one; Evert Van Wagenen, two; Johan Van Wagenen, one; Peter DeWitt, four; Jogham Reddely, two; Mathew Sleight, two; Hendrick Sleight, one; Jacobus Van Etten, Jr., one; Col. Hendrick Beekman, eight; Lea Van Wagenen, one; Herry Hendricks, two; William Traphagen, one; Joe Croffert, one; Arie Hendricks, one; Charles Crooke, one—altogether thirty-four.　In the precinct, fifty-two slave-holders, one hundred and sixteen slaves.

THE REVOLUTION.

After the battle of Lexington, on the 19th of April, 1775, the people of Dutchess County were asked to sign the following pledge:

" Persuaded that the rights and liberties of America depend, under God, on the firm union of its inhabitants in a vigorous prosecution of the measures necessary for its safety, and convinced of the necessity of preventing anarchy and confusion, which attend a dissolution of the powers of government, we, the freemen, freeholders and inhabitants of Dutchess County, being greatly alarmed at the avowed design of the ministry to raise a revenue in America, and shocked by the bloody scene now enacting in Massachusetts bay, do, in the most solemn manner, resolve never to become slaves, and do associate under all the ties of religion, honor and love to our country, to adopt and to carry into execution whatever measures may be recommended by the Continental Congress, or resolved upon by our provincial convention for the purpose of preserving our constitution, of opposing the several arbitrary acts of the British Parliament, until a reconciliation between Great Britain and America, on constitutional principles, which we most solemnly desire, can be obtained ; and that we will, in all things, follow the advice of our general committee respecting the purposes aforesaid, the preservation of peace and good order, and the safety of individuals and property."

The people in the precinct of Rhinebeck who thus repudiated the British Government, and placed themselves under the power of new men and new measures, were as follows:

Petrus Ten Broeck,	Peter Hermanse,	Samuel Green,
P. G. Livingston,	Zach. Hoffman, Jr.,	Peter Traver,
George Sheldon,	Martin Hoffman,	Andrew Simon,
William Beem,	Zacharias Hoffman;	Jacob Fisher,
John Van Ness,	Abraham Cole,	Samuel Elmendorf,
Herman Hoffman, '	James Everett,	Zacharias Backer,
Ananias Cooper,	William Pitcher, Jr.,	Johannes Hannule,
David Van Ness,	Jacob More, Jr.,	Johannes Richter,
Egbert Benson,	Christian More,	Levi Jones,
Jacob Hermanse,	Lodowick Elseffer,	Isaac Cole,
Andries Hermanse,	Isaac Walworth,	Hendrick Miller,

Simon Cole, Jr.,
Frederick Weir,
John Banks,
John Garrison,
Nicholas Hermanse,
Philip Bonesteal,
Simon S. Cole,
Andries Michal,
John Davis,
Christian Miller,
Will.elmus Pitcher,
John Hermanse,
Godfrey Gay,
Henrich Tetor,
Johannes Smith,
Jeab Meyer,
William Harrison,
Christoffel Schnei-
der,
Christopher Fitch,
John Schermerhorn,
Henry Waterman,
Jr.,
Jeab Waterman,
Henry Beekman,
Evert Van Wage-
nen,
Art Van Wagenen,
H. J. Knickerbacker,
William Tuttle,
Stephen Sears,
Joseph Elsworth,
Jacob Thomas,
Philip Feller,
Harman Whitbeck,
Evert Vasburgh,
John Moore,
Petrus Backer,
Johannes Backer,
Conradt Lescher,
Michael Sheffer,
Goetlieb Mardin,
Hendrick Mardin,
David Martin,
Cornelius Swart,
James Adams,

Daniel Ogden,
Joseph Funck,
Christian Fero,
Ryer Schermerhorn,
Wilhelmus Smith,
Frederick Moul,
George Reystorf,
Joseph Rogers,
Benjamin Bogardus,
Hans Kierstead,
Isaac Kip,
Jacob Kip,
Philip J. Moore,
Nicholas Hoffman,
John Williams,
Joseph Lawrence,
Jeab Vosberg,
James Douglass,
William Klum,
Johannes Miller,
Jacob Schermer-
horn,
C. Schermerhorn,
Reyer Hermanse,
Jacob Hermanse,
William Pitcher,
Jacob A. Kip,
John Tremper,
Henry Shop,
John Balist,
Helmes Heermanse,
Cor. Elmendorph,
Philip Staats,
Isaac Beringer, Jr.,
William Waldorf,
Johannes Benner,
George Sharp,
Christian Backer,
William Radcliff,
H. Waldorph, Jr.,
Henrich Benner,
Philip Hermanse,
Thomas Lewis,
Hendrick Livey,
Everhart Rynders,
Henry Kuncke,

George Stetting,
Elias Hinneon,
Samuel Haines,
Peter Ledwyck,
Jacob Elmendorph,
Jan Elmendorph,
Patt Hogan,
Evert Hermanse,
John Cole,
Petrus Pitcher,
Zacharias Root,
Edward Wheeler,
Peter Hoffman,
William Beringer,
Conrad Berringer,
Henry Klum, Jr.,
C. Osterhout,
Peter Cole,
Simon Kole,
Jacob Maul,
Everardus Bogardus,
Simon Westfall,
Jacob Tremper,
Henry Titemor,
John Mares,
James Ostrander,
Christover Weaver,
Peter Westfall, Jr.,
Henry Gissebergh,
W. Van Vraden-
burgh,
Jacob Kip,
James Lewis,
Peter DeWitt,
John Pawling,
Alburtus Sickner,
Andrew Bowen,
Martinus Burger,
Johannes Scutt,
Jacob Sickner, Jr.,
Barent Van Wage-
nen,
William Dillman,
Cornelius Miller,
Simon Millham,
John Weaver, Jr.,

Benjamin Osterhout,
Henry Burgess, Jr.,
Uriah Bates,
William McClure,
Joshua Chamber,
Jacob Sickner,
J. Van Aken,
Peter Van Aken,
Jacob N. Schryver,
Peter Radcliff,
C. Wenneberger,
Jacob Folant,
Abraham Kip,
Peter Brown,
Jacob Schultz,
John Hoffman,
Jacob Maul, Jr.,
B. Van Steenburgh,
Johannes Van Rensen,
Tobias Van Keuren,
John Klum,
Godfrey Hendrick,
Jacob Beringer,
John Bender,
Zacharias Whiteman,
Joseph Hebert,

William Schultz,
John Blair,
Thomas Greves,
Michael Schatzel,
Peter Schopp,
Hendrick Moore,
Herrick Berger,
Johannes Turk,
John White, Jr.,
John Cowles,
Herman Duncan,
John Denness,
William Waldron,
Cornelius Demond,
S. Van Benschoten,
B. Van Vradenburgh,
Peter Scoot,
Jonathan Scoot,
John Mitchell,
Simon Scoot, Jr.,
William Scoot, Jr.,
Jacob Lewis,
Jacobus Kip,
William Skepmus,
Johannes P.V. Wood,
John Haas,
P. Vradenburgh,

R. J. Kip,
David Mulford,
Lemuel Mulford,
Paul Gruber,
Solomon Powell,
Henry Bull,
George Bull,
William Powell,
Casper Haberlan,
Thomas Humphrey,
Christopher Denirah,
Abraham Westfall,
John McFort,
William Carney,
Philip Feller, Jr.,
Nicholas Bonesteel,
Philip Bonesteel,
Zach. Neer,
Nicholas Stickel,
Abraham Scott,
William Troophage,
Alexander Campbell,
R. Van Hoverburgh,
John Rogers,
Nicholas Stickel,
Jacob Teil,
John Satin,
Henry Fraleigh, Jr.

CHAPTER X.

THE BEEKMAN FAMILY.

WILLIAM BEEKMAN, the father of the patentee of Ryn Beek, we are told by those who ought to know, came to New Amsterdam, now New York, with Governor Stuyvesant, in 1647; that he was born in Holland, of German ancestry, on the 28th of April, 1623; that he married Catherine DeBough, in the city of New York, on the 25th of September, 1649, by whom he had seven children—three sons and four daughters; and that he died in the city of New York in 1707, in the 85th year of his age. In 1653, '54' '55' '56' '57 he was elected one of the schepens (assistant aldermen) of New Amsterdam. On the 18th of October, 1658, he was appointed vice-governor on the Delaware; on the 4th of July, 1664, he was elected sheriff of Esopus, now Kingston.   On the 16th of August, 1647, he was elected burgomaster of New Amsterdam, the Dutch having recovered, and restored the old name to the city during this year.   He was alderman at twelve different dates under the English, until 1696, when he withdrew from public life.   The old New York records tell us that the business by which he lived and prospered was that of a brewer.   His sons were Henry, Gerard and John.   Henry, the eldest, was the patentee of Ryn Beek, and therefore the one with whom we have specially to do.

Henry Beekman married Joanna DeLopes, and settled in Kingston, Ulster County, where he became county judge, member of the legislature, colonel of the militia, and deacon and elder of the Reformed Dutch Church.   Having a son Henry, he has been mistaken for his own father by Peter A. Jay and others.   He never lived in Rhinebeck, but it was he who laid out the land for the " High Dutchers," and settled on his patent the Palatines who founded Rhinebeck, and gave the name to the town.   He died in 1716, certainly not above sixty-six years old ; and there are very few deeds over his own signature extant.   The lands to the German families were laid out as early as 1714, but the deeds were given on the 20th of October, 1718, by the heirs.   He had four children, as follows : William, born at Kingston in 1681, died in Holland, aged eighteen ; Catharine, born September 16, 1683, married John Rutsen, of Kingston ; Henry, born in 1688, married Janet Livingston, the daughter of Robert, a nephew of Robert, the patentee, and first lord of the manor of Livingston ; Cornelia, born 1690, married Gilbert Livingston, son of Robert, the lord of the manor.

John Rutsen was living in 1720, and witnessed a deed in this year as justice of the peace in Kingston, from Hendricus Heermance to Gerrit Aartsen.   There is no evidence that he ever had a residence in Rhinebeck ; he died before 1726.   In this year his widow, Catharine Beekman, at the age of forty-three, married Albert Pawling, of Kingston.   Albert Pawling died in 1745.   We have no evidence that he lived or died in Rhinebeck, and presume he did not, his name not being found among the freeholders in the census of 1740. We have a letter in Dutch from Henry Beekman, in New York, to his sister, Mrs. Catharine Pawling, in Rhinebeck, dated 1746. We assume, therefore, that she was a resident in Rhinebeck at this date; but in what particular locality we have not learned.

John Rutsen and Catharine Beekman had four children baptised in Kingston, as follows: Johanna, born April 11, 1714; Jacob, born April 29, 1716: Hendrick, born March 9, 1718; Catharine, born May 24, 1719. Albert Pawling and Catharine Beekman Rutsen had no children.

Jacob Rutsen, son of John Rutsen and Catharine Beekman, married his cousin Alida, daughter of Gilbert Livingston and Cornelia Beekman. We are told that he built the mill known as Rutsen's mill, on the premises now owned by Mrs. Mary R. Miller. This mill was in existence in 1750 as Rutsen's mill. How much, if any earlier, we have not learned. Jacob Rutsen died before 1755, and, therefore, before he was forty years old. He was not a freeholder in the town in 1740, when he was twenty-four years old. If he built the mill after he became of age, he built it after 1737. We assume that he built it when he became a resident of the town, and, therefore, after 1740.

Jacob Rutsen and Alida Livingston had two children, as follows: John, born October 23, 1745; Cornelia, born May 31, 1746. He died after this date, and his widow, after 1755, married Henry Van Rensselaer, of Claverack, by whom she had seven children.

Catharine Rutsen, daughter of John Rutsen and Catharine Beekman, married Peter Ten Broeck. They lived in Rhinebeck as early as 1751, he being a road master here at this date. He and his mother-in-law, Catharine Pawling, lived in the same district when the census was taken in 1755, and may have lived together. They did not live in the same district with the widow Alida Rutsen. In 1765 he lived on the Barrytown road, his gate being the end of the road district from the post road, William Feller being road master. He, therefore, lived north of the Feller homestead. He was supervisor of the precinct in 1763, '64, '65, '66, '67. He and his wife, Catharine Rutsen, stood sponsors at the baptism of Catharine, the daughter of

John Rutsen and Phebe Carman, in the German Reformed
Church at Pink's Corner, in 1768. This church was on the
lands which fell to Mrs. Pawling in the division of the Beekman estate, and we presume it had the support of her family.
In 1775 Peter Ten Broeck and his wife conveyed to William
Schepmoes part of the farm now occupied by Thomas Reed;
and in the same year we find him colonel of a regiment of
Dutchess County soldiers. If they had children, we have not
learned the fact. And beyond their baptism, we have no
knowledge of Johanna and Hendrick, the other two children
of John Rutsen and Catharine Beekman.

John Rutsen, son of Jacob Rutsen and Alida Livingston,
married Phebe Carman. They had two children, as follows:
Catharine, born September 18, 1768; Sarah, born 1770. John
Rutsen, we are told, died aged twenty-eight years, and therefore in the year 1773. His widow married Robert Sands, January 25, 1779, by whom she had five children, as follows: Christina, Joshua C., John R., Eliza, Grace. Phebe Carman died
November 23, 1819, aged seventy-two years. Robert Sands
died March 3, 1825, aged eighty years.

Catharine Rutsen. daughter of John Rutsen and Phebe
Carman, married George Suckley, an English merchant in the
city of New York, by whom she had seven children, as follows:
Rutsen, Mary, Elizabeth, George, Sarah, Catharine and Thom-
as. George died at nine, and Catharine at nineteen years.
George Suckley was a widower when he married Catharine
Rutsen, with two children, George and John L. Suckley.

Sarah Rutsen, daughter of John Rutsen and Phebe Carman, married Philip J. Schuyler. He was the son of General
Philip Schuyler; built the mansion now the property of his
niece, Mrs. Mary R. Miller; was a resident of Rhinebeck, and
a member of Congress from Dutchess County in 1817, '18·
They had five children, as follows: Philip P., John Rutsen,
Catharine, Robert, Stephen. Sarah Rutsen Schuyler died October 24, 1805, aged thirty-five years. Philip J. Schuyler married for a second wife Mary Anna Sawyer, by whom he had
three children, as follows: William, died aged twenty-two
years; George, married Eliza Hamilton; Sybel, died aged four

years. Philip J. Schuyler, born January 21, 1768; died in the city of New York, February 21, 1835.

Philip P. Schuyler married Rosanna, daughter of Abraham Livingston, and thus a great granddaughter of Robert, the nephew, and a distant relative of the late Hon. Peter R. Livingston, of this town. A gentleman at our elbow says he fought a duel with a British officer, and killed his antagonist. He died May 6, 1822, aged thirty-three years. Livingston Schuyler, a gentleman well known in Rhinebeck as " Lev. Schuyler," was his son. John Rutsen Schuyler died, unmarried, June 22, 1813, at the age of twenty-two; Catharine Schuyler married Samuel Jones. She died November 20, 1829, aged thirty-six years. Robert Schuyler, distinguished as a railroad operator and officer, married, we do not know whom, and died, we do not know where. Stephen Schuyler married Catherine M. Morris. He was born April 18, 1801. He was a local Methodist preacher. He was at one time the owner of the farm now the property of John H. Lambert. He was highly respected, and died in Livingston street, this village, in a house now owned by Henry Clay Williams, November 1, 1859. And thus far do we trace the descendants of Catherine Beekman, daughter of Henry, the patentee.

Henry Beekman and Janet Livingston had two children, as follows: Henry, baptised May 13, 1722, died young; Margaret, baptised March 1, 1724, married Robert R. Livingston, the grandson of Robert, the lord of the manor. Janet Livingston, the wife of Henry Beekman, born in 1703, died in 1724, and thus at the early age of twenty-one years. Born in 1688, Henry Beekman was fifteen years her senior when he married her, and thirty-six years old when she died. He married a second time, and took for his second wife Gertrude Van Cortlandt, by whom he had no children. He became a resident of Rhinebeck after 1728, and probably not until after his second marriage. The old Kip house, of which he became the owner in 1726, was, in the meantime, greatly enlarged, and became his mansion when he became a resident of Rhinebeck. He died January 3, 1776, aged eighty-eight years. There is a tradition among the people here that he died in Rhinebeck, and was buried under the old edifice of the Reformed Dutch Church. His first wife was certainly not buried in Rhinebeck, and if his second wife was, we have no knowledge of the fact. His sisters, Catherine and Cornelia, were not buried here, so far as we can learn. There is a tradition that he had a residence in Kingston as well as Rhinebeck, and that he spent his winters there. He died in the winter, and we deem it probable that he died in Kingston and was buried there in a family vault or burying plot. If he was buried under the Rhinebeck church, there should have been, and, we think, there would have been, a tablet or monument stating the fact. We have not learned who became the occupant of the Rhinebeck mansion immediately after Henry Beekman's death. Pero Van Cortlandt was road master "from the Hog-bridge to Beekman's mills, and from thence to Kip's ferry," in 1778. We assume that he was a relative, if not a brother, of Mrs. Henry Beekman, and that he was living in the Rhinebeck mansion, in charge of her affairs, at this date. We infer from documents that have come under our notice, that Henry Beekman made a will; that he left all his Rhinebeck estate to his daughter during her life, and *allotted* it to her children at her death. Col. Henry Beekman Livingston, his grandson, was road master from the Hog bridge to Livingston mills, and from thence to the river, in 1786; and we assume that from this date on to that of his death, he was the occupant of the Beekman mansion, and the owner of the Beekman mills. The lands attached to the mills, embracing about forty acres, were surveyed and laid out for him in 1796.

We have not learned the day or year of Margaret Beekman's birth. She joined the Reformed Dutch Church on Rhinebeck Flatts, in 1742, as Margaret Beekman, and, therefore, before her marriage. We are told she married at eighteen years of age. Assuming that she married in the same year in which she joined the church, we get 1724, the year of her mother's death, as the year of her birth. She, therefore, never knew a mother. Mrs. Delafield says: "The orphan child found another mother in her aunt Angelica (her mother's sister), and another home in Flatbush." We have said that Robert R. Livingston, her husband, was the grandson of the older Robert.

He was the only child of his father.   He and his father died
in the same year—1775.   His father, born in 1688, attained the
age of eighty-seven; he, born in 1719, attained the age of fifty-
six years.   By the death of his father, he became the owner of
all the land of Clermont, and, Mrs. Delafield says, "of one-fifth
of the great Hardenburgh patent."   He was a justice of the
Supreme Court of the colony, and a member of the Stamp Act
Congress.   He was a man of prominence and influence in the
affairs of State in his day.   Having espoused the cause of the
people against the government, he was greatly distressed at the
loss sustained by the patriots at Bunker Hill, receiving a shock
which carried him to his grave.   Mrs. Delafield says: " In December, 1775, Mrs. Robert R. Livingston was summoned to the
death-bed of her father, Col. Beekman. He had not yet
breathed his last, when a message arrived from Clermont that
the judge was alarmingly ill.   She hastened to her husband,
but she was too late." An intelligent old lady in our town
says, " Margaret Beekman (Mrs. Robert R. Livingston) told her
father the judge was dead when the messenger left, and she
compelled him to tell her the fact as soon as they got on the
road."   Mrs. Delafield says he died intestate, and that, according to the English law of descent, his eldest son, Robert, afterward the chancellor, succeeded to his landed estate; and, as
soon as circumstances permitted the division to be made, " the
youthful heir gave thirty thousand acres to each of his three
brothers, and twenty thousand to each of his six sisters in the
Hardenburgh patent."   He thus disposed of two hundred and
ten thousand acres of land, retaining the thirteen thousand
contained in the town of Clermont, and we do not know how
many more in the great Hardenburgh patent, in his own possession.

    We are told when General Vaughn had burned Kingston,
on his way up the Hudson, in 1777, to succor General Burgoyne
on his way down from Canada, he landed a portion of his army on
the east side of the Hudson, who, when they had burned Rhinebeck, proceeded by land as far as Clermont, where they burned
the mansion of Margaret Beekman Livingston.   We do not
think they came up as high as the Flats, and cannot conceive

where they found a Rhinebeck to burn. We are told shots were fired at the Beekman mansion from the fleet; that one of them pierced the wall and left the hole still to be seen in the west gable; and that others lodged in the hillside near the river, where they were afterward plowed out. We do not learn that they were preserved in the archives of the town, or that they are now anywhere on exhibition. We have learned that Barent Van Wagenen, who lived on the Hutton place, abandoned the premises when the fleet came in sight, being an earnest patriot. Returning, on horseback, a few days later, to look after his stock, he discovered a boat-load of Britishers approaching the shore, and at once showed them the heels of his horse in a rapid retreat. The speed of his horse being insufficient to satisfy his supposed necessities, he abandoned it and took to his own heels. If they burned his houses and barns, and carried off his stock, the fact has not been recorded.

Robert R. Livingston and Margaret Beekman had ten children, as follows: Janet, born in 1744, died on November 6, 1828, and thus in the eighty-fourth year of her age; Robert R., born in 1747, died on February 25, 1813, and thus in the sixty-sixth year of his age; Margaret, born in 1749, died on March 19, 1823, and thus in the seventy-fourth year of her age; Henry B., born in 1750, died in 1831, and thus in the eighty-first year of his age; Catharine, born on October 14, 1752, died on July 14, 1849, and thus in the ninety-seventh year of her age; John. R., born in 1754, died in 1851, and thus in the ninety-seventh year of his age; Gertrude, born in 1757, died in 1833, and thus in the seventy-sixth year of her age; Joanna, born on September 17, 1759, died on March 1, 1829, and thus in the seventieth year of her age; Alida, born in 1760, died on December 25, 1822, and thus in the sixty-second year of her age; Edward, born in 1764, died on May 23, 1836, and thus in the seventy-second year of his age.

MRS. JANET MONTGOMERY.

Janet Livingston, the daughter of Robert R. Livingston and Margaret Beekman, married General Richard Montgomery in July, 1773; he in the thirty-seventh year of his age, and she in the twenty-ninth year of her age. Very soon after their marriage they moved to Rhinebeck Flats, on the domain of her grandfather, Colonel Henry Beekman, and occupied the house on the premises of Thomas Edgerley, which he took down and re-erected on East Livingston street, in 1860. This was their residence when the general took command of the expedition against Canada, and lost his life in the assault on Quebec, December 31, 1775. And this is why the part of the post road on which this house stood is now Montgomery street, in the village of Rhinebeck.

THE HOUSE THE GENERAL BUILT.

Before the war, the general had commenced the erection of a mansion on the premises which are now the property of Lewis Livingston, south of this village.

Mrs. Martha J. Lamb, in her "Homes of America," has made the mistake of assuming that the house built by Mrs. Montgomery above Barrytown, in Red Hook, after the death of her mother, and, therefore, after 1800, and known as "Montgomery Place," was the house built by the General before he entered the army. This is corrected in the history of the Rhinebeck house, which follows:

"The place now known as 'Grasmere' originally formed part of the Beekman patent, and was included in the part of it which fell to Henry Beekman, Jr., when, after his father's death, the property was divided among him and his two sisters. Through what hands the property may have passed before we find it in possession of a descendant of Colonel Beekman we do not know, as there are no deeds to be found, and there are none on record in the county office at Poughkeepsie, relating to this property. The first we certainly learn of it is in 1773, when General Montgomery was in possession, and built mills upon it and caused it to be laid out and planted by his nephew, Mr. Jones, a son of Lord Ranelaugh, who married General Montgomery's sister. The house was planned and begun under the General's auspices, but he did not live to see it finished.

"In the notes written by Mrs. Montgomery to serve as material for a memoir of her husband, which we have in a pamphlet edited by Miss Louise L. Hunt, now in possession of the family papers by the will of their inheritrix, the late Cora Livingston Barton, daughter of Edward Livingston, of New Orleans, brother and heir of Mrs. Montgomery, we find these lines: 'In July, 1773, he was married. He then removed to Rhinebeck and laid the foundation of a house.'* From the same source, in a letter to his wife, dated at camp near St. John's, October 9th, he says: 'You must not go into the house until I return.' And again, Montreal, November 24th: 'I long to see you in your new house. If the winter sets in soon, don't forget to send for the lath to fence the garden, and, also, to have chestnut posts cut for the same purpose. I wish you could have a stove fixed in the hall, they are the most comfortable things imaginable.' And, from Holland House, near Quebec, December 5th, in the last letter he ever wrote, he says: 'I am glad to hear your house is in such forwardness. May I have the pleasure of seeing you in it soon.' In his will, copied still from the same pamphlet, he says: 'I leave to my said wife, the farm I purchased from Shaver, at Ryn Beek, with horses and everything upon it.' Dated, August 30, 1775.

"After the General's death, the house was occupied by Mrs. Montgomery, who was accustomed to walk around the farm with the seeds of the locust (pseudacacia), then a new tree in this country, in her pocket, and strew them along the fences. From these seeds have come the numerous fine locusts now on the place. After a time she desired a house on the river bank, and built the house known as 'Montgomery Place,' above Barrytown, where she resided until her death.† Grasmere, then called Rhinebeck House, as we find from the date of a letter written by Mrs. Montgomery, was rented to Lady Kitty Duer (Lord Sterling's daughter) and her family. And here was born the late William Alexander Duer, some time president of Columbia College, in New York. After that it was rented to

---

*A part of a house, said to have belonged to General Montgomery, is still standing at King's Bridge, Westchester Co., N. Y.

† "Montgomery Place * * * the house which Mrs. Montgomery erected about the beginning of the present century."—*Hunt's Life of Edward Livingston*, pages 355-6.

Mrs. Montgomery's brother-in-law, General Morgan Lewis, who occupied it nine years. After the expiration of General Lewis' lease, Mrs. Montgomery sold the property to her sister Joanna, the wife of Peter R. Livingston, who lived here five and twenty years. During their occupancy, the house burned down, in 1828. It was rebuilt; but Mrs. Peter R. Livingston died before the new building was finished.

"Peter R. Livingston died here in 1847, and, having no children, bequeathed all his property to his brother, Maturin, who, dying the following year, left it to his wife, Margaret Lewis Livingston, who gave the Grasmere estate to her son, Lewis Livingston, who has lived on it since 1850. In 1860 he inherited from his mother a farm of two hundred and eighty acres adjoining the Grasmere farm, and incorporated it with it, the whole property now including eight hundred and ninety-eight acres. In 1861-2 the house was rebuilt and enlarged, and a third story added."

In a spacious and elegantly-furnished room in this now very handsome and stately mansion, are to be seen the hangings of Gobelin tapestry brought out by Chancellor Livingston when he returned from his mission to France.

Mrs. Montgomery's death and funeral obsequies are well remembered by the old residents of Rhinebeck. All who could do so attended, and all who wished had access to the larder and wine cellar; and all who were predisposed to excess came home intoxicated. Her remains were deposited in the vault at Clermont, and we presume the funeral sermon was preached by the Rev. George W. Bethune, who was the pastor in charge of the church at the Flats at the time.

MRS. MONTGOMERY'S WILL.

Mrs. Montgomery had no children. By the will of her mother, and probably her grandfather, Henry Beekman, she owned the Rhinebeck Flats and adjacent lands; and by her will, dated September 19, 1823, and proved April 29, 1829, she thus disposes of them:

"And I do further devise and bequeath to my said brother, Edward Livingston, all the real estate I may own at Rhinebeck

Flatts, at the time of my decease, extending to the south so far as to include the farm of Thomas Hyslop, and to the north so far as to include all my land at the Flatts; and to extend to the eastward to include the farm of Conrad Lasher, the lands occupied by Henry Norris and Peter A. Ackert; the farm held under lease by the heirs of Isaac Davis; the lot occupied by Paul Dixon; and the several farms occupied by Andrew Teal."

CHANCELLOR LIVINGSTON.

Robert R. Livingston, second child of Robert R. Livingston and Margaret Beekman, having received a thorough education, graduating at Kings, now Columbia College, in the city of New York, studied law under his kinsman, William Livingston, and was admitted to the bar in 1773. He was, for a short time, a business partner of John Jay. He was appointed recorder of the city of New York under the crown in 1773, retaining the office two years, when he lost it on account of his sympathy with the revolutionary spirit of his countrymen. He was a delegate from New York to the Congress of 1776, and was one of the committee to draft the Declaration of Independence, which failed to receive his signature because he was absent in New York, of the convention of which he was a member. He was a member of Congress again, and appointed Secretary of Foreign Affairs in 1781. He was appointed the first Chancellor of the State of New York, in 1785, and held the office until 1801, when he resigned it to accept the office of Minister to France, where he was one of the commissioners who negotiated the purchase of Louisiana; out of which we now have the States of Louisiana, Arkansas, Missouri, Iowa, Minnesota and Kansas. He was a member of the convention held in Poughkeepsie, in 1788, to decide on the adoption of the Constitution of the United States, and administered the oath of office to George Washington, as the first President thereunder, in the city of New York, on the 30th of April, 1789.

While in France he made the acquaintance of Robert Fulton, whom, from this time on, he assisted with his money and practical intelligence in the invention and construction of the steamboat. In 1807 they put the first steamboat afloat on the Hudson river, and named her "Clermont," after the chancellor's country seat, a short distance north of Tivoli. His is one of the statues of its two most eminent citizens placed in the capitol of the nation, at Washington, by the State of New York. He is represented as standing erect, his form mantled by his robe of office, which . falls in graceful folds from his shoulders, the right hand bearing a scroll inscribed "Louisiana."

He married Mary Stevens, daughter of John Stevens, of New Jersey, by whom he had two children, as follows: Elizabeth S., married Edward P. Livingston ; Margaret M., married Robert L. Livingston.

Hamilton Child, in his Gazetteer of Columbia County, says the chancellor's grandfather, after receiving his estate (after 1728), "built a large stone house at Clermont, which he gave to his son, Robert R., in his old age." This house, he says "was located at the mouth upon the north side of Roeliff Jansen's creek." If this were true, the house had been built in the town of Livingston instead of that of Clermont. He confounds the old manorhouse built by the first Robert, in 1699, with that built by his son, north of Tivoli, and, which was burned by the British in the Revolution. The house was rebuilt at once, the old side walls being used, and, we presume, the old plan retained. And yet, the writer, in the same paragraph in which he gives us this information, says: " Mr. Livingston also built another house, after the close of the war, a little north of the ruins of the former one." The old house having been rebuilt at once, there were no ruins of the former one left ; and Mr. Livingston dying two years before the old one was burned did not build another after the close of the war. The second house was built by the chancellor, *south* of the old one, in what was then the town of Rhinebeck, and, therefore, in Dutchess County. We remember very well when the two houses were occupied by the chancellor's sons-in-law—the north and older one by Edward P., and the south one, the chancellor's homestead, by Robert L. Livingston. They are both on the banks of the Hudson, and charming for situation. The view of the Catskill Mountains is very fine, and, though in different counties, they are near together, and in view of each other. They are nearly opposite to what was then Bristol, and is now Malden, in Ulster County, on the opposite side of the river.

General Lafayette stopped at Robert L. Livingston's on his visit to the United States, in 1824, and gave a reception on his lawn to the people of the surrounding country. We are told they came in thousands, from both sides of the river, and from distant places. We have people still living in Rhinebeck who helped to swell the crowd, and shook the General's hand.

MARGARET LIVINGSTON,

the third child of Robert R. Livingston and Margaret Beekman, was married to Dr. Thomas Tillotson, of Maryland, a surgeon in the Revolutionary Army, by Rev. Stephanus Van Voorhees, of the Rhinebeck Reformed Dutch Church, on the twenty-second of February, 1779. It is said, we think on the authority of the late Miss Mary Garrettson, that they were at one time the occupants of the Grasmere mansion as the tenants of Mrs. Montgomery. If this be true, it must have been before 1794, when our old town records place them at Linwood. Mrs. Dalafield says the Linwood farm was once the property of her grandmother, for which she received a lamb per year rent; and that she sold it to her sister, Mrs. Tillotson. We do not see how this could be. Mr. Tillotson purchased the land on which he erected the Linwood mansion from Isaac Van Etten, in 1790. The Van Etten land was on the patent of Arie Roosa & Co., which never paid rent to the Beekmans. The older Henry Beekman built a mill on the creek which enters the river at this point, and his son purchased six acres of land, on what is called the "Neck" in old deeds, from Arie Roosa, immediately about the mill. He deeded the mill to his son, Henry, in 1713; and it may, through him, have become the property of his granddaughter, Mrs. Morgan Lewis, and been sold by her to her sister, subject to the rent named, of a lamb a year. We presumed Mr. Tillotson had purchased the Van Etten farm because his wife was the owner, or to become the owner, of the mill and the adjacent lands by the deed of her mother. If the mill had fallen to General Lewis, we think he would have retained it;

for he built another on the same creek, in the immediate vicinity, before 1806.

Thomas Tillotson was a prominent man in the politics of the State, soon after the close of the war. He was State Senator from 1791 to 1800, when he became Secretary of State, and Robert Sands was elected Senator in his place. He retained the office of Secretary of State until 1805, and held it again in 1807. He died in May, 1832.

Mrs. Tillotson was the best known, and is the best remembered, of all Margaret Beekman's children by the old people of Rhinebeck. Though a member of the Reformed Dutch Church, her good will and kindly deeds were not limited to the brotherhood and sisterhood of her church, and her praises are spoken by all who remember her. Her funeral sermon was preached by Rev. David Parker. It was printed in pamphlet form, and copies of it are still preserved among the things cherished by families in the town. Her body, and that of her husband, were deposited in the vault in the rear of the Dutch Reformed Church, in this village. They had five children, one dying young. The others were: Jannette, born in 1786; married Judge James Lynch; died on August, 26, 1866, and was buried in Rhinebeck. Robert L., born in 1788; died in Rhinebeck, July 22, 1877; was buried in New York. John C., born May 16, 1791; died in New York, December 18, 1867; was buried in Rhinebeck. John C. retained Linwood; Robert L. built the house at Tivoli, now owned by Johnson Livingston; Howard, the youngest son, entered the navy as a midshipman and was killed in battle on Lake Erie, in the War of 1812.

COLONEL HARRY.

Henry B. Livingston, the fourth child of Judge Robert R. Livingston and Margaret Beekman, was the first Livingston in what is now the town of Rhinebeck. Among the warrants issued by the Provincial Congress in June, 1775, to persons in Dutchess County to recruit for the Revolutionary Army, we find the following: Henry B. Livingston, captain; Jacob Thomas, first lieutenent; Roswell Wilcox, second lieutenant.

In Holgate's genealogy of Leonard Bleeker, we are told that on the first of January, 1777, the army being newly organized he was appointed first lieutenant in the fourth New York Regiment, under Col. Henry B. Livingston.

Mrs. Delafield says: " Congress voted him a sword in compliment to his bravery. He was a fine-looking man, and not even his brother, the chancellor, surpassed him in the manly courtesy of his address. He married Miss Ann Horn Shippen, niece to Henry Lee, president of the first Congress. The peculiarities of this unhappy lady, which led to her separation from her husband, became in time, insanity." His only child, by his wife, Margaret B., inherited the old Beekman homestead and farm, and leased them to Andrew J. Heermance, in 1832, for ten years. Before the expiration of this lease she sold them to her cousin, John Armstrong, Jr., who, in turn, sold them to Mr. Heermance, the lessee. She died in Philadelphia in 1864. Colonel Harry's remains, we are told, were deposited in the vault in the rear of the Reformed Dutch Church in this village.

Colonel Harry was also the owner, from 1796, of the two grist mills in the south of the village, and also of an oil mill on the site of the grist mill below the " Sand hill, now in the occupation of Mr. P. Fritz.

When Margaret Beekman gave to her son, Henry B., the land includin the mills below the village, she made a deed to cover sixteen hundred and thirteen acres in lot No. 16 in the Beekman grant in the south of the county; also four acres of meadow land at the Buco bush, reserved in a former conveyance for the use of the Miller and Kelder farm; also a piece of land on the west side of the road near the house formerly occupied by Wm. Van Vredenburgh, containing about four acres. On the Rhinebeck premises she reserved the rents to herself during her life. He also received from his brother, the chancellor, a deed for 3,000 acres in the Hardenburgh patent (on record in Poughkeepsie).

MRS. CATHARINE GARRETTSON.

Catharine Livingston, the fifth child of Judge Robert R. Livingston and Margaret Beekman, married the Rev. Freeborn Garrettson, celebrated in his day as an earnest and devoted preacher in the Methodist Church. We are told that he came to Rhinebeck on the invitation of Dr. Thomas Tillotson, who knew him in their native State of Maryland; and that while a guest at the doctor's house, which was at this time the Grasmere or Montgomery mansion, he preached to the people of the neighborhood in the stone house on the post road, which is now the property of Mrs. Ann O'Brien. It was on the occasion of this visit that he made the acquaintance of Catharine Livingston, she being on a visit at her sister's residence, which ripened into love and marriage, in the year 1793, and brought Mr. Garrettson permanently into the town of Rhinebeck.

Mr. and Mrs. Garrettson commenced housekeeping on a farm, which was a gift from her mother, east of Mrs. Mary R. Miller's. Having tarried here for four or five years, and built a small Methodist church on the main road, near their residence, they exchanged farms with Mr. Johannes Van Wagenen, father of Captain William Van Wagenen, of this village, whose farm was on the Artsen & Co.'s patent, and thus with a frontage on the Hudson River, and in the near vicinity of the residence of her sister, Mrs. Tillotson. They at once built a new, large and handsome house on these premises, and entered it in the month of October, 1799. It is now "Wildercliff," on the banks of the Hudson, and one of the celebrated country seats in the town of Rhinebeck. Mrs. Olin says: "How many who have enjoyed the genial hospitalities of this house will recall the dignified form of the hostess, with her marked features, her soft, hazel eyes, the brown hair parted under the close-fitting cap, with its crimped muslin border, and the neatly-fitting dress, always simple and yet always becoming! No one would have imagined that this was the gay young lady that had been asked for in the dance by General Washington."

An intelligent old lady in the neighborhood says " Mrs. Garrettson was the most aristocratic of all her sisters." Of course, by her birth and position, Mrs. Garrettson was excluded from familiar intercourse with the mass of the people, and it did not fall to their lot to know to what extent the unfortunate and suffering engaged her sympathies. The working man and woman, who are self-supporting, never in need or distress, have no points of contact with the higher grades of society, and of

necessity know very little of them. *They* come *down* only to
visit the sick, feed the hungry and clothe the naked; and to the
working people, who are neither sick, hungry or naked, they are
of no *earthly* account, when they are not customers. From
what we have seen and heard of, and read about Mrs. Garrettson, we infer that she was, by the strength of her faith, under
the power of the unknown world to a greater extent than falls
to the common lot of religious people; and we think this fact
is amply attested by her marriage with the Rev. Freeborn Garrettson, who is remembered among our people for nothing save
the simplicity of his faith, and the fervor of his piety. He was
in nothing like the husbands chosen by Mrs. Garrettson's bril-
liant sisters. They were all earnest patriots and intelligent
politicians, and thus more under the power of the world that
now is, and the things that are present and real. Mr. and Mrs.
Garretson married when they were both above forty-one years
of age, and had one only child—the late Miss Mary Garrettson
—who was dwarfed in stature, but possessed of a mind of full
strength, which had been thoroughly and, we presume, system-
atically cultivated. She never married, and died on the 6th of
March, 1879. Born on the 8th of September, 1794, she was in
the eighty-fifth year of her age. She was burried with her
father and mother in a vault attached to the Methodist Episcopal Church in this village, of which she was a member and
liberal supporter.

JOHN R. LIVINGSTON.

John R. Livingston, the sixth child of Judge Robert R.
Livingston and Margaret Beekman, was twice married: first to
Margaret Sheafee, of Boston, by whom he had no children;
and, second, to Eliza McEvers, by whom he had eight, as follows
—Robert Montgomery, married Sarah Bache, granddaughter
of Leonard Lispenard, of New York; Angelica, died unmar-
ied; Dr. Edward, married Sarah Suckley, daughter of George
Suckley; John R., married Mary McEvers, daughter of
Charles McEvers, of New York; Charles, died, unmarried;
Serena, married Col. George Croghan, of the United States
Army; Eliza, married Captain Benjamin Page, of the United
States Army; Margaret, married Captain Lowndes Brown, of
the United States Army.

So far as we can learn, John R. Livingston was never an officer, civil or military, in the service of the government. We are told that he was a merchant in the city of New York, and, as such, not very successful. " Massena," the beautiful country seat at Barrytown, now the property of Mrs. Aspinwall, was built by him, probably in 1797. Mrs. Delafield says this house, in the early part of the century, " disputed with Clermont the honor of being considered the show-place of the Hudson River." He purchased the land on which it was built, some two hundred acres, from Peter Contine, Jr., on the third of June, 1796.

We cannot learn that John R. Livingston obtained a share of the land which fell to his mother in what are now the towns of Rhinebeck and Red Hook. The Beekman grant in the south-east of the county, which comprised the present towns of Beekman, Pawling, Dover, and a part, if not all, of Lagrange, was obtained by the elder Henry Beekman in the same year in which he obtained that of Rhinebeck, and is included in the same royal patent; and in the former, as in the latter, he deeded to his son a large number of the best acres before his death. Dying intestate, the son obtained a third of what was left, and thus the lion's share of the two grants. In 1780 his daughter, and only child, Margaret, had the lands falling to her in the south-east of the county surveyed and subdivided into ten equal shares, one for each of her children, in fulfillment of her father's will. In May, 1785, she set over to her son, John R., the portion, or a part of the portion, falling to him in this division.

GERTRUDE LIVINGSTON.

Gertrude Livingston, the seventh child of Judge Robert R. Livingston and Margaret Beekman, married Morgan Lewis, in May, 1779. They had one child, Margaret, born on the fifth of February, 1780. This was Margaret Beekman's first grandchild. She married Maturin Livingston on the twenty-ninth of May, 1798.

Morgan was the son of Francis Lewis, a member of the Continental Congress, in 1776, and a signer of the Declaration of Independence. He was aid to General Gates and Quartermaster-General of the Northern Army in the Revolutionary War. He received a thorough education, and became a lawyer. He was a member of the lower house in the State Legislature in 1789-90-92, from the city of New York; Attorney-General in 1791, and Chief Justice in 1801, from Rhinebeck. In 1804, he was elected Governor over Aaron Burr, and in 1807 was defeated by Daniel D. Tompkins.

Governor Lewis was State Senator for the Middle district, which included Dutchess County, in 1811-12-13-14. He was made Quartermaster-General of the United States Army in 1812 by President Madison; resigned the office in March, 1813, and accepted that of major-general; and as such participated honorably in the war with England, which was then waging.

The deed from Margaret Beekman to her daughter, Gertrude, for the Rhinebeck lands, bears date January 5, 1790, and covers nearly, if not quite, all the lands deeded to Henry Beekman by his father, in 1713; and in the same year, Morgan Lewis bought from Johannes Van Wagenen, for five dollars, the privilege to build a dam in the creek where it ran against his premises. He did not build the mill at once, and we do not think before 1800. The road through Fox hollow was not in existance in 1798, and there was no mill there at this date. The road to Governor Lewis' landing is first named in our old town records in 1806.

Governor Lewis' Staatsburgh mansion was not built on his wife's Rhinebeck lands. It was built several miles further south, in the town of Clinton, becoming Hyde Park in 1821. He purchased these lands from the executor of Mrs. Lewis Morris, of Morrisania, who was a daughter of Dr. Samuel Staats, under a mortgage foreclosure, in 1792. We have not learned when he built his house, but we have learned that it was destroyed in 1832 by fire.

Governor Lewis died in the city of New York, on the 7th of April, 1844, in the 90th year of his age. His remains were interred in the Episcopal graveyard at Hyde Park, where a unique and massive granite monument marks his resting place.

JOANNA LIVINGSTON.

Joanna Livingston, the eighth child of Robert R. Livingston and Margaret Beekman, married Peter R. Livingston, brother to Maturin Livingston, who married her niece, Margaret Lewis. They had no children. She was the owner of the Montgomery house below the village. The house burned, and they moved into the village. It was rebuilt at once, but she died before it was complete, in the house now owned by Matthias Wurtz.

Peter R. Livingston was prominent in his day as a politician, and, if not a statesman, he had taken an active part in State affairs. He was a State Senator from Dutchess County in 1820-21-22, and again in 1826-27-28-29. He is named as a member of Assembly in 1823 in the civil list of the State. He was president of the Whig National Convention which nominated General William H. Harrison for President in 1840. He was Secretary of Legation to General Armstrong, while the latter was minister to France, and, we are told, married on his return with the General, and settled in Rhinebeck, in the old Montgomery mansion, which had become the property of his wife by purchase from her sister, Mrs. Montgomery. This would bring him into Rhinebeck in 1812. We find his name in our old town records for the first time as a roadmaster in 1813. We do not know what property his wife owned in Rhinebeck besides the Montgomery farm. Whatever it was, he had a deed for it from her, and disposed of it by will, to the disappointment of some of her relatives. He had lent Col. Harry money on the mills, and obtained them by foreclosure of a mortgage in 1832. He died in 1847, and was buried in the vault in the rear of the Reformed Dutch Church in this village.

ALIDA LIVINGSTON.

Alida Livingston, ninth child of Robert R. Livingston and Margaret Beekman, married John Armstrong in 1789. They had five children, as follows : Horatio Gates ; Henry Beekman ; John ; Kosciusko ; Margaret, married William B. Astor. These children are all dead except Colonel Henry B., who is living at an advanced age in the village of Red Hook, in the paternal homestead. He served with distinction in the last war with England.

Gen. Armstrong was born at Carlisle, in Pennsylvania, on the twenty-fifth of November, 1758. He left the college at

Princeton at seventeen years of age, and joined the Revolutionary army as a volunteer, in a Pennsylvania regiment. He became aide-de-camp to Gen. Horatio Gates, and served in the
campaign which ended in the capture of Burgoyne. He was
appointed adjutant general of the Southern Army, but falling
sick of a fever on the Pedee river, was succeeded by another.
Resuming his place as aide, he remained with General Gates to
the close of the war. He was Secretary of State, Adjutant General, and a member of the old Congress for the State of Penn.
sylvania, before 1787. After his marriage, in 1787, he took up
his residence in the State of New York.

He is named in a deed of land conveyed to him by Heermance and Van Benthuysen, as a resident of Kingston. We
presume it was the land which is now the Bard place, at An--
nandale. He owned these premises with the mill at Cedar
Hill, in 1797, and occupied the mansion, which we are told was
built by him. Of the three falls in the Sawkill, with eight acres
of adjacent lands, which were reserved by the three partners
who became the owners of three-fourths of the Schuyler patent,
and divided it among themselves in 1725, the one near the river
fell to Henry Beekman. In 1747 he conveyed this fall to his son-
in-law, Robert R. Livingston, who in the same year purchased
a second fall and four-fifteenth of the creek from Andrew Heermance. Judge Livingston owned a mill at the river in 1770,
which, we are told, was burned by General Vaughan in October,
1777, when he burned the mansion of Margaret Beekman at
Clermont. At this date Judge Livingston and Henry Beekman had both been dead nearly two years, and Margaret Beek.
man Livingston, the widow of the former, and daughter of the
latter, was the owner of the mill at the mouth of the Sawkill,
and also of that in Tillottson's cove, and the Beekman house, in
this town. A New York loyalist writer blamed Vaughan for
" amusing himself burning residences on the river bank" when
he 'should have hastened to Albany. Lossing says : " A de-
tachment crossed the river and marched to Rhinebeck Flatts,
two miles to the eastward, where they burned several houses. "
We have never been able to learn from authentic sources that
anything but mills aud storehouses were burned on this side of

the river. It is incredible that they would pass the Beekman house at the river and proceed two miles into the interior to burn the harmless houses of comparatively innocent parties. The storehouse of Colonel Petrus Ten Broeck, at Barrytown, and the Livingston mill, a short distance above, were burned, and they were in the precinct of Rhinebeck.

The falls in the Sawkill, with the mill at the river, were deeded by Margaret Beekman to her daughter, Alida, in 1793, subject to a rent during her life, but to become absolutely hers at her death. John Armstrong at about the same time became the owner of the Bard farm, and built himself a mansion thereon. The map in the Starr Institute, made in 1797, shows him the owner of this mansion and of the mill at Cedar Hill; while that at the river is put down to Mrs. Margaret Livingston, and the Hendricks mill, in the interior of the town, to Chancellor Livingston. After 1800, the mill at the river and the mill at Cedar Hill are both in the possession of General Armstrong, and they both apparently continued so until 1812, when our town record says John C. Stevens is roadmaster " from General Armstrong's gristmill door at the river easterly *   * ."

Gen. Armstrong, we are told, declined all invitations to public office in the State of New York until 1801, when he was tendered the office of United States Senator by an unanimous vote of both branches of the Legislature, and accepted it. ' He was re-elected in 1803, and retained the office until the following year, when he resigned it, and accepted the mission to France, as successor to his brother-in-law, Chancellor Livingston. He remained in this position seven years. When he returned from France, he purchased the farm and built the mansion which are now " Rokeby," on the banks of the Hudson, south of Barrytown, in Red Hook. In 1812 he was appointed Brigadier-General in the United States Army, and, in 1813, secretary of War, by President Madison.

He sold Rokeby to his son-in-law, William B. Astor, and built the house in Red Hook Village in which his son, Colonel Henry Beekman Armstrong, the last survivor of Margaret Beekman's grandchildren, is now residing. He died in this house on the 1st of April, 1843, in the eighty-fifth year of his age. His

remains are reposing in the Armstrong vault in our village cemetery, with those of his wife and his son John.

EDWARD LIVINGSTON.

Edward Livingston, the tenth child of Judge Robert R.
Livingston and Margaret Beekman, married twice: first, Mary
McEvers, in April, 1798; second, Louise Moreau de Lassy, the
young widow of a gentleman from Jamaica, in June, 1805, her
maiden name being D'Avezac.· He had three children by the
first, and one by the second wife. Those by the first were: .
Charles Edward, born in 1790; Julia Eliza Montgomery, born
in 1794; Lewis, born in 1798; all died young and unmarried.·
The child by the second wife was Cora L. She married Thom-·
as P. Barton, of Philadelphia, in April, 1833. They had no
children. Mary McEvers, the first wife, died in March, 1801;
Louise D'Avezac, the second, died in October, 1860. Thomas
P. Barton died in April, 1869; Cora Livingston Barton died in
May, 1873; and thus passed away the family of Edward Living-
ston, the last child of Margaret Beekman.

Edward Livingston was elected to Congress from the city
of New York, in 1794, re-elected in 1796–'98, and appointed Attorney-General of the United States for the district of New
York in the same year, and filled both offices. He was Mayor
of New York in 1798. He moved to New Orleans, in Louisiana·
He was elected to Congress from New Orleans in 1822, and re-
elected twice thereafter. He was made Senator for the State of
Louisiana in 1829; Secretary of State for the United States in
May, 1831; resigned the office on the 29th of May, 1833, and
on the same day was appointed Minister to France. He accepted the office, retained it until 1835, when he returned, arriving
in the city of New York on the twenty-third of June, 1835.
He retired to Montgomery place, in Red Hook, where he proposed to spend the remnant of his life in the pursuits of the
farmer, and died, as before stated, on the twenty-third of May,
1836, leaving all his property to his wife.

On the 1st of October, 1836, Mrs. Louisa Livingston sold
all the lands in the village of Rhinebeck, which became her
property by the will of her husband, to William B. Platt, John
T. Schryver, Freeborn Garrettson, Rutsen Suckley, John Arm-

strong and Walter Cunningham, for nineteen thousand six hundred dollars. These parties are known in the history of our village as the " Improvement Company." Why, we have not learned. They divided the land into shares, and assigned to each his portion by deed. The design of the purchasers was doubtless to lay out the land in village lots, and thus dispose of it at a large advance on the cost.

CORNELIA BEEKMAN.

Cornelia Beekman and Gilbert Livingston had fourteen children, as follows: James, Henry, Robert Gilbert, Margaret, Johanna, Alida, Catherine, John, Philip, William, Samuel, Cornelius, Gilbert, Gilbert. Of these children, we learn from Helgate's genealogies, that John, Philip, William, Samuel, Cornelius and the first Gilbert died unmarried.

James Livingston married Judith Newcoomb. They had three children, as follows: Cornelia, Judith, Gilbert James. He was sheriff of Dutchess County, and resided in Poughkeepsie.

Henry Livingston married Susan Conklin. They had eleven children, as follows: Beekman, Robert, Henry, John H., the celebrated Reformed Dutch minister; Catherine, Johanna, Susan, Alida, Cornelia, Helen, Gilbert. He was county clerk under the English government, and also under that of the United States, until his death, 1799, in the eighty-fifth year of his age. He resided in Poughkeepsie.

Robert Gilbert Livingston married Catherine McPheaders. They had five children, as follows: Gilbert R., Henry G., Helen, Catherine, Robert G. He resided in New York.

Margaret Livingston married Peter Stuyvesant.

Johanna Livingston married Pierre Van Cortlandt.

Alida Livingston married, first, Jacob Rutsen; second, Henry Van Rensselaer. She resided in Rhinebeck in 1755.

Catherine Livingston married Thomas Thorn.

Gilbert Livingston married Joy Darrell.

Robert G. Livingston, son of Robert Gilbert and Catherine M. Pheaders, and thus grandson of Gilbert Livingston and Cornelia Beekman, married Margaret Hude, and settled in Rhinebeck near the mills which were once called Robert G. Livingston's, and afterwards Hake's and Crook's mills, near Rock City.

He was roadmaster from those mills to the Rhinebeck Lutheran Church in 1789. They had six children, as follows: Catherine, married twice; first, M. Brissac; second, Claudius G. Massonneau, of Red Hook; Helen, married Jeremiah Tronson, of New York; Cornelia, married John Crooke, of Poughkeepsie; Margaret, married Augustus C. Van Horn, of New York; Robert G., married Marthe de Reimer, of Poughkeepsie; Henry G., married Catherine Coopernail, of Milan, on December 26th, 1703.

Of the last named we know that he had no children; that he spent part of his life in Schoharie; that he spent his last days in a house near Rock City belonging to his brother-in-law, John Coopernail, sustained by his bounty; and that he died on September 29, 1868, in the eighty-fourth year of his age. His wife died a year later, and they repose, side by side, in the old graveyard of the Rhinebeck Lutheran Church, which was a gift to the church by his great-grandparents in 1729. He was a tall man, of large stature, measuring fifty inches around the waist, and having a striking countenance. We had not traced his genealogy, but on seeing a picture of Dr. John H. Livingston in an old Dutch Church hymn book, found the likeness so striking that we at once pronounced them of the same blood. He was never awed by the dignity of a merely human position, or the state or style of a human being, however exalted. He would not have given the emperor more than half of the road, and if he had met the empress on the street would have hailed her with a gracious salutation, and commended her for her beauty; and if he had asked her for a kiss in return, it would have been just like him. He was a temperate man, and constitutionally religious.

Jeremiah Tronson and Helen Livingston had a son, Robert, who married a daughter of Isaac Davis, of Rhinebeck. He is well remembered by our old people as the keeper of a grocery store in this village many years ago. Jeremiah Tronson, a well-known resident of this town, is his son.

Cornelia Beekman never resided on her Rhinebeck estate. Except her daughter, Alida, the wife of Jacob Rutsen, it is not certain that any of her children ever resided here.

The book of the old German Reformed Church has this

record, in German: "Baptized on profession of their faith, Robert Livingston's neger and negerin, January 2d, 1743." On the following page we have this record of a baptism: Child, Gysbert; parents, Henry Livingston, Susan Conklin: sponsors, Jacob Rutsen, Alida Livingston; January 30th, 1743." This record is doubtless in Henry Livingston's own handwriting, and of a baptism by Rev. George Michael Weiss. It may be inferred from this, that Robert G. Livingston, with his slaves, was a resident of Rhinebeck at this date. But it is just as likely that they were the slaves of Robert, of Clermont. And Henry Livingston, county clerk, and probably a resident of Poughkeepsie, may have been on a visit to his sister when he had his son baptized.

We insert the following genealogy because the town of Rhinebeck, and Cornelia Beekman are distinctly touched by it:

Robert Livingston, the first lord of the manor, had a son, Philip, who married Catherine Van Brough;

Philip Livingston and Catherine Van Brough had a son, Robert, who married Mary Tong;

Robert Livingston and Mary Tong had a son, Peter R., who married Margaret Livingston, a grand-daughter of Robert Livingston, the nephew, and thus, aunt of Peter R. and Maturin Livingston, both at one time residents of Rhinebeck;

Peter R. Livingston and Margaret Livingston had a son, Walter Tryon, who married twice—first, Eliza Platner; second, Elizabeth McKinstry;

Walter Tryon Livingston and Eliza Platner had a son, Peter R., who married Jane Thorn, a great-grand-daughter of Cornelia Beekman; and a daughter, Helen, who married Leonard W. Ten Broeck;

Peter R. Livingston and Jane Thorn had a son, Walter T., who married Elizabeth Wager, of this town; and Leonard W. Ten Broeck and Helen Livingston had a son, Walter Livingston Ten Broeck, who married Helen U. Shultz, also of this town. We believe the title to the Scottish Livingston lordship belongs to the line of Robert, the nephew, some of whose blood has thus found its way into the veins of our Walter L. Ten Broeck, and our late Walter T. Livingston, but flows in a larger measure in those of some other branches of the family.

CHAPTER XI.

THE HOFFMAN FAMILY.

THERE was a family of Hoffmans in the north end of the precinct of Rhinebeck who became prominent at an early date in our history. Whether they obtained their lands directly from Peter Schuyler, the patentee, or from other parties who had thus obtained them, we have not learned. We have seen a reference somewhere to Nicholas Hoffman as the owner of lands in that locality as far back as 1725. In 1722, Peter Schuyler sold lands there to "Lawrence Knickerbocker, Cornelius Knickerbocker, Evert Knickerbocker, all of Dutchess County ; Anthony Bogardus, of Albany, and Jan-itje, his wife ; and Jan Vosburg, of the said Dutchess County, and Cornelia, his wife ; sons and daughters of Harme Jans Knicker-bocker, late of Dutchess County aforesaid, deceased." In 1766 John Vosburgh, and Cornelia, his wife ; Laurence Knickerbock-er and Hans Jury Loundert, all of Rhinebeck precinct, in Dutchess County, of the one part, and Anthony Hoffman, of Kingston, Ulster County, Zacharias Hoffman, of Rhinebeck, of the other part, agree to divide a certain tract of land lying ad-jacent to the south of the manor of Livingston, apparently be-longing to them in common. Whether by this division, at this time, or at an earlier date, and in an another manner, the Hoff-mans became the owners of lands at the river, about Tivoli, and about the old Red Church and the Hoffman mills, northeast of Tivoli ; and they were freighters, store-keepers, and millers before and after the Revolutionary War.

Holgate, in his genealogies, says these Hoffmans were de-scendants of Martinus Hoffman, of Sweden, who settled at Shongum, in Ulster County. His son, Nicolas, married Jannitje Crispell, daughter of Antonie Crispell, a Huguenot, one of the patentees of New Paltz, and thus transmitted some of the best blood of France in the veins of his descendants. He says he settled in Kingston. He was evidently the Nicholas Hoffman who owned land in the precinct of Rhinebeck as early as 1725, and was a freeholder here in 1740. He had no son Nicholas, and his grandson of that name was not born at this date.

Nicholas Hoffman and Jannitje Crispell had five children, as follows: Martinus, born in 1706; Anthony, born in 1711; Zacharias, born in 1713; Petrus, born 1727; Maria, born 1730. There is here a space of fourteen years between Zacharias and Petrus, which Holgate ought to have accounted for.

Martinus Hoffman married Tryntje Benson, daughter of Robert Benson and Cornelia Roos, for a first wife, and the widow, Alida Hansen, daughter of Philip Livingston, the second lord of the manor, for a second; and was thus brother-in-law to Rev. Dr. John H. Livingston. By Tryntje Benson he had nine children, as follows: Cornelia, born in Kingston, August 13, 1734; Robert, born in Kingston, September 17, 1737; Anthony, born in Red Hook, August 1, 1739; Maria, born June 20, 1743; Martin, born in Red Hook, January 12, 1847, baptized in the Camp Church, July 3, 1747; Zacharias, born in Red Hook, May 10, 1749; baptized in the Rhinebeck German Reformed Church, at Pink's Corner, June 2, 1749; Jane, born February 14, 1752; Harmanus, born January 3, 1745; Nicholas, born 1756. He had one child by Alida Hansen Livingston, Philip L., born December 28, 1767.

Philip Livingston Hoffman married Helen Kissam. They had seven children, as follows: Catharine Ann, Alida, Helen Hannah, Philip, Richard Kissam, Adrian Kissam. The latter had several children, among them John T. Hoffman, ex-Governor of New York.

Martinus Hoffman was a Justice of the Peace for Dutchess County in 1750–51. In 1755, he owned ten slaves, the largest number held by any one person in the precinct. He was doubtless a man of large property and influence. His son, Anthony, was Superviser of the town of Rhinebeck from 1781 to 1785. He was Colonel, and member of the first, third and fourth Provincial Congresses.

Anthony, brother to Martinus, resided in Kingston. His son, Nicholas, married Edy Sylvester, of New York, and resided in Red Hook. The latter's son, Anthony, married, first, Miss Pell; 2d, Ann Cornelia, daughter of Isaac Stoutenburgh and Ann

Heermance, aunt to Rev. H. Heermance, of Rhinebeck. By his first wife his children were: Jane, born March 15, 1808; Laura, born November, 1809; Nicholas, born October, 1811; Mary Ann, born January, 1814, married Andrew Pitcher.   By the second wife the children were: Edward, Cornelia, Charles, Augustus, Elizabeth, Francis, Frederic, Anna, Catharine, Howard, Caroline.   Cornelia, of this family, married John M. Keese, and had two children, Charlotte Suydam and Anthony Hoffman Keese.

Col. Martinus Hoffman's wife was Tryntje Benson. Egbert Benson was a member of Congress from Red Hook from 1789 to 1793.   We assume that he was a relative, if not a brother, of Mrs. Martinus Hoffman.   John S. Livingston bought land of Egbert Benson in 1715, and we assume they were the premises on which he resided, and on which Egbert Benson resided when he went to Congress from Red Hook.

The ministers of the Reformed Church here made a record of baptisms in Red Hook as early as 1751.   After 1787, when the Church in Upper Red Hook was built, it was called the " New Red Hook Church," and the one near Hoffman's Mills was called the " Old Red Hook Church."   It is clear, then, that the vicinity of this mill was the point to which the name of Red Hook was applied as early as 1751.   In our old town records, in 1789, " Mickle More " is roadmaster, " from Henry King's to Col. Hoffman's."   In 1790, it is " from Henry King's to Red Hook Landing," and so again in 1791.   In 1792, Henry Lyle being Town Clerk, it is " from Henry King's to Reed's Store," and it is to Read's store until 1799, when the road district is as follows: " From the River road to James Wilson's, to manor line, and from Zacharias Hoffman's to Red Hook Landing road."   It is never to " Read Hook."   In 1774 William Davies gave a receipt to Johannis Smith for " twenty skepples wheat and four fowles for James Bogardus," and dated at " Red Hook."   *Hoek* is the Dutch for corner, and Red Hook simply means Red Corner; and we have no doubt the corner occupied by Hoffman's Mill had its buildings painted red, and that this was the origin of Red Hook.   In those days the farm building went unpainted, and when the Hoffmans painted they used red, as most everybody else did.   The Hoffmans were an important people, and we have no doubt their corner was, in its day, an important one to the neighborhood.   The name of Red Hook was applied to the Upper several years before it reached the Lower village of Red Hook.   But we have seen no evidence that it reached the Upper village in advance of the church.

There were Palatine Hoffmans, and there were many people of the name in Red Hook, not related to those concerned in this history.

CHAPTER XII.

THE VAN BENTHUYSENS AND HEERMANCES.

BARENT VAN BENTHUYSEN, who bought one-fourth of the present town of Red Hook from Peter Schuyler, in 1725, was a native of Albany.   He married in Kingston, April 17, 1699, Altje, daughter of Jan Elting, and widow of Aart Gerritse, eldest son of Gerrit Aartsen.   He was thus related by marriage to two of the patentees of the tract of land in this town called Kipsbergen in the beginning of our history.   He became a widower, and married for a second wife Jannetje, daughter of Gerrit Aartsen, and thus sister to the wives of Hendricus and Andries Heermance, on the 21st of April, 1701.   As we have learned, the children of Gerrit Aartsen took Van Wagenen for a family name.   And we learn from the Kingston Church records that Barent Van Benthuysen and Jannetje Van Wagenen had children baptized as follows: Gerrit, January 25, 1702; Jan, February 6, 1704; Catryntje, September 28, 1707; Anna, May 7, 1710; Peter, February 24, 1712; Jacob, October 3, 1714; Abraham, August 24, 1718.

Barent Staats, another of the partners to the purchase of the Schuyler patent in 1725, disposed of most, if not all, of his lands to other parties, some of it passing into the possession of the Van Benthuysens and Heermances, who seem to have moved out of Kingston to Red Hook together, at an early date, and simultaneously with the Hoffmans and Elmendorfs. Hendricus Heermance, whose wife was Annatjen Van Wagenen, settled in Rhinebeck, and had six children; Andries Heermance, who married Neeltje Van Wagenen, remained in

Kingston later, and had fourteen children.   It is probable that nearly, if not quite all their children settled on the lands of Barent Van Benthuysen and Barent Staats, in the north part of the precinct of Rhinebeck.

Jacob Heermance, born in Kingston, and probably son of Andries Heermance and Neeltje Van Wagenen, married Catherine Vosburgh, probably daughter of Jan Vosburgh and Cornelia Knickerbocker, on the 30th of December, 1747.   He lived in and probably built the stone house occupied in our recollection by Lewis Beckwith, west of Henry Benner's, on the road from Henry Cotting's (near the post road), to the river, in 1762.   They had four sons and four daughters, as follows: Jacob, John, Andrew, Martin, Cornelia, Anna, Dorothea, and Eleanor.

Martin Heermance married the daughter of Dr. Hans Kiersted, who owned the farm now the property of Eugene Wells, in this village.   Martin Heermance succeeded his father-in-law in the possession of this property, and built the present spacious and substantial brick mansion in 1793.

Eleanor Heermance married Peter Contine.   They lived in the village of Upper Red Hook from 1785 to 1791, the road east of the village during the time being from Warachkameek to Peter Contine's.   We assume that his pursuit was that of a merchant, for we find him, after this date, keeping a store at what is now Barrytown Landing, and in 1798 in the same pursuit at the Hoffman's, or Red Hook Landing.

Jacob J. Heermance was found by the road district in 1792– and 1793, where it found Peter Contine, and he was probably his successor in business.   He was his brother-in-law.

Dorothea Heermance married Henry DeWitt, and in 1794– 5–6–7 he was found by the road district from Warrachkameek where it had found his brothers-in-law, Peter Contine and Jacob J. Heermance, and probably in the same employment.

Anna Heermance married Isaac Stoutenburgh, Jr., and they were found at the same corner in 1798.

Cornelia Heermance married David Van Ness.   From 1790 to 1798 we find him in the house which became Stephen Holmes' Inn, in 1798, Ebenezer Punderson's house in 1802, and the residence of Wilhelmus Benner, at Punderson's death, about 1836.

What were known to us as the Kittle, the Lyle, and the Punderson houses in 1838 were large and stately edifices, with gambrel roofs, and two stories high. They were the most important houses, and doubtless occupied by the most important personages in the vicinity in their day. We assume that the Punderson house was built by David Van Ness, and it is a well authenticated tradition that the Lyle and Kittle houses were built by one person. A daughter of Harry Lyle says they were both built by the same person, and by a man whose name was Heermance. She says when he had completed the Lyle house, he found the ceilings too low to suit his taste, disposed of it for this reason, and at once built the Kittle house, of brick, and with a higher ceiling. The builder, if a Heermance, was probably either John, Jacob, or Andrew, of the sons of Jacob Heermance and Catherina Vosburgh.

Jacob Thomas was Lieutenant in the company of soldiers enlisted by Henry B. Livingston as Captain in 1775. He was roadmaster on the King's highway from the manor line to the Sawkill, in 1764. He was found in the village of Upper Red Hook, by the Warachkameek road district from 1767 to 1784, a period of seventeen years. His wife was Margaret Teator, and she was sister to the wife of John Fulton, who lived on Turkey Hill, a short distance east of Warachkameek. There is a tradition among the Teators that he built the Kittle house, that he kept a tavern during the Revolutionary War, and sold a great deal of liquor for a great deal of money. He may have been the builder of the two houses with the proceeds of his traffic, and built the second for the reason stated by Mrs. Smith, the daughter of Harry Lyle. It is stated, on the authority of the late Judge Rowley, that he contracted with the father of the late Henry Staats for the brick, at a price which fell greatly below their market value, before the house was completed, and that Staats importuned him in vain, and with liberal offers, for a release from his engagement.

The Lyle House, with the adjacent lands, are now the property of Edward Mooney, the artist, and the Kettle House, which was the residence of Captain Isaac Stoutenburgh in 1798, is now the stately and substantial residence of Dr. John Losee,

In 1768 Janetia Bratt was the owner of a mill in the Cove at the mouth of the White Clay Creek, Thomas Louis being road-master therefrom to the post road. In 1769 the road is from John Van Ness' mill, and it continues thus until 1779, when it is from Widow Van Ness' mill. From this it appears that John Van Ness married Janetia Bratt, and thus became the owner of the mill. The road from the river to the post road, from 1762 to 1778, was from Hoffman's to John Van Ness', and from 1779 to 1787 from Colonel Hoffman's to Widow Van Ness'. In 1789 it is from Widow Van Ness' to Henry King's, and from Henry King's to Red Hook landing, and it is from Henry King's to Widow Van Ness' until 1796. It thus appears that the residence of John Van Ness and his widow, for all these years, was the house near the post road, east of Henry Benner's old place, and which was the residence of Henry Cotting before he purchased the Nicholas Moore Farm, near the village of Upper Red Hook, and which house is not now in existence.

There was a store at the corner north of the residence of Thomas Elmendorf, kept by a family of Heermances, we think from 1802 to 1812, and who were the owners of the property as far back certainly as 1790.

Our old records, commencing in 1748, apply the name of Red Hook nowhere except to the Tivoli landing, and to that for the first time in 1789.

CHAPTER XIII.

OUR PALATINE SETTLERS.

THERE were three immigrations of Palatines to our State in the first quarter of the eighteenth century. The first came in 1709, under Joshua Knockerthal, their minister, and consisted of "fifty-one poor Lutherans from the Lower Palatinate in Germany"—viz.: ten men, ten women and twenty-one children. They settled at Quasek creek, now called Chamber's creek, in Orange County. The second came with Governor Robert Hunter in 1710, and the third in 1722 under Governor Burnet.

It concerns our present purpose to deal with those only who came here with Governor Hunter.

The first installment of these people came in the ship, Lyon, which arrived in the port of New York in June, 1710. Having contagious diseases among them, they were detained on Governor's Island. On the 24th of July, 1710, Governor Hunter wrote to the Board of Trade, in England, that "all the Palatine ships, separated by the weather, are arrived safe except the Herbert Frigat, where our tents and arms are. She was cast away on the east end of Long Island, on the 7th of July; the men are safe, but our goods much damaged. We still want the Bercly Castle, which we left at Portsmouth. The poor people have been mighty sickly, but recover apace. We have lost above four hundred and seventy of our number. Soon after our arrival, I sent the surveyor with some skilled men to survey the land on the Mohaks river, particularly the Skohare. * * * These lands, however, I believe will be noways fit for the design in hand, being very good lands which here bears no pines, and lyes very remote. I shall, however, be able to carry it on elsewhere, for there is no want of pines; but the pine land being good for nothing, the difficulty will be in finding such a situation as will afford good land for their settlement near the pine lands. I am in terms with some who have lands on the Hudson River fit for that purpose, which I intend to view next week with Dr. Bridges, who is now with me, and gives me good encouragement."

On the 3d of October, 1710, he wrote to the same parties: " I have been obliged to purchase a tract of land on Hudson's River from Mr. Leviston, consisting of 6,000 acres, for £400 of this country money, that is £266 English, for the planting of the greatest division of the Palatines. It has these advantages, that, besides the goodness of the soil, it is adjacent to the pines, which by the conveyance we are entitled to, and a place where ships of fifteen feet water may go without difficulty. Over against it, but a little further, I have found a small tract of about a mile in length along the river, which has, by some chance, not been granted, though pretended to have been purchased of the Indians by some, where I have planted the remainder.   They are not all transported as yet, but I am making all possible dispatch that I may prevent the Winter.   This tract also lies near the pines."

The object in settling these people on good land near the pines, with their families, was to enable them to make tar and pitch for the English Navy from the pines, and support themselves by cultivating the land on which their tents were pitched.

On the 14th of November, 1710, Governor Hunter again addressed the Board of Trade as follows: "I have now settled the Palatines on good lands on both sides of the Hudson River, about one hundred miles up, adjacent to the pines.   I have planted them in five villages, three on the east side of the river, upon the 6,000 acres I have purchased of Mr. Levingston, about two miles from Rowlof-Jansen's Kill, the other two on the west side, near Sawyer's Creek.   *   *   *   The land on the west side belongs to the Queen, and each family hath a sufficient lot of good arable land, and ships of fifteen foot draught of water can sail up as far as the plantations.   In the Spring I shall set them to work preparing the trees according to Mr. Bridges' directions."

The settlement of these people on this side. of the river was known as East Camp, and that on the other as West Camp. Robert Livingston, besides selling Governor Hunter the lands on which they were settled on this side, entered into a contract with him to subsist them on both sides until they could support themselves.

In reference to these contracts by the Governor, Lord Clarenden wrote to Lord Dartsmouth on the 8th of March, 1711: "I think it unhappy that Colonel Hunter, at his first arrival, in his government fell into.so ill hands, for this Levingston has been known many years in that Province for a very ill man.   He has a mill and a brew-house upon his land, and if he can get the victualling of these Palatines, who are so conveniently posted for his purpose, he will make a very good addition to his estate, and I am persuaded the hopes he has of such a subsistence to be allowed by her Majesty were the chief if not the only inducements that prevailed with him to propose to Colonel Hunter to settle them upon his land, which is not the best place for pine trees. * * * My Lord, upon the whole matter, I am of opinion that if the subsistence proposed be allowed, the consequence will be that Levingston, and some others, will get estates, the Palatines will not be the richer."

Mrs. Lamb, in her History of New York, says of our Palatine settlers: " These earlier German emigrants were mostly mere hewers of wood and drawers of water, differing materially from the class of Germans who have since come among us, and bearing about the same relation to the English and Dutch and French settlers of their time as the Chinese of to-day to the American population of the Pacific coast."   This opinion is the opposite of that expressed by Macauley in his History of England.   He says of these same people: " With French Protestants who had been driven into exile by the edicts of Louis,ı were now mingled German Protestants, who had been driven into exile by his arms.   Vienna, Berlin, Basle, Hamburg, Amsterdam, London swarmed with honest, laborious men, who had once been thriving burghers of Heidelburg or Mannheim, or who had cultivated vineyards on the banks of the Necker and the Rhine.   A statesman might well think that it would be at once generous and polite to invite to the English shores, and to incorporate with the English people, emigrants so unfortunate and so respectable.   Their ingenuity and their diligence could not fail to enrich any land which should afford them an asylum ; nor could it be doubted that they would manfully defend the country of their adoption against him whose cruelty had driven them from the country of their birth."

While the bill to naturalize these people in England was under debate in the British Parllament, Sir John Knight, member for Bristol, said of the Dutchmen whom Mrs. Lamb distinguishes by her preference: " The bill was evidently meant for the benefit, not of French Protestants and German Protestants, but of Dutchmen, who would be Protestants, Papists or Pagans for a guilder a head, and who would no doubt be as ready to sign the declaration against transubstantiation in England as to trample on the cross in Japan.   They would come over in multitudes. They would swarm in every public office. They would collect the customs and gauge the beer barrels. 　*　* For Hans, after filling the pockets of his huge trunk hose with our money by assuming the character of a native, would, as soon as a press gang appeared lay claim to the privileges of an alien."

It is perfectly understood by those who have given the matter a thought, that the English, the French and the Hollanders, with whom Mrs. Lamb attempts to disparage our early German settlers, came here to make money in commerce and trade, while the latter were here to maintain the freedom and purity of their consciences. They had attained that moral and intellectual elevation in which they knew that their masters and rulers were tyrants—men who had been debased by luxury, and lost the sense of human responsibility by the long exercise of usurped or hereditary power—and that it had become their duty to God, to themselves, and to their fellowmen to resist them, and, failing of success, to escape the yoke by flight into God's wilderness, and, if need be, beyond the seas. They had thus developed within them a power of will and purpose to which unjust governments, and the world of conceit, cunning and venality must, sooner or later, succomb. While they were hewing wood and drawing water, and subduing the earth, in fulfillment of God's requirements, cunning, avaricious and domineering men were absorbing their lands, limiting their opportunities, crippling their skill, appropriating the profits of their toil, and hoping to secure in their bondage the source of a princely and perpetual income. But they had within them the elements of a perpetual growth, and they soon "swelled beyond the measure of their chains," and they are now the owners of the soil they have conquered, and the masters of their own persons. Whole counties and townships of land were acquired by the patentees for nothing save a trifling quit rent at the end of seven or ten years. And when the exiled Palatine took fifty of their acres in the wilderness, and agreed to fence them, and build houses and barns upon them, fell the trees and dig out the stumps, and pay an annual rent of a schepel of wheat to the acre during his and his wife's lives, their children to lose the fruit of their toil thereafter, it was with the hope of winning a heavenly reward for earthly sacrifices. But God has put a limit to the profit which the fortunate and strong man may make out of the weak and unfortunate.

Governor Hunter's plan of setting the Palatines to making tar and pitch, and raising hemp for the British Navy, in order to indemnify the Government for the expense of sending them over here, and maintaining them until they could be settled and set to work, proved a failure, not because the men proved intractable, but because the scheme was, in its nature and circumstances, wholly impracticable. The Palatines were greatly distressed, and complained, and the Government received very small return in tar, pitch and hemp for its outlay. They blamed Governor Hunter, and he blamed them, and they made a mutual defence before the English Board of Trade, in 1720. Their defence is on record in the third volume of the Documentary History of New York, p. 423

Now, whatever may have been the other sides of these questions, there was evidently a purpose, favored by Governor Hunter, that the land of Schoharie, which they claimed, and whither they had gone, should not be owned by these people, but that it should be owned by some non-resident favorites, perhaps for a personal consideration, to whom they should forever remain mere " hewers of wood and drawers of water." The fact that they saw and resisted the doom that was preparing for them, proves that they had attained a development of mind and soul beyond the reach of the measure which Mrs. Lamb was able to apply them.

CHAPTER XIV.

GERMAN REFORMED CHURCH.

THE first church in Rhinebeck, and probably in Dutchess County, was the " High Dutch Reformed Protestant Church," which, until the year 1800, stood near the old cemetery, on the post-road, three miles north of the present village of Rhinebeck, at what is now known as " Pink's Corner." It came into the town with the German Palatines, and probably as early as 1715. There were among these people both Lutherans and Calvinists, and they built the first church together, and remained joint owners until 1729, when " contentions arising between them, they thought best for both parties to separate, and to have each a church to themselves," and the Lutherans sold out to the " Reformed Protestants " on the 10th day of December, 1729, receiving for their interest in the church and four acres of ground, " twenty-five pounds current money of New York." The money was paid by Hendrick Shever, Joseph Rykart, Barent Siperly, and Karell Neher, for the Lutherans, and received by France Kelder, Cœnradt Bearinger, Wendell Polver and Jacob Wolleben for the Reformers. In a bond given by the Lutherans to the Reformers, they say, " in a deed from Henry Beekman, son of Col. Henry Beekman, deceased ; John Rutsen and Catherine, his wife, daughter of Col. Henry Beekman ; and Gilbert Livingston and Cornelia, his wife, another daughter of Col. Henry Beekman, to Barent Siperly, Jr., for a farm at Rhynbeek, on the fifth day of March, 1721, containing fifty-six acres of land, was reserved four acres of land whereon the Church of Rhynbeek *then stood*, for the use of a church and church-yard, and so to remain forever for that use ; " and, also, that " Gilbert Livingston and his wife, with the consent of the said Barent Siperly, Jr., did, on the first day of August, 1724, lease the said farm unto Hendrick Beam, with the said reservation of the said four acres for the church."

We learn from this that four acres had been assigned for the church, and the church built thereon before 1721 ; that the reservation was again made in 1724, when the land changed owners; and that joint ownership continued to 1729, when the German Reformers became sole proprietors. On the fourth of December, 1747, "Catherine Pawling, of Rinebeek Precinct, in Dutchess County, Province of New York, widow," gave to Nicolas Stickell, Jacob Sickener, Philip More, Hendrick Berringer, Jacob Drum, and Jacob Berringer, "being the present Elders and Deacons of the High Dutch Reformed Protestant Church of Rinebeek," a deed for this church and lands, in which she again recites the leases to Siperly and Beam, and says: "Whereas, by the above recited leases there is no provision made or liberty given to the inhabitants of Rinebeek aforesaid to lett, ride or make use of any wood on the commons of Rinebeek aforesaid; and whereas, the farm above menrioned is lying in lott number two (in Rinebeek patent) belonging unto the said Catharine Pawling, who has caused the said four acres for the use of the Church aforesaid to be surveyed, and is beginning on the west side of the King's road, next to and bounding on the land of Zacharias Smith, by a stone set in the ground; from thence south twenty-six degrees east, twelve chains and forty-four links to a stone set in the ground; then north fifty degrees east, four chains and nine links; then north, twenty-two degrees west, three chains fifty-nine links; then north, thirty-four degrees west, seven chains eighty-eight links; and then north, sixty-eight degrees west, three chains and twenty links, to the place of beginning, containing four acres, the breadth of the road being first deducted." The four acres thus described she deeded to the elders and deacons named, with the privilege " to cutt, ride and carry away all sorts of wood and stone for the use of said ground, and for fire-wood for the minister and the church, on the waste ground or commons, or unimproved lands of the said Catharine Pawling, her heirs and assigns, for the only proper use and benefit and behoof of the inhabitants residing in Rinebeek professing and practising the Protestant religion (according to the rules and method as is agreed and concluded by the Synod National held at Dortreght in the year 1618 and 1619), as it is now used to exercise their worship in said church, and to bury their dead in the cemetery or burying-place forever; and also for the use of a minister, when one shall be called there, as aforesaid, and that the same ground and premises and privileges shall be converted to no other use or uses whatever," signed by Catharine Pawling, December 24, 1747, in presence of Alida Rutsen and Henry Livingston. When the church was discontinued on these premises, in 1800, the land reverted to the heirs of Catharine Pawling, or to the sole use of the cemetery. It is now, with the exception of about one-fourth of an acre, appropriated for farming purposes, and cattle are herded among the tombstones. By what right this is done we have not learned, except it is by the right of possession.

The records of this church while in union with the Lutherans, if any were kept, are lost. Johannes Spaller, a Lutheran, was minister at the " Kamps and Rinback," in 1723, and doubtless ministered to the Lutherans in the Union Church at this date. We have no positive knowledge of the minister who served the German Reformed people during the union. John Frederick Hager came to the Camps with the German people in 1710. On the 8th of October, 1715, he, with John Cast and Godfrey de Wolven, on behalf of themselves and upwards of sixty families of the Palatines in Dutchess County, petitioned Governor Hunter for license to build a church in Kingsbury. Corwin, in his Manual, classes him with the Reformed ministers. This being so, he probably served both the Kingsbury and Rhinebeck people. And the Rhinebeck may have been the Kingsbury church.

After the separation, in 1730, a book of records was opened in the Reformed Church, which is now in our possession. The first baptisms were recorded on the 5th of April, 1730, and the first in the list is Johannes, the son of Zacharias Schmidt. The writer of this history is the grandson of this Johannes Schmidt. The title page to the book, in German, is in the hand-writing of George Michal Weiss, and is as follows, in English : " General Church Book of the Reformed Congregation in Reyn Beek, Organized and Established by G. M. Weiss, Preacher for the time being for the Two Low Dutch Congregations at Kats Kill and Kocks Hocky. Ao. Christi, 1734, May 23d."

From this period on to 1742, there were one hundred and

forty baptisms by George Michael Weiss and George Wilhelm Mancius, a large majority by the latter. On the 27th of June, 1742, the record is again in the unmistakable hand of Dominie Weiss, and this is the beginning of a pastorate of four years in the German church at Rhinebeck, and the Dutch church on the Flats, the churches being a joint charge during this period. His record in the German church terminated on the 22d, and in the Dutch, on the 29th of June, 1746. He baptized two hundred and thirty-three children in the former, and one hundred and twenty in the latter.

Casper Ludwig Schnorr, of the Camp Reformed Church, installed the officers of the Rhinebeck church on the 2d of May, 1747, and presided at the reception of members therein on the 26th of April. The baptisms from 1746 to 1748 are in his hand. He evidently served both churches during this period, and thus established a union which endured for a century.

At the close of Schnorr's labors, Mancius resumed the charge of the church, and did all its work until February 15, 1755. He recorded one hundred and seventeen baptisms in this period, and added eighty members to the church.

Johan Casper Rubel came into the pastorate of the Camp and Rhinebeck churches in 1755. He recorded his first baptism in Rhinebeck on the 18th of May, 1755, and his last on the 30th of September, 1759. He baptized two hundred and twenty children, and added eighty members to the church. His records are those of an easy and rapid writer, and the most orderly, in a well-kept book. He always wrote " Rein Beek " for the name of the precinct.

At the close of Rubel's pastorate, Mancius again came to the help of the church; and, with the exception of three baptisms in the hand of Johannes Casparus Fryenmoet, of Livingston's Manor, on the 25th of October, 1761, he did all the work of the church to May 31st, 1762.

On the 27th of September, 1764, there was a single baptism recorded by Rubel; and on the 25th and 26th of October there are six baptisms and four additions to the church recorded in the hand of Dominie Fryenmoet. On the 25th of June, 1763, Rubel recorded thirteen baptisms and four additions to

the church.   And this is the last we find of his hand in the
records of the church.   Corwin says he was on Long Island
from 1759 to 1783, a violent Tory, calling the American soldiers
" Satan's soldiers "; was deposed in 1784, and died in 1797.

Gerhard Daniel Cock came to America, on invitation of
the Camp church, in November, 1763, and at once took charge
of both churches.   He recorded his first baptism in the Rhinebeck church on the 11th of December, 1763, and his last on
the 24th of July, 1791.   In this pastorate of twenty-eight years,
his record is unbroken,—kept in a legible hand, and in a clear and
orderly manner.   He baptized one thousand eight hundred and
nineteen children, seven hundred of them between the years
1775 and 1785, the period which embraced the seven years of
the Revolutionary War.   In his list of baptisms there were ten
pairs of twins, and eight children born out of wedlock.   He died
at the Camp, now Germantown, in Columbia County, and was
buried under the pulpit of the church there.   The balance of
salary due him was paid to his widow, who gave the receipt
which follows:

" Received German Kamp, October 9th, 1791; from Johannes
Schmid, Gered Halsabel, Elders and Drostis of the Reverend
Gurch of Rinebeck, the sum of Thirty seven pound Eith shil-
lings Tenn Pens in full upon all Demands for Dominie Gered
Daniel Koock Sellere.

I say Received By Me,

Hendrick Benner.   Christina Cok."

At the close of Cock's pastorate, between July 24, 1791,
and June 15, 1794, there are twenty-four baptisms in an unknown hand.

Johan Daniel Schefer came into the pastorate in 1794, and
kept an orderly record in German.   He recorded his first baptism on the 26th of August, 1794, and his last on the 9th of
October, 1799.   He baptised two hundred and nineteen children, of whom the following were twins:

Johannes and Jacob, children of Jacob Berringer and Elis-
abath Reinhard, his wife.

Elisabeth Martha, and Catharine Ann, children of Ezecheal
Valentine and his wife, Catherine.

We find Henry, son of Thomas DeLamater and Christina Pulver, his wife, among Schefer's baptisms, on July 2, 1798. And
we may here remark, that while the German Reformed Church
remained at Rhinebeck, it seemed a matter of indifference to
Van Ettens, Van Wagenens, Van Keurens, Van Vradenburgs,
Van Deusens, Van Hovenburgs, DuBoises, DeLamaters, De-
Witts, Ten Broecks, and the Kips, whether their children were
baptized in the Dutch or German church.

Between July 8, 1800, and September 26, 1802, there are
nine baptisms in an unknown hand; and we think in this
period the new edifice was built, four miles further north, in
what is now Red Hook, on land donated by General
Armstrong, and the church moved to it. But it should be
borne in mind that it did not cease to be the Rhinebeck German
Reformed Church, by this change of location. The precinct of
Rhinebeck, organized in 1734, extended to the Columbia
County line until 1812, when Red Hook received a separate
organization.

Valentine Rudiger Fox came into the pastorate in 1802,
and doubtless commenced it in the new church. He recorded his first baptism in a new book, on the 20th of October,
1802, and his last, on the 27th of July, 1823.*

In this pastorate of twenty-one years, he baptized seven
hundred and twenty-five children, of whom the following were
twins:

Elisa Caroline and Lena Lavinia, children of Abraham
Duft and his wife, Cornelia.   '

John Rudy succeeded Dominie Fox, coming into the pastorate in 1823. His first baptism was recorded on the 2d of
October, 1823, and his last on the 18th of October, 1835. In
this pastorate of thirteen years he baptized two hundred and
forty-eight children, of whom the following were twins: Sally
Margaret and Christina, children of Henry Allendorf and his
wife, Rebecca.

---

* A gentleman who resided in Red Hook when Dominie Fox was the pastor there,
says he was a penurious man, and at the end of his ministry there returned to Germany with considerable money ; that his charge for baptizing a child was two shillings ; and that on one occasion, having been sent for to baptize a child "sick unto
death," he arrived too late, but baptized the dead child, nevertheless, and took the
two shillings.

Up to the pastorate of John Rudy the services of this church were all in German. Rudy preached in both the German and English languages, on alternate Sundays.

Cornelius Gates succeeded Rudy in the pastorate of the Red Hook church, the Camp church having passed under the care of the classis of Poughkeepsie on the 25th of April, 1837, during the pastorate of Rev. Jacob William Hangen, who served thenceforth in connection with the Upper Red Hook Dutch Reformed Church. This church having thus taken the Camp, the Lutherans in a short time thereafter took the Red Hook charge ; and this was the end of the German Reformed Church in Dutchess Connty. All there is left of it in Rhinebeck, where it had its birth, and passed the most prosperous period of its existence, is the old grave-yard, now a cow-yard, at Pink's Corner, within the limits of the old Palatine village of Rein Beek. Stranded between the Dutch Church on the Flats and that erected in the village of Upper Red Hook, in 1785, it fell a very easy prey to the Lutherans, with whom its people had freely inter-married, and toward whom they naturally gravitated. From first to last, its ministers resided at the Camp, now the Germantown church.

CHAPTER XV.

THE RHINEBECK LUTHERAN CHURCH.

THIS church came into being simultaneously with the German church at Pink's Corner. If it kept any records while in union with the latter, before 1729, they are not now in existence. It sold out its interest in the church at Pink's Corner on the 10th of December, 1729. On the 4th of November preceding, it had applied to Gilbert Livingston for a lot for a church and cemetery, and received the response which follows :

" MEMORANDUM.—This 4th day of November, 1729, have Francis Near and Michael Bonestell asked of me, in behalf of the Lutheran congregation in Rhinebeck, Dutchess County, a piece of ground for the purpose of building a church and making a burying-place for the said congregation, which ground, so said, lies by Barent Sipperly's. For the encouragement of so good a work, I promise in this the same ground in my lot lying, and at a convenient time to measure off to them and to give a transfer for the Lutheran congregation dwelling on land of the late Col. Henry Beekman. In witness whereof I have under-signed this, date as above, at Kingston, Ulster County.

"GILBERT LIVINGSTON."

"The above promissory note was translated from the origi-nal Low Dutch by me, the undersigned, at Clermont, Columbia Co., N. Y., this 2d day of May, 1857.

"AUGUSTUS WACKERHAGEN."

The fruit of this promise was the present church lot and cemetery, containing five acres, three roods and eighteen perches. We do not find a deed for it among the church pa-pers, but possession was doubtless at once obtained. There are tombstones in the graveyard dating back to 1733. The follow-ing letter is also found among the archives of the church:

"NEW YORK, ye 12 Feby., 1759.
"GENTLEMEN:
"I recd. yours of ye 5th inst. concerning that piece of ground I gave for a parsonage. I find your inclinations are to appropriate it for ye use of a schoolmaster, which is also a charitable use. Therefore I freely grant your request, and wish you a great deal of success in your undertakings. I am, with respects, Gen'l, Your Very Obt. Servt.,

"ROBERT G. LIVINGSTON,
"Messrs. FRANZ NEHER, ADAM SCHEFER, DAVID REICHERT."

The farm of twenty-nine and one half acres, sold to Hans. Adam Frederick by the Beekman heirs, on the 20th of October, 1718, was sold by Frederick to Barent Sipperly, on the 1st of April, 1726, for fifteen pounds, New York money. On the 1st day of May, 1768, Michael Sipperly, the son of Barent, sold this land to Henry Tator, Loedewick Elseffer, and Philip Bonesteel, trustees of the Rhinebeck Lutheran Church, forever, for two hundred pounds, New York money.

On the 1st day of May, 1768, Robert G. Livingston, of New York, gave the same parties a life lease for two pieces of ground, both pieces to contain seventeen acres, subject to a rent of six bushels of wheat a year, and to continue during the term of the lives of George Tator, Jr., David Elshever and Frederick Sipperly, the son of George Sipperly.

On the 1st day of June, 1798, John Crooke deeded to Peter Traver, Jost Neher, Frederick Pister, John Seaman, David Lown, Jr., and George Elsheffer, trustees, and their successors, forever, two acres of land for fifty dollars, subject to an annual rent of three pecks of wheat.

On the 8th day of December, 1807, Robert G. Livingston, of Clinton, and his wife, Martha, sold to Nicholas Bonesteel, Zacharias Traver, Johannes Simmon, Zacharias Feller, Andries Teal, and John F. Feller, of the town of Rhinebeck, trustees of St. Peter's Church, for the sum of fifty dollars, three acres and three roods of land for a parsonage lot.

We found also a map of the church lot, for five acres, three roods, eighteen perches, with a map of seven acres, two roods, five perches, on the east side of the road, for a parsonage lot. These maps are without date, and were probably made in 1760.

A lease, dated May 1, 1797, given by the trustees of the church, to Charles Reinold, says he is to have all the lands lying on the east side of the post road, belonging to the church, and the house, until the 1st day of May next, for which he must pay the rent to the landlord, keep the fende in good repair, and transact the business of a clerk of said church. But he is not to cut or carry away any timber or wood from said land, except to make or repair the fence; and when he shall have brought a receipt from the landlord for the rent, he shall have the liberty to cut and carry away such grains as he sows, " providing it be no more than one-third part of the land ;" that is, providing not more than one third part of the land has been put in grain. The church now owns no lands on the east side of the road. Why not, we find no documents to tell us. They were either sold or held under leases which expired, and were not renewed.

On the 8th of January, 1808, the church lands, independently of the church lot, were the property of Robert G. Livingston and his wife, Martha, and they disposed of them in a

conveyance bearing this date, to Samuel Hake, and are described as being now in the possession of the church, and containing thirty-two acres. The church held these lands under a
perpetual lease, and paid an annual rent of ten bushels and
twenty-eight quarts of wheat. On the 1st day of May, 1857,
this rent was due to James De Peyster, Frederick De Peyster
and Robert G. L. De Peyster, heirs and devisees of Samuel
Hake; and they released the land from this incumbrance at
this date, in a deed of absolute ownership to Henry Cotting,
Michael Traver, John A. Traver, Stephen Traver, Jacob Teal,
Philip Sipperly, John H. Rikert, Henry A. Cramer, and Lewis
D. Elseffer, trustees of the church, for two hundred and seventy-
five dollars.

The first church edifice was undoubtedly built in 1730; for
we find in the archives of the church the following statement
and receipts: "Anno, 1730, cost of glass for the Lutheran
church, four pounds twelve shillings, Received from Carl Nier
two pounds." This is in the handwriting of Petrus Bogardus.
"Kingston, June 14, 1731, Received from Carl Nier three pounds
eight shillings in part payment for plank for the church in
Dutchess county, For Juryan Tappen, G. Hends. Slecht," " September 21, 1731, Received from Carl Nier the sum of forty
golden for hinges for the church. Benjamin Van Steenburgen."
This is the English of papers written in Dutch. They tell us
that the Carl Neher whose tombstone tells us that he died on
the 25th of January, 1733, and is the oldest in its burying ground
was actively employed in the erection of the edifice of the
church in 1730. Of the cost and character of this house there
are no records to give us information. " The Stone Church,"
the name by which it has been distinguished for more than a
century, was built some time before the Revolution. In 1824
this was remodeled and enlarged, and embellished with its present tall and handsome tower. The expense of this improvement was about three thousand dollars, and we recall the name
of Philip Schuyler, Esq., as one of the building committee, and
that of Stephen McCarty as the builder. In 1843 it was stuc-
coed and otherwise improved at an expense of some eleven
hundred dollars.

The present parsonage house was built in 1798, for Dominie Quitman. It is therefore more than eighty years old. It is a commodious dwelling, well preserved for its years. When Dominie N. W. Goertner added the Red Hook church to his charge, or soon after, he took up his residence in that village, and the church let the parsonage until the two churches became independent charges. It was at one time let to Coert DuBois, at another to Rev. Stephen Schuyler, and we think to Cornelius Nelson, and others.

Where the parsonage was located before 1798, if there was one, we can find no one to tell us. The following receipt was found among its papers:

" Received Red Hook, 12th April, 1793, of the Rev. George Henry Pfeiffer seventeen and a half bushels wheat on account of back rent due before the death of Robert G. Livingston (the elder), Esq.

"17 1-2 Bu. Wheat.   JNO. READE."

ITS BOOK OF RECORDS.

The oldest book in the possession of the church has lost a number of its pages, and is an imperfect record.

At one time it evidently contained a list of all the families, with the names of all the children in each, who constituted the Lutheran populations of Queensburg and Rhinebeck, the church in the former, in later days, becoming the Camp Church. The Queensburg record seems complete. It contains fifty-four families, numbering three hundred and twenty-five persons. From the Rhinebeck list a number of leaves are missing, and it is not possible now to tell how many families there were, or how many persons they contained. A paper written by Christoval Hagadorn, at Queensburg, in 1734, shows that these records were made by his hand.

The record of baptisms is also incomplete. Thirty-six baptisms by Johannes Spahler are missing. He baptized one hundred and eighty-four children. The first on record was that of Peter Berg, son of Christian Berg, on Nov. 20, 1733, numbered thirty-seven; and the last, that of P. Dederick, on March 28, 1736. Dominie Hartwick bears testimony in a record at the head of one of the pages, that these baptisms were by Dominie Spahler.* He records no marriages, confirmations, or communion services, in this book. From March 28, 1746, to July 6, 1758, the record is complete, and all in the hand of Johan Christoval Hartwig. In this period of eleven years, there is not one in which he is not present and at work with the people of this church. In 1746, he records twenty-eight baptisms, six in Ancram; in 1747, thirty-nine, two in Ancram; in 1748, forty-six, two in Ancram, six in Staatsburg; in 1749, forty-nine, two in Ancram, two in Staatsburg; in 1750, fifty-six, ten in Ancram, one in Staatsburg; in 1751, thirty-one; in 1752, forty-five; in 1753, thirty; in 1754, thirty-three; in 1755, five; in 1756, twenty-seven; in 1757, five. There are here three hundred and ninety-two baptisms. At the head of one of the pages, in 1751, he makes a note of the fact that he has returned from Pennsylvania; but there is no evidence that he surrendered the charge of the church here when he went there. He records sixty marriages and thirty-four confirmations. Of ten persons confirmed by him in 1748, one had been baptized by Van Dreissen, six by Berkenmeyer, one by Vas, one by Maucius, and one by Spahler. Of seven confirmed in 1749, one had been baptized by Van Dreissen, one by Mancius, two by Spahler, and three by Berkenmeyer. It does not follow that any of these persons were baptized in Rhinebeck, though it is probable some of them were. Vas and Mancius were in Kingston, and Van Dreissen in Columbia County, and, so far as we can learn, had never been in Rhinebeck. Spahler served the Camps, and Rhinebeck, as early as 1723; and he may have baptized the children in one place or the other. Berkenmeyer had been at the Camps frequently, and the following document shows that he had made at least one visit to Rhinebeck.

" REYNBECK, 1744, June 6.

" Received from ye vestry of Rynbeck two pounds tenn and

*A deed to Johannes Spaller, dated 1723, for land now in the possession of Samuel Ten Broeck, calls him "minister at the Kamps and Rinbach." This was when the Lutherans were united with the Reformers, at Pink's corner.

six shillings, in behalf of ye money for ye minister and ye assurance ; I say Received by me.

"£2 : 16 : 0.   W. C. BERKENMEYER."*

Spahler and Hartwick † both served the Camp and Rhinebeck churches.   Johannes Frederick Reis succeeded the latter
in 1760 and became the pastor of the Wertemburg, as well as
of the Camp, Churchtown and Rhinebeck churches.   He died
in 1791, and was buried at Churchtown.   Whether he served
the Tarbush church also, we have not learned.   That he did an
efficient work in the Rhinebeck church, his record clearly testi-
fies.   His pastorate commenced on the 7th day of March, 1760,
and ended on the 5th of January, 1783.   We find no record of
marriages or burials in his hand.   On a Sunday in 1783, he had
one hundred and fifty persons with him at the communion
table.   He recorded the baptisms of eight hundred and fifteen
children.

George Henrich Pfeiffer succeeded Reis in the pastorate.   He
recorded his first baptism on the 17th of May, 1784, and the
last on January 29, 1798, serving the church fourteen years.
He baptised six hundred and sixty children, and recorded the
marriage of three hundred and thirty-eight couples.   He wrote
a legible but peculiar hand, and kept a complete record.   A
tombstone in the Rhinebeck churchyard closes his history, as
follows :

   "*Sacred to the memory of* GEO. H. PFEIFFER, *a native of Germany, pastor of the Lutheran congregation in Rhinebeck, who
died Oct. 26, 1827, aged about 80 years.*"

Frederick Henry Quitman succeeded Pfeiffer in the pastorate,
in 1798.   He recorded his first baptism on the 18th of February,
1798, and his last on the 23d of August, 1830.   The last in his

---

* On page 594, the Documentary History of New York tells us that William
Christov Berkenmeyer was a protestant Lutheran minister "in ye city and county
of Albany in 1746."

† John Christover Hartwick obtained a grant of 21,500 acres of land from the
government in 1754.   He died at the residence of Mrs. Judge Livingston, in Clermont, on the 17th of July, 1796, aged 82 years and 6 months, and was buried at the
Camp Lutheran Church.   His remains were subsequently removed to Albany and
buried under the pulpit of the Ebenezer Lutheran Church of that city.   Hartwick
Seminary, at Cooperstown, is named in his honor ; was erected and is largely sup-
ported with means left for that purpose in his will.

own hand bears date September 21, 1826. Between this date and the former, there is a record of 69 baptisms, evidently by him, but entered by another. There are thus one thousand five hundred and twenty baptisms to his credit. His marriages number seven hundred and eight couples. Among these we find that of Rev. Augustus Warkerhagen to Mary Mayer, and that of Rev. Frederick G. Mayer to Margaret Kirk. Among the baptisms we note those of Robt. Clermont, and Edward, sons of Edward, and Fitz William Pitt, son of Philip Livingston George Bethune, son of Benjamin Schultz, and Walter, son of William Scott. Under the head of "Solemn Interments," he records that on the 27th of September, 1809, Philip Coopernail died from a fractured skull, occasioned by being thrown from a horse; and that on the 21st of August, 1809, Jane Van Keuren, wife of Frederick Berringer, was instantly killed by a stroke of lightning. He was buried in the cemetery of the Rhinebeck church, and his tomb bears the following inscription;

"*Frederick Henry Quitman, born in the Duchy of Cleves, Westphalia, Aug. 7, 1760. Died at Rhinebeck, June 26, 1832.*"

A tablet in the church tells us that his wife, Elizabeth Hueck, died Feb. 24, 1805, aged 37 years. Gen. John Quitman, the distinguished soldier, and Governor of Mississippi, was his son.

Rev. William J. Eyer succeeded him in the pastorate. His first baptism was recorded on the 24th of October, 1828, and his last on the 17th of March, 1836. He recorded the baptism of one hundred and forty-six children, and four marriages, the last dated February 28th, 1833. We presume it was about this date when he ceased to minister to the Rhinebeck church, and devoted himself exclusively to his Wertemburgh charge.

Rev. N. W. Goertner succeeded Dominie Eyer. He recorded his first baptism in January, 1837, and his last, on the 24th of October, 1845. He baptized one hundred and seventeen children, and buried ninety-eight people. We find no record of his marriages. It was during his ministry that the Red Hook German Reformed church was brought into the Lutheran fold, and added to his charge. He took up his residence in Red Hook, and we presume the record of his marriages in both churches is to be found there.

Rev. Dr. Charles Shaeffer succeeded Goertner, and the only record of his work we can find is the following, "transferred from the book of Zion Church, Red Hook, by Frederick M. Bird."

Confirmations: Seven in 1846; ten in 1847; two in 1848; four in 1849; nine in 1850.

Rev. Dr. Strobel succeeded Dr. Schaeffer, and, like him, left his records in Red Hook, and, therefore, beyond our present reach. There are thirteen confirmations transferred out of the Red Hook to the Rhinebeck book by Frederick M. Bird, the first dated on Whitsunday, 1852, and the last on May 16, 1858. After Dr. Strobel's pastorate, the Red Hook and Rhinebeck churches became independent charges.

Rev. Frederick M. Bird succeeded Dr. Strobel. His first baptism is dated December 6, 1860, and his last in June, 1862. He baptized twenty-two children, married eight couples, confirmed ten, and buried ten persons. He states the membership of his church, "as near as can be computed," at one hundred and two persons.

Rev. George W. Schmucker succeeded Mr. Bird. He recorded his first baptism on the 25th of December, 1862, and the last on the 1st of April, 1871. He baptised twenty-two children, married twenty-two couples, confirmed thirty-three, and buried seventy-three persons.

Rev. Charles Koerner succeeded Mr. Schmucker. He recorded his first baptism on the 1st of May, 1870, and his last on the 18th of October, 1880. He baptized six children, married six couples, confirmed eleven, and buried seventeen persons.

Rev. Samuel G. Finkel succeeded Dominie Koerner, commencing his pastorate in 1871. He recorded his first baptism on the 11th of August, 1871, and his last on the 24th of March, 1878. He baptized twenty-seven children, married four couples, confirmed forty-five, and buried seventy-two persons.

Rev. J. A. Earnest is the present incumbent. He has the confidence and affections of his people, and there is no reason why, having long life and adequate support, he should not be in the beginning of a long pastorate.

P. S.—A baptism recorded in the Pultz family says it took place in "Stadtsburger Kircke," in Rhinebeck. This was in 1756. Whatever was done in Staatsburg was recorded in Rhinebeck. The church at Staatsburgh has passed out of the recollection of the oldest people living. Whether the Rhinebeck minister ceased to go to Staatsburgh when he went to Wittenburgh, nobody knows. The Staatsburgh church had no records except in Rhinebeck. It is certain the Wittenburgh church grew out of the Rhinebeck, not the Staatsburgh church.

CHAPTER XVI.

REFORMED DUTCH CHURCH.

THE first step in the history of the Reformed Dutch Church on the Flatts was taken when Henry Beekman presented to Lawrence Osterhout, Jacob Kip and William Traphagen, for themselves and "the rest of the inhabitants of the North Ward, in Dutchess County," the following deed:

"To all Christian people to whom this present writing shall or may come, Henry Beekman, of the city of New York, gentleman, sends greeting: Know *yee* that the said Henry Beekman for the love, good will and affection which he hath and bears toward the inhabitants, and those that shall hereafter be the inhabitants, of the North Ward in Dutchess County and province of New York, hath given, granted, and by these presents doth freely, clearly and absolutely give and grant unto the said inhabitants, being of the profession as is practiced in the Reformed Church of Holland, all that certain lot of land in Dutchess County, in the north ward, situated on the southwesterly side of a large plain near the now gristmill of the said Henry Beekman, lying in the corner of the King's road, and that which parts therefrom easterly to the neighborhood of Sepascot, where now Simon Westfall lives, being the southwesterly corner of 'the arable land now in the occupation of said Henry Beekman, to contain there, in one square piece, two acres of land ; and also another tract of land, situate, lying and being in the north ward, in Dutchess County aforesaid, on the north side of a certain creek, called Landsman's Kill, near the

house of William Schut, beginning at a stone put in the ground
on the north side of the said creek; from thence, running north
twenty chains, to a stone put in the ground; then east, one degree south, nineteen chains, to a white oak saplin, marked;
then south twenty chains to the said creek; then along the
same as it winds and turns to the first station; being bounded
to the south by the creek, and on other sides by land of the
said Henry Beekman; containing forty and four acres, two
quarters and thirty and seven perches:—To have and to hold
the said two parcels of land to be hereby granted, and every
part and parcel thereof, unto the inhabitants aforesaid, which
now are, or hereafter forever shall be the inhabitants of the
said ward, for the use, and in the manner following: that is to
say, that two elders and two deacons shall annually be chosen
and appointed by majority votes of the said inhabitants being
of the profession aforesaid, and shall be approved of by the
Dutch Reformed minister, elders and deacons of the Dutch
Reformed Church of Kingston, in the county of Ulster, every
year, to act as trustees until they shall be in quality to call a
minister of their own, who then, with the other two elders and
two deacons so chosen and appointed as aforesaid, shall and
may act according to the establishment of the Reformed Church
of Holland; and that the said congregation may in the meanwhile, and likewise hereafter, erect and build on said two acres
of land, such church or meeting house, and other buildings as
to them shall seem meet and convenient; and that the remainder of said two acres of land they may appropriate for a com
mon burying place according to the custom and discipline of
the said church and such lands, and not otherwise; and the
other tract shall be Imployed to the benefit and behoof of the
church forever; and the said congregation shall maintain and
keep the said two acres of land, or such part thereof as they shall
think convenient, in a good and sufficient fence, and shall
build thereon some or one building as is hereby intended, within the space of three years now next ensuing, and in neglect
whereof, or that any time hereafter the said two acres of land
and premises hereby granted or intended to be granted, shall
be neglected and abolished, contrary to what it is intended to

be given for, that in any such case or cases, the before recited tracts or parcels of land to *Revoline* its property to the said Henry Beekman, his heirs and assigns, as if such instrument as these presents had never been made. And the said inhabitants being of the profession as aforesaid; or such minister, elders and deacons as shall hereafter be called, chosen or appointed, shall have liberty to cut, break or carry away any stone, or wood, or timber from any part of the unimproved lands of said Henry Beekman: that is to say, for the use of said land and premises, and toward the building of such buildings as shall be erected and made on the said land, or any part thereof.

"In witness whereof, the said Henry Beekman put his hand and seal, this 26th day of August, Anno Dom. 1730.

"Provided, nevertheless, and it is the true intent and meaning of these presents, and of the parties to the same, that nothing herein contained shall extend, or be construed to grant to any person or persons whatsoever, the liberty or lysense to cut or carry away any timber, wood or stone, or other things whatsoever, on or off from the wood called Book Boss, or any other of the lands of said Henry Beekman, but where the same shall be necessary or convenient and used for building a church, school house, chapel, meeting house, or building on the lot of ground aforesaid, and for no other use or purpose whatever; neither shall any person sell any wine, rum, brandy, beer, cider, or other spirits, nor peddle, trade merchandise on the hereby granted premises, or any part thereof; and in case anything shall be done contrary to the meaning of these presents, this deed to be void, and the estate to revert to the said Henry Beekman, his heirs and assigns, as if the same had never been made.

"HENRY BEEKMAN, [L. S.]
"Witnesses,
"BARRENT VAN WAGENEN,
"ALBERT PAWLING."

The first election of church officers under this deed was held on the 28th of June, 1731. Two elders chosen were Hendricus Heermance and Jacob Kip, and the deacons, Jacobus Van Etten and Isaac Kip. The elders and two deacons were thus elected annually and approved by the minister and consistory of the Kingston church, as required by the terms of this deed, until 1742, when the church on the Flatts found " itself in quality" to support a minister in connection with the German Reformed Church, at Rhinebeck.   All the records in this period of eleven years, of the election and installation of church officers, are in the handwriting of Dominie Petrus Vas, of Kingston.   Besides these, there are receipts for money paid him, over his own signature, for every year from 1733 to 1742 ; and there were persons received into the membership of the church here in every other year, in the same period, and a record made of their names, in every instance in the hand of Dominie Vas. There is a record in the same period of one hundred and twenty-five baptisms and thirty-eight marriages.   Of the baptisms ninety-two are in the hand of Dominie Vas, twenty-eight in that of Dominie George Wilhelm Mancius, also of Kingston, and five in that of Dominie Cornelius Van Schie, of Poughkeepsie.   Of the marriages a large majority are, also, in the hand of Dominie Vas.

That a house was built as early as 1733 we think quite certain.   The deed required it to be built by this time, and old monuments, still to be found in its graveyard, tell us that the ground was appropriated for burial purposes in this year.   It is not probable that this step would have been taken in advance of the erection of the edifice necessary to secure the title to the property.   We assume, therefore, that the house was built in due time, and that services were conducted in it, as occasion required, by the minister from Kingston, for the baptism of children, the publication of intended marriages, the reception of church members, and the installation of the officers required by the deed.

The first meeting of the consistory on record was held on the 11th of July, 1741, and its proceedings, recorded in the Dutch language, were as follows, in English :

" Proceedings of a meeting of the consistory of the church on the Flatts, by coll. Henry Beekman's mill, in Dutchess county, July 11, 1741.

"After mature deliberation, we have thought good for weighty reasons that the men should purchase their seats for each family for one pound ten shillings each place. The four places on the left hand of coll. Beekman's Bench, near the door, shall be let for two shillings yearly, each place, as long as the consistory think right. The justices of the peace shall be next. When it happens that the gallery shall be made in the church, then the males in the two first pews in the right and left hand in the church shall leave their places for women's benches, and shall have their places again in the gallery. All the first comers in the benches must make room for the next."

The elders at this time were Andries Heermance, Roeloff Kip, Gose Van Wagenen, and Gysbert Westfall; the deacons, Juyre Tremper, Jan Van Etten, Hendrick Kip, and Mathews Earnest. They held a second consistory meeting on Oct. 1, 1741, the proceedings of which were as follows;

"Proceedings in a meeting of the consistory of the church on the Flatts by coll. Henry Beekman's mill, in Dutchess county.

After mature deliberation, we have thought good for weighty reasons that the females shall have their places for life for six shillings, and at their deaths their daughters, or any of their near relatives, shall have their places for the same price of six shillings. Moreover, the first comers in the bench must make room for the next. We have thought good that no women let any man sit in their places, or they shall forfeit their seats."

George Michael Weiss came into the pastorate of this church in 1742, and served it, in connection with the German Reformed Church, until 1746. In this period there is a record of one hundred and twenty-six baptisms, and one hundred and fifteen additions to the church membership.

From the 15th of April, 1746 to 1750, there is apparently no settled pastor. There were in the mean time sixty-one baptisms; fifty-five of these were by George Wilhelm Mancius, and six by Dominie Goetschius. There were in this period thirty marriages recorded in a strange hand; but since nearly all the baptisms were by Mancius, the marriages were probably also by him, and recorded from slips by the church clerk. There were six additions to the membership of the church in the same time. Their names are recorded in the unmistakable hand of Mancius, who seems to have stood this infant church in good stead, as he did the German church at Rhinebeck, in the day of its need.

Eggo Tonkens Van Hovenburg came into the pastorate of the church, it appears, on the 23d of December, 1750, and continued therein to the 26th of February, 1763. There are eight hundred and sixteen baptisms, and seventy-six marriages recorded in his hand.

From the close of Van Hovenburgh's pastorate to March 26th, 1769, there was no settled pastor, the church being served at intervals by Gerhard Daniel Cock, of the Camp and Rhinebeck German Reformed churches, Johannes Casparus Fryenmoet, of Livingston's Manor, and Isaac Rysdyk, of Poughkeep_ sie and Fishkill. There was but one marriage in all this time, and that is recorded in the hand of Freynmoet, the parties being Tunis Turpenning and Breehje Van Akin ; there were forty-five baptisms, and twenty-six additions to the membership of the church.

On the 26th of March, 1769, Warmaldus Kuypers came into the pastorate, and remained therein until September 29th, 1771. He married twelve couples, baptised one hundred and seven children, and added fifty members to the church.

From the termination of Kuyper's pastorate in 1771 to 1776, the church was again without a settled pastor. At this period the country was in the throes of the Revolution ; and it is interesting to note the condition of the churches. The officers in this church were regularly elected in 1772, and 1773, and installed by Gerhard Daniel Cock, still of the Camp and Rhinebeck German Reformed churches. On the 2d of August, 1772, the elders elected were Jan Van Etten and Tunis Van Benschoten, and the deacon Petrus Stoutenburg.

In 1773 Johannes Van Wagenen and Johannes Krepser were elected elders, and Christoval Weaver and Jacobus Kip deacons. On the 19th of June, 1773, Isaac DeLamater was received into the church, and on the 20th, Jacomintje Turck, wife of Wilhelm Sehepmus, both by Dominie Cock. There were six baptisms on the 31st of August, also by him. This is all the work done until December 12, 1774, when there are twelve baptisms, apparently in the handwriting of Stephen Van Voorhees.

On the 2d of June, 1776, one month before the Declaration of Independence, he is evidently the pastor, and continue thus until December 18, 1785, one year after the close of the war. During this pastorate of nine years he recorded two hundred and ten marriages, three hundred and sixty-four baptisms, and a large addition to the membership of the church. He made the record of his addition to the membership of the church on the fly-leaves, in the front of the book, two of which are evidently missing, carrying with them the records for 1776 to 1777. Those left contain sixty-eight names, probably not more than three-fourths of those recorded by him. His records are in English, and very orderly.

From December 18, 1785, to October the 28th, 1787, there is no pastor. In 1786 there are nine baptisms by Gerhard Daniel Cock, still of the Camp and Rhinebeck German churches. On the 28th of October, 1787, Dominie Petrus DeWitt commences his record in Dutch, as follows:

"Children baptized by Do. Petrus DeWitt, preacher at Rhinebeck Flatts and Red Hook New church." This Red Hook church was the Dutch Reformed church in the village of Upper Red Hook, founded in 1785. He recorded the baptism of two hundred and seventy-one children in the Rhinebeck Flatts church.

On the 7th of March, 1788, the Legislature of the State of New York passed an act making alterations in the act for the incorporation of religious societies, rendering it more convenient to the Reformed Protestant Dutch congregations. On the 6th day of June, 1789, this church took the steps required to become a body corporate under this new act, and took the name of "The Reformed Protestant Dutch Church of Rhynbeek Flats."

John Broadhead Romeyn succeeded DeWitt, coming into the pastorate in 1799 and going out in 1803. He served the church three years and nine months, baptizing one hundred and two children.

On the 1st day of October, 1801, Mrs. Montgomery presented the church with an acre of ground to take the place of that taken by the extension of East Market street through the church lands, which was done in this year.

This acre of ground lies on the north side of East Market street, opposite the Episcopal church, and tells us why the church land extends farther west on the north than on the south side of the said street. And this acre is all the land ever given to the church by Mrs. Montgomery. We have conversed with people in the church who believed that all the lands owned by the church were a gift from Mrs. Montgomery. We have seen that they were a gift from her grandfather, Henry Beekman, the son of Henry the patentee, twelve years before she was born, and seventy years before the lands of the village of Rhinebeck Flatts fell to her lot by the gift or death of her mother.

It was also during the pastorate of Dominie Romeyn that 'the church lands were released, or attempted to be released, from the restriction forbidding their occupancy by liquor sellers, shopmen and pedlars, in an indenture bearing date September 2, 1801.

This document is sealed for fourteen signatures, and fourteen persons are named therein as the parties of the first part. Why the signatures of Chancellor Livingston and his sister, Mrs. Montgomery, alone were obtained, and why the document was not at once put on record, we have not learned. Mrs. Montgomery having fallen heir to the lands on the Flatts within the limits of which the church lands are included, perhaps her signature alone was required to give the release desired.

John Broadhead Romeyn was succeeded in the pastorate by Rev. Jacob Broadhead, who served the church from 1804 to 1810. His first baptism was dated August 26, 1804, and his last, April 3, 1809. He recorded the baptism of forty children, and five adults, three of the latter being slaves.

The present substantial church edifice was built in 1807–8, and therefore during the ministry of Rev. Jacob Broadhead. The building committee were Jacob Schultz, William Radcliff, Abraham Van Keuren and John Van Etten. The work was done by contract, the church furnishing all the material. John Coddington, of New York, did the mason work, and Cornelius C. Welch the carpenter work ; John Cox built the window frames ; John Wilson and Robert McCarty built the sash ; John

Wilson, Stephen McCarty, Daniel Tittemore, Henry Teal and Robert McCarty did the joiner work, according to the plan made by John Wilson; James Dunham burnt two hundred thousand brick on the lot of Abraham DeLamater, at $2.50 per thousand; and Aaron Camp superintended all the work at ten shillings a day, and found himself. The largest subscriptions to the building fund came from the heirs of Henry Beekman, the children of his daughter Margaret. Janet Montgomery gave $200; Thomas Tillotson, $200; Morgan Lewis, $200; John R. Livingston, $100; Peter R. Livingston, $100; Robert R. Livingston, $50; Philip Schuyler, $100; William Radcliff, Jacob Schultz, Henry Pells, Aldert Smedes, and Abraham Adriance, gave $100 each; Peter Brown gave $70; and, seemingly, the whole community took an interest in the enterprise, and the subscriptions were generally liberal. It was at this date the only church in the village of Rhinebeck Flatts, and six miles distant from the German Reformed church, rebuilt in what is now Lower Red Hook.

Among those who took pews at the completion of the church, we find the names of Governor Lewis, Chancellor Livingston, Mrs. Montgomery, Peter R. Livingston, Thomas Tillotson, John R. Livingston, Philip Schuyler, Henry Beekman Livingsston. These people are long since dead, and their descendants are no longer found among the members and pew holders of this church.

Jacob Broadhead was succeeded in the pastorate by Dominie McMurray. He served the church from 1812 to 1820, and baptized one hundred and ninty-four children, and three adults. He is credited with a pastorate of eight years and seven months.

William McMurray was succeeded by David Parker, who served the church from 1820 to 1827, and is credited with a pastorate of six years and six months. He baptized one hundred and eighteen children, and one adult. David Parker was succeeded by Rev. George W. Bethune, who served the church from 1827 to 1830, and is credited with a pastorate of two years. His first baptism is dated, November 11, 1827, and his last, November 8, 1829. He baptized thirty children and three adults.

The present parsonage was completed during the pastorate of Dominie Bethune, and he was the first occupant. The old parsonage, a stone building, stood near the site of the present parsonage barn. The premises, we are told, were laid out and the trees planted under his direction; and the internal arrangement of the house was mainly of his planning. He was fond of horses, kept an excellent span, which he took great delight in driving. He kept a colored man to groom and take care of them. He was as genial as he was talented, and his pastorate is remembered with pride by a good many people still to be found in the community.

George W. Bethune was sueceeded by James B. Hardenbergh, who came into the pastorate in 1830, and went out in 1836, serving the church for six years and seven months. His first baptism is dated, September 19, 1830, and his last, November 6, 1836. He baptized one hundred and twelve children, and six adults, and is credited with a pastorate of six years and seven months.

Dominie Hardenburgh was a good financier, lived on his salary, and it is said, "saved money." He left the savor of a good name and a good record with the community.

James B. Hardenburgh was succeeded by Rev. James Lillie, who came into the pastorate in 1837, and went out in 1841. His first baptism is dated, August 20, 1737, and his last, August , 1841. He has a record of twenty baptisms, and is credited with a four years' pastorate. He kept an unclerkly record, and that of his baptisms is a meagre one; perhaps so because he declined to baptize the children of parents who were not themselves members of the church.

Dominie Lillie's pastorate was a short but memorable one. He was a Scotchman, and a graduate of the Edinburg University, a profouud scholar, and, warmed by his theme, an eloquent and magnetic speaker. He had a good body and a large brain, and was thus by nature a strong man. He was self conscious, and not always politic, but thoroughly honest. He never quailed before an antagonist, and, of course, when he met a Greek "there was the tug of war." His controversies with the agent of the Dutchess County Temperance Society, on the Wine

Question in his own church, and with the champions of the Ladies Benevolent Society, when they diverted their funds from the support of the missionary, Thompson, to the repair of the church and parsonage, are events never to be forgotten in the history of Rhinebeck by those who witnessed them. He held that the wine commended in the Bible was fermented, and that the husbands of pious wives who were not themselves members of the church, put "untempered mortar in the walls of Zion," when permitted to meddle in its affairs.

Dr. Lillie was succeeded by Rev. Brogan Hoff. He came into the pastorate in 1842, and went out in 1851. His first baptism was recorded on the 23d of March, 1841, and his last on the 11th of July, 1851. He baptized thirty-three children and eighteen adults, and is credited with a pastorate of nine years and one month.

Brogan Hoff was succeeded by Rev. Peter Stryker. He came into the pastorate in 1851, and remained in it until 1856. He recorded his first baptism on the 30th of January, 1852, and his last on the 1st of February, 1856. He baptized fifty-two persons, of whom thirteen were adults; married thirty-two couples, and added one hundred and sixty-two members to the church. His pastorate embraced four years and three months and he left the country for a city charge.

The recess and new pulpit were built, the heaters put in, and the church edifice otherwise greatly improved in convenience and appearance during Dominie Stryker's pastorate.

Peter Stryker was succeeded by Rev. William A. Miller, who came into the pastorate in 1856 and went out in 1859. He recorded his first baptism on the 12th of October, 1856, and his last on the 15th of September, 1859. He recorded the baptism of seven children and five adults, married seventeen couples and added twenty-one persons to the membership of the church.

Dominie Miller came among us an invalid, and hoped by a change of air and employment to regain his health. This hope was not realized, and he tried the experiment of a sea voyage and tour in Europe, with the consent and assistance of his people. After an absence of several months he returned, apparently improved in health, but, as the sequel showed, really no

better.   He soon relinquished his charge and tried the effect of
different localities and climates in his own country, but all to
no purpose.   He died in 1863.

William A. Miller was succeeded by Rev. Heman R. Timlow, who came into the pastorate in 1759, and went out in
1766.   He recorded his first baptism on the 25th of March,
1860, and his last on the 3d of August, 1866.   He baptized seventeen children and two adults, married thirty-five couples, and
added fifty-nine members to the church.

Heman R. Timlow was succeeded by Rev. Goyn Talmage.
He came into the pastorate in 1867, and went out in 1871, and
is credited with a pastorate of four years and seven months.
He recorded his first baptism on the 2d of August, 1867, and
his last on the 1st of December, 1871.   He baptized fifteen persons, of whom ten were adults, married twenty-nine couples, and
added fifty-nine members to the church.

Goyn Talmage was succeeded by Rev. Alonzo P. Peeke.
He came into the pastorate in 1872, and went out in 1879, serving the church for seven years and two months.   He recorded
his first baptism on the 3d of August, 1872, and his last on the
10th of July, 1879. He baptized twenty-seven persons, of whom,
it appears, twenty were adults. He married fourteen couples,
and added forty-eight members to the church.

Rev. L. Walter Lott is Dominie Peek's successor.   He
was ordained, and installed pastor of the church, on the 7th of
October, 1879.   He is thus on the threshold of his career as a
Christian minister, and in the beginning of his pastorate.

THE CHURCH LANDS.

Excepting the Episcopal Church property, and the Francisco premises, all of the village of Rhinebeck lying east of
Mulberry street and south of Chestnut street, is built on church
land.   It is traversed by South, East Market, Livingston, Parsonage and Beach streets.   On the laying out of these streets, this
land was laid out in lots.   These lots have all been sold under
durable leases, subject to a yearly rent.   On some of the lots
the rents are low, and on others higher, according to the prices
paid for the leases, and the time of purchase.   We count over

ninety houses on this land. On the church and cemetery lot of two acres, the houses of William Bergh Kip, Levy Leroy, and Mrs. John Killmer, on Mill street, pay rent to the church.

THE CEMETERY.

The old cemetery was abandoned in 1845, not because it was full, but because it lies near the centre of the village, and interments were prohibited by the corporate authorities. There is a tradition among the people of this church that Col. Henry Beekman, the donor of the church lands, was buried in its cemetery, near the old church, and that the new edifice was built over his grave. His descendants have no knowledge at variance with this tradition. And yet it is singular there is no tablet or monument to be found, to establish the fact. He died on the 3d of January, 1776, six months before the Declaration of Independence by the American Congress. His daughter and only child, Margaret, widow of Judge Robert R. Livingston, died in June, 1800.

CHAPTER XVII.

ST. PAUL'S OF WURTEMBERGH.

On the 20th of March, 1759, two farmers residing in the part of the precinct of Rhinebeck, called at that time " Whitaberger Land," addressed a letter to Henry Beekman, the proprietor of said land, and received the following answer:

" NEW YORK, April 17, 1759.

" MESSRS. WAGER & BOLTZ :—Having received your letter of the 20th ult., concerning leave to build a church, &c., which reasonable request I willingly grant, and give you what further assurance that shall be adjudged for such purpose necessary, wishing you good prosperity in the meanwhile, am and remain,

Your well wishing friend,

HENRY BEEKMAN.

To conduct a church in those days, required a government license, and to receive and collect subscriptions for the erection of a church edifice, a special charter. That these were at once obtained and the edifice erected is certain. And it is equally certain the edifice was erected and a graveyard opened on the premises of said Wager and Boltz. On the 5th of September, 1774, Henry Beekman conveyed to Johannes Markwat, Michael Pultz and Adam Dipple, trustees, for the time being, of said church, nineteen acres and three-quarters of land lying adjacent to the lands of Leonard Wager and the "Jacomintie Fly convey-ance," "for the sole and only proper use, benefit and behoof of the Protestant Church now erected on the southeast part of Rhinebeck, commonly called the ' Whitaberger Land.' "

On the first day of June, 1785, George and Sebastian Pultz, and Paul and Sebastian Wager, deeded to the church two acres of ground, one acre each, "together with all and singular the buildings, church and churchyard thereon erected and belonging, the said church being now commonly distinguished as the " Wir_ temburg church." The trustees named in this conveyance were David Traver, Peter Traver and George Marquart, of Charlotte precinct, now the town of Clinton. The deed states that the conveyance is for " the use and benefit of the Protes-tant congregation or society of said church, * * * só as they do not occupy any part of the said two acres of land for any other purpose than for a church and burying ground." On the 7th of February, 1796, George and Sebastian Pultz re-leased the north half of the lot, the acre given by themselves, from this restriction, giving their own consent, and binding their heirs to give theirs to the trustees of the church to erect school house, and conduct a school thereon. It will be n' that neither of these deeds refers to the church as " St. F or " Lutheran." It was certainly not known by these ·i꜡ until some time after the Revolution.   ·i

A new church building was erected in 1802 ; and in   ꜄. the church sold the 19 3-4 acres obtained from Henry Beekn   ·꜡ and employed the proceeds in the payment of a debt incurre in the erection of the new edifice. Morgan Lewis, and Gertrude Livingston, his wife, the granddaughter of Henry Beekman, in whom the fee of the Wurtemburg lands vested at the death of her mother, gave their consent in proper form to this disposi-tion of the said land ; and they were sold under an order from

Chancellor John Lansing, Jr., dated at Albany, February 27, 1807, in response to a petition of the trustees of the "Lutheran St. Paul's Church in the town of Rhinebeck called Wertembergh." The church edifice was thoroughly repaired in 1832; and in 1861 it was enlarged and remodelled and put into the shape and condition in which it is found to-day.

The first baptism in the church was recorded on the 22d of October, 1760. The first pastor named in the record was Rev. J. F. Ries. He served the church from 1760 to 1785. George Henrich Pfifer served as pastor from 1785 to 1794, and was succeeded for a short period by John Frederick Ernst. Dr. Fredrick H. Quitman came into the pastorate in 1798. His contract, bearing date February 8, 1798, requires him to preach to the people of the church at Rhinebeck eighteen Sundays and three festival days; to the people of the church at East Camp, sixteen Sundays and two festival days; to the people of the church at Wertembergh, nine Sundays and one festival day; and to the people of the church at Tarbush, seven Sundays and one festival day. For these services the Rhinebeck people agree to pay him thirty pounds New York current money, ten bushels of wheat, and grant him the use of the parsonage and church lands, he to be responsible for the ten bushels rent-wheat thereon; the East Camp* people £35 in money, and eight bushels of wheat, fire-wood, and the free use of the parsonage and church lands, or £25 in money instead, if he shall choose not ·e them; the Wertembergh people £30 in money and eight ' of wheat; and the Tarbush* people £25 in money and shels of wheat.

of the 4th of February, 1815, Dr. Quitman agreed to preach
re Wertembergh Church "on every third Sunday during
a ar, one Sunday excepted—namely, during the winter season
ermon—and from May until October, two sermons—namely,
ie in the German and one in the English language," upon con-

* East Camp and Tarbush were in Columbia County. The former is now Germantown; the latter in the Town of Livingston, near Johnstown, and is now the "Manor Church," in the new locality, farther east and south. The German Camps were so called because they were the camping grounds of the Palatines brought over by Governor Hunter in 1710, at the expense of Queen Anne, of England; and the Tarbush is the name given to the pine woods in which they were employed in making tar for the British government.

dition that they will pay him "every year, in semi-annual pay-
ments, $200, and between twenty-five and thirty loads of wood,"
the congregation in Rhinebeck to make up what will pay for the
remaining Sundays.   They do this at his request, that he may
be "freed in his advancing age from the tedious task of continued travelling." It thus appears he relinquished the East Camp
and Tarbush churches in 1815. He continued to serve the
Rhinebeck and Wertembergh churches until 1825.   Toward
the close of his ministry he had to be carried to the pulpit, and
retained his seat while preaching.   He died in the parsonage
of the Rhinebeck church, and was buried in the Rhinebeck
graveyard.   He is well and reverentially remembered by all
who knew him.

William J. Eyer was Dr. Quitman's successor, entering on
the pastorate of the church in September, 1825, and continuing
therein until September, 1839.   Rev. George Neff says,"shortly
after his settlement he preached altogether in the English language, and ministered exclusively to the Wurtembergh church."

A. T. Geissenhainer came into the pastorate in 1838, and
retained it until 1840.   He kept his record in a clerkly hand
and in an orderly manner.

Rev. Charles A. Smith succeeded Dominie Geissenhainer
in the pastorate, and retained it until 1850.

Rev. W. N. Scholl succeeded Dominie Smith, and remained pastor of the church until 1855.

Rev. George Neff succeeded Dominie Scholl, and took
charge of the congregation in July, 1855, retaining it until July,
1876, a period of twenty-one years.

Rev. J. G. Griffith took the pastorate on the 1st of September, 1876, and is the present efficient and popular incumbent.

The first baptism by Rev. Charles A. Smith bears date
June 19, 1842 ; the last, December 25, 1849.   He baptized forty-
nine children.

The first baptism by Rev. W. N. Scholl bears date April
13, 1851, and the last, February 18, 1855.   He baptized forty
two children.   The first baptism by Rev. George Neff bears
date August 29, 1855, and the last, April 8, 1874.   He
baptized eighty-seven children.   The first name on the record

of the church is Salome, daughter of Wilhelm Berger, baptized October 22, 1760; the second, Rosina, daughter of Henrich Buis, baptized June 8, 1760; the third, Mathias, the son of Mathias Marshall; the fourth, Margaretha, daughter of Eberhard Wager. These are all there are in 1760. At this date the Ackerts were Eckers, the Ashers, Eschers; the Travers, Trebers; the Pultzs, Boltzs; the Waltermeyers, Waldemires; the Cookinghams, Kuckenheims; and the Marquarts, Marckworths.

CHAPTER XVIII.

RED HOOK REFORMED CHURCH.

We have found no evidence that there was a church organ-ization or church edifice anywhere in what is now the town of Red Hook before 1766. Before this date, Red Hook people had their church membership in the German Reformed and Lutheran churches at Rhinebeck, and the Dutch Reformed church on the Flatts. The first knowledge we get that there was a Red Hook, is in the records made in the Dutch Reformed Church here, by Ego Tonkens Van Hovenburgh, of baptisms in "Roode Hoek," in 1751. Precisely where he went when he went to Red Hook has not been definitely settled. We assume it was in the vicinity of Tivoli, because it was here, near the river, where the Hollanders from Kingston and Albany·made their first settlements, and had their most considerable popula-tion at this early date.

On the 5th of October, 1766, a book of records was opened in Dutch, in the old Red Church near Madalin, the title page to which reads as follows: "Church book of the congregation of Roode Hoek, beginning on the 5th of October, 1766, when, at the same time, the church was consecrated by the Rev. John Casper Fryenmoet, minister of Livingston manor, &c., from the words out of 1 Kings, viii, 30, whereto God gave his blessing."

Dominie Fryenmoet received into the membership of the church, on the same day, by certificate from the church on the Flatts, the following persons: John Vosburgh and his wife, Cor-nelia Knickerbacker; Martinus Hoffman; Louwrentz Knicker-backer and his wife, Maryke Dyke; Barent Van Benthuysen; Pe-

ter Van Benthuysen; Jacob Heermance and his wife, Catharina
Vosburg; Volkert Witbeck and his wife, Dorothea Vosburg;
Thomas Lewis and his wife, Dorothea Elig; Maria Kip, widow
of Jan Benthuysen; by letter from Kingston, Zacharias Hoffman; by ditto from Do. Cock, Benjamin Knickerbacker and his
wife, Aletta Halenbeck; by letter, on the 13th of February,
1767, Alida Livingston, wife of Col. Mart. Hoffman; and the
Honorable Robert R. Livingston and his wife, Beekman; ditto,
on the 23d of January, 1768, Anna Christina Phillipena de Haes.

A register of the seats disposed of, and their cost, dated
1766, in the hand of Dominie Kuypers, is as follows:

1	5 places, Pieter Benthuysen. - - . . .	6s.
2	10 places, Gerritt Van Benthusen and his son, Barent,	10s.
3	8 places, Barent J. Van Benthuysen, - - -	22s.
4	8 places, Catharine Ten Broeck, - - - -	12s.
5	8 places, Zacharias Hoffman, - - - -	12s.
6	8 places, Martinus Hoffman, - - - -	12s.
7	8 places, Robert R. Livingston, - - - -	12s.
8	8 places, D. Van Ness, 4; J. Schermerhorn, 2; W. Heermanse, 2, - - - - - - -	10s.
9	8 places, G. Heermanse, 4; E. Vosburg, 2; W. Colom, 2,	9s.
10	8 places, J. Heermance, 4; D. Van Ness, 4, - -	12s.
11	10 places, F. Witbeck, 5; M. Vosburg, 5, - -	9s.
12	5 places, Benjamin Knickerbacker, - - -	7s.
13	5 places, Nicholas Hoffman, - - - - -	5s.

This is followed by a record in Dutch, dated June 12, 1771,
which seems to us to say, the consistory, consisting of W. Kuypers, V. D. M.; Gerritt Heermans, John Van Ness, Martin Vosburg, elders; Zacharias Hoffman, Volkert Witbeck, deacons,
have resolved that all in the habit of attending church in this
house, who have not rented seats, will be asked to pay two shillings each per annum for the seats they will occupy.

This is followed by an order made on the 28th of June,
1775, by Martin Vosburg, Egbert Benson, Nicholas Hoffman,
elders: Thomas Lewis, John Van Ness, Cornelius Swart, deacons, that all who use the " Dodt Kleet " (dead cloth or pall)
shall pay therefor the sum of three shillings.

From 1769 to 1771 the record of additions to the church
is in the hand of Warmaldus Kuypers, who served the church
on the Flatts for the same period. He added thirteen members

to the Red Hook church, and recorded the baptism of eleven children, one in 1774. Among those added to the membership, we find the names of Jacob Elmendorf, Cornelius Swart, Mallie Beekman and Annatje Burhans. Mallie Beekman was the wife of Cornelius Swart, and Annatje Burhans of Jacob Elmendorf. The last parties were married in Kingston, January 11, 1751, and had children baptized in Kingston, as follows: Cornelius, July 12, 1751; Samuel, July 14, 1754; Jan, May 30, 1757; Abraham, Aug. 12, 1759; Engeltje, November 8, 1761; Jacob, Aug. 12, 1764; Annatje, Aug. 16, 1772; Tobias, January 15, 1775. Jacob Elmendorf was the son of Cornelius Elmendorf and Engeltje Heermance, and Annatje Burhans, daughter of Samuel Burhans and Jenneke Brink. Johannes Beekman and Lydia Beekman were sponsors at the baptism of a son, Cornelius, of Cornelius Swart and Mallie Beekman, on the 30th of December, 1770. From 1773 to 1775, the records are in the hand of Dirck Romeyn. He added ten to the membership of the church, and baptized fifteen children. Among his additions to the church, we find the names of Egbert Benson, Harmanus Hoffman and Catharina Dow, his wife; Nicholas Hoffman and Ede Sylvester, his wife; Zacharias Hoffman, Jr., and Junnetje Hoffman, his wife. From 1780 to 1783 there were seventeen additions by Dr. John H. Livingston. Among these are the names of Margaret Tillottson, in 1780, Ryer Heermanse and his wife, Maritje Heermanse; Cornelius Elmendorph; Harmon Whitbeck and his wife, Mary Sylvester; Eleanor Heermanse, wife of Peter Contine; Elizabeth Heermance, wife of John Heermance; Cornelia Vredenburgh, wife of Harmon Hoffman.

From 1783 to 1807, when Dominie Andrew N. Kittle came into the pastorate, there were no additions to the church recorded in this book. There were baptisms in every year from 1766 to 1810. They number, in all, one hundred and ninety-four. Among the clergymen who served the church for short periods during this time, we find the names of Fryenmoet, Kuypers, Rysdeck, Van Voorhees, Livingston, Ladley, Samuel Smith, of Saratoga, Dirck and Jeremiah Romeyn, and Andrew N. Kittle, of the Dutch Reformed Church, and Dominie Cock, of the German Reformed Church. Among those who had children baptized, we find the names of Robert G. Livingston, Edward P. Livingston, Philip H. Livingston, Peter Ten Broeck Meyer and Lendert Ten Broeck.

The book contains but sixteen marriages, all by Dominie Kittle. Among these we find that of Hubert Van Wagenen, of New York, to Mary Wheeler, of Red Hook; William M. Smith, of Sharon, Connecticut, to Miss Helen Livingston, daughter of G. R. Livingston, and George W. Cuyler to Miss Catharine Livingston, daughter of G. R. Livingston.

Two Dutch records in this church, rendered into English, read as follows.:

" On the 18th of July, 1780, reckoning was done by the deacons and elders, and found in the chest £36, 12s, 2d. Continental money, and £2, 1s. hard money, which is in the hands of William W. Gilbert.   CORNELIUS SWART."

" On the 30th of June, 1785, reckoning was done by the deacons and elders, and found in the chest £92. 10s. 9d. Continental money, and £5. 12s. 9d. hard money, which is in the hands of Martin Vosburgh.   CORNELIUS SWART."

CHAPTER XIX.

THE UPPER RED HOOK CHURCH.

THE title page to its oldest book of records tells us in the handwriting of the Rev. Andrew N. Kittle that this church was " organized, Anno Domini, 1788, and a union formed with the Lower Red Hook Church." The Lower Red Hook here named was not what is now known as Lower Red Hook. It was the neighborhood of the Old Red Church, northeast of Madalin, near Hoffman's mills, the history of which was briefly sketched in the preceding chapter.

Andrew N. Kittle did not come into the pastorate of this church until 1807. The union between the two churches was not formed until 1794, and the organization of the Upper Red Hook Church was evidently of an earlier date than 1788. The record of baptisms in its book commences on the 15th day of December, 1785, and the first record of an election of officers, in Dutch, reads as follows, in English : " Red Hook, November

9, 1788. Were chosen members of the consistory the following persons : Elder, Peter Heermance, in place of Cornelius Swart, who goes out ; Deacon, Cornelius Elmendorf in place of David Van Ness, who goes out." Cornelius Swart and David Van Ness had thus served a term of office each at this election ; and Jacob Elmendorf and Ryer Hermance were in office, also by a previous election. Andrew N. Kittle also gives 1788 as the year when the Rev. Petrus DeWitt came into the pastorate. We find in the old book of the Reformed Dutch Church on Rhinebeck Flatts, a record in his own hand in Dutch, which reads as follows, in English : " October 8, 1787. Children baptized by Do. Petrus DeWitt, preacher at Rhinebeck Flatts and Red Hook New Church."

REV. PETRUS DEWITT.

From the 15th of December, 1785, to May 8th, 1791, the baptisms are in the handwriting of Henry Lyle. They are all in the same ink, were probably all recorded in one sitting, and, therefore, copied from slips, or some book not suited to the taste of the consistory, or in a condition to receive other necessary records. From July 17, 1788, to August 26, 1791, the records are all in the hand of Dominie DeWitt. He served the church on Rhinebeck Flatts until 1796. We think he closed his pastorate in the Red Hook church on the first of July, 1791. A record in the book of the latter, over his own signature, dated September 26, 1791, says he made a settlement on this day with Hendrick Heermanse, David Van Ness, Andrew Heermanse, and Andrew G. Heermanse, " elders and deacons of the New Church at Red Hook," and found them in his debt " for salary, as minister of that congregation until the first day of July last, the sum of fifteen pounds, eight shillings and two pence." By writing " that " instead of *this* congregation he indicates that he did not reside in Red Hook ; and we assume that he resided in the old stone parsonage of the church in this village. If he received a regular call to these charges, we have not found it on record in either church.

Giving him credit for all recorded in the hand of Henry Lyle, Petrus DeWitt baptized eighty-three children in the Red Hook church, twenty-one of whom had a Heermance for

father or mother.   He added thirteen members to the church, ·
all of whom, with one exception, were Heermances and their
wives.   The exception was Catharine Verplank, wife of Harmanus Hoffman, who became a member on profession of her
faith, on the 19th of June, 1790.   He baptized Philip Verplank
Hoffman, their son, on the 10th of May, 1791.   There are no
marriages recorded during his pastorate.

JEREMIAH ROMEYN.

We find the record of a call to Rev. Jeremiah Romeyn,
which tells us that " by reason of the many deaths and remov-
als from the congregation of the Linlithgow church, they are
rendered incapable of paying the salary promised to the said
Romeyn," and united with the two Red Hook congregations
in a call to him to serve the three churches at a salary of one
hundred and fifty pounds, to be paid half-yearly, eighty pounds
by the church of Linlithgow, and seventy pounds by the two
Red Hook churches, the church at Linlithgow to provide him
with a convenient dwelling house and outhouses and with a
glebe of forty acres of land, to be put in good and lawful fence,
and he be provided with sufficient and necessary firewood at
his door.   On his part the Rev. Jeremiah Romeyn promised to
perform divine services among them, " according to the received
doctrine and discipline of the Low Dutch Reformed churches
as established in the Synod of Dort ;" to preach one half of his
time to the church at Linlithgow, and the other half, on alternate Sabbaths, to the two churches in Red Hook ; to preach
twice a day from the first Sabbath in April to the first Sabbath
in October ; and in either the Dutch or English language, as
the consistory in either church shall, from time to time, deter-
mine.

This call was agreed to in a united meeting of the three
consistories, held at Clermont, December 14, 1793, the Rev.
Petrus DeWitt acting as moderator.   The composition of the
respective consistories was as follows :

Consistory of the Linlithgow church : James Van Deusen,
Barent Ten Eyk, Johannes Stieber, George Snyder, elders ;
John Stall, Peter Wagener, Conrad Petrie, Henry Stall, deacons.

Consistory of the church at the road : (Upper Red Hook)

David Van Ness, elder; Andrew Heermans, Simeon Heermans, deacons.

Consistory of the Old Red Hook Church: Martin Vosburgh, Thomas Lewis, elders; Nicholas Hoffman, Harmon Whitbeck deacons.

The approbation of this call by the classical assembly was signed by Isaac Labaugh, president, pro tem., and John Demarest, scribe, pro tem. "In consequence of this call," the Rev. Jeremiah Romeyn was installed over the church on the 2d of February, 1794, the Rev. Petrus DeWitt preaching the sermon. He remained in the charge until 1806, a period of twelve years. He added fifty-one to the membership of the church, baptized one hundred and eighty-four children and married seventy couples. Among those added to the membership of the church we find the names of Wilhelmina Vredenburgh, wife of Dr. Wheeler, June 10, 1802; Elizabeth Van Benschoten, wife of Henry Benner, June 3, 1803; John Knickerbocker, Jr., November 1, 1805; Hendrick Benner, John W. Pitcher, Philip Pitcher, Peter Rypenburgh and Lawrence Hendricks, by certificate from the church at Rhinebeck, September 24, 1806 (the church at Rhinebeck here means the German Reformed Church, then in what is now Lower Red Hook, of which John W. Pitcher was a deacon in this year). Among the children baptized, we find the names of John Van Alen Lyle, James Kosciosko Armstrong, Philip Henry Knickerbocker and Cornelius E. Elmendorf. Among the marriages we find those of John W. Pitcher, of Red Hook, with Catharine Kip, of Rhinebeck, November 4, 1797; Anthony Hoffman with Jannet Bostick, both of Mount Ross, September 3, 1797; John Radcliff, with Jane Van Ness, both of Rhinebeck, October 24, 1798; Garret Cock, of Germantown, with Catharine Benner, of Red Hook, November 8, 1801; Henry G. Livingston, Jr., of Rhinebeck, with Catharine Coopernail, of Little Nine Partners, December 26, 1803; John Knickerbacker, Jr., of North East, with Mary Benner, of Red Hook, January 8, 1804; John Davenport, of New York, with Eliza Wheeler, of Red Hook, February 10, 1806; Jacob Vosburg, with Hannah Shoemaker, both of Red Hook, February 10, 1806.

ANDREW N. KITTLE.

Andrew N. Kittle came into the pastorate under a regular call from the Old and New Red Hook churches, which was accepted by him on the first day of February, 1807. These being his first charges, he was ordained in the Lower or Old Church, on the 26th of April, 1807, by Dominies Broadhead and Vedder, Broadhead preaching the ordination sermon. The oldest book of records, which is all we have to consult, ends 1813. In this period of six years he added twenty-five to the membership of the church, baptized eighty-six children, and married sixty couples. Among the additions to the church we find the names of Phebe Pugsly, wife of Peter Van Alen, May 30, and Peter Van Alen, November 30, 1807: Annatie Moore, from the German Church at Rhinebeck; Garret Cock, from the German Church at the Camp; Abraham Kip and his wife, by certificate from Rhinebeck Flats; Miss Sally Livingston, on confession; and Miss Nancy Corie, on certificate from the Episcopal Church in New York. Among the children baptized we find the names of Francis, daughter of Thomas Broadhead and Maria Curtis; Robert L., son of Robert L. and Margaret Livingston, with Chancellor Robert R. Livingston and Mary Stevens, his wife, as sponsors; Margaret Elizabeth, daughter of John Radcliff and Jane Van Ness; Andrew N. Kittle, son of John W. Pitcher and Catharine Kip; Thomas, son of Jacob C. and Ganetye Elmendorf. Among the marriages we find those of John Benner to Miss Hannah Schryver, of Rhinebeck, September 3, 1808; Gamaliel Wheeler, to Miss Mary Panderson, both of Red Hook, November 15, 1810; Jacob Benner to Miss Margaret Fero, both of Rhinebeck, December 25, 1810; John Constable, of Schenectady, to Miss Susan Maria Livingston, of Red Hook Landing, June 9, 1811; John Du Bois, merchant, of Red Hook Landing, to Miss Gitty Broadhead, of Clermont, June 23, 1811; John Elting, Jr., to Miss Margaret Jones, both of Clermont, March 14, 1813; Thomas Mesick, of Clavarack, to Miss Betsey Maule, of Red Hook, August 22, 1813; and on the same day, Tom and Bet, servants of General Ten Broeck.

The pastorate of Dominie Kittle extended to 1833, covering a period of twenty-six years. The writer remembers very well listening to his farewell sermon, and recalls the emotion with which he alluded to the fact that he had grown gray and spent the vigor of his life in the service of the people he was addressing. The church at this time was paying a small salary, and we think his reason for leaving was that it did not suffice for the support of his family. He was living in the large brick house, now the residence of Dr. John Losee. His wife was sister to the Rev. Dr. John Gosman, and his father-in-law was living with him. Corwin, in his Manual, says he was a grandson of Dominie Fryenmoet. We remember him as a good preacher; a good-looking, good-tempered, very intelligent, and very affable gentleman " of the old school."

FREDERICK W. THOMPSON.

The Rev. Frederick W. Thompson, of New Brunswick, N. J., was Dominie Kittle's successor. His pastorate was a very short one, lasting from 1834 to 1836. We have no record of his work in the book before us. He left the church to go abroad as a missionary. The beautiful and lovely woman whom many of us remember as his wife, died at Batavia, in the island of Java, November 16, 1839. He married again, on the 9th of November, 1840, Cecelia Combe, a Swiss lady who was teaching a Christian school at Batavia. She died on the river, on a journey from Karangan to Pontianak, in December, 1844. He died, March 3, 1848, at Berne, in Switzerland, whither he had gone for the recovery of his health.

JACOB W. HANGEN.

The Rev. Jacob W. Hangen succeeded Mr. Thomson. He came into the pastorate in 1838, and went out in 1840. The German Reformed Church, of Germantown, in Columbia County, called the " Sanctity Church," joined the Poughkeepsie classes of the Dutch Reformed Church on the 14th of January, 1837, while Jacob W. Hangen was serving it as pastor ; and, we think, after this date he served it in connection with the Red Hook church to the end of his pastorate. He died in 1843. We have not learned where.

JOHN W. WARD.

The Rev. John W. Ward succeeded Dominie Hangen. He

served the church from 1841 to 1845. He went from Hed Hook
to Greenpoint, serving there from 1849 to 1854. He died in
1859.

JOHN G. JOHNSON.

The Rev. J. G. Johnson succeeded Dominie Ward. He
served the church from the 1st of January, 1846, to July 3, 1874,
on the evening of which day his labors were terminated by his
death. He died in the fifty-seventh year of his age, the thirty-
first of his ministry, and the twenty-fourth of his Red Hook
pastorate. His remains were interred at Peekskill, in the village cemetery. He was universally esteemed as a man and a
pastor, and the church extended its influence, and was greatly
prospered by his ministrations.

HENRY VAN SCHOONHOVEN MYERS.

The Rev. Henry V. S. Myers succeeded Dominie Johnson,
and served the church from 1871 to 1874. He went from Red
Hook to South Brooklyn. He is an eloquent and able preacher.

JOSEPH SCUDDER, M. D.

The Rev. Joseph Scudder, a doctor of medicine, and an India
missionary for a number of years, was Dominie Myers' successor. He came into the pastorate in 1875, and was taken out
by the hand of death on the 21st of November, 1876. His remains were interred in Greenwood Cemetery.

EZEKIEL CARMAN SCUDDER, M. D.

The Rev. Ezekiel Carman Scudder, also a doctor of medicine, and at one time an India missionary, is Dominie Joseph
Scudder's successor, and the present efficient, intelligent, and
popular incumbent.

THE CHARACTER OF THE PEOPLE.

The pastors of the Red Hook Dutch Reformed Church
have all displayed more than an ordinary degree of intelligence
and influence, because they were always the choice of an intelligent, self-reliant, and well ordered people. We think the land
of Upper Red Hook falls within a tract of three thousand acres,
assigned to Barent Van Benthuysen in the division of the Schuyler patent, and was disposed of by him to his children, and those
of the families of Heermances in Kingston and Rhinebeck; and

that the Dutch Church of Upper Red Hook, in its first inception, was the creation, and located on the land of some of these Heermances, who, though now nearly extinct, were at the beginning of the century very numerous, and very influential in the town.

REAL ESTATE.

When, from whom, and on what terms the two Red Hook Reformed Dutch Churches obtained their first grants of land for church and cemetery lots, we have not been able to learn. The oldest tradition in reference to the two acres comprised in the church lot and graveyard of the old Red Church, near Madalin, is, that it was a gift from Zacharias Hoffman, about 1760. The graveyard is still in the care of trustees, and the burial place for families in the neighborhood. The oldest graveyard in the town, long disused, we are told, lies on a hill back of the Farmers' Hotel, at Tivoli.

The Upper Village Church has no deed for its first church and cemetery lot, and there is no one living who knows from whom, or on what terms it was obtained. In 1802 Andrew G. Heermance and his wife gave a deed for four-tenths of an acre for an addition to the cemetery ; and in 1822 Jacob Heermance and his wife gave a deed for five-tenths of an acre for another addition to the cemetery. The deed for the parsonage and lot was given by Henry Pulver and his wife, in 1835 ; and there is a later deed from Robert Almstead and his wife for another addition to the cemetery.

CHURCH EDIFICES.

The Old Church is of wood, and painted red ; and, if it is not the same edifice dedicated by Dominie Fryenmoet, on the 5th of October, 1766, we have not learned when it was reconstructed, or its place taken by another.

The new, or Upper Red Hook edifice, was in existence in 1787, and probably built in this year. It was built of stone, quarried out of the "Styler Barrick," a rocky hill northeast of the village. Tradition says Peter Ryfenburgh was the master mason. There is a resolution in the book before us, passed on the 21st of September, 1813, presenting thanks " to the Reformed German Church for the use of their church this summer.

We presume the Dutch edifice in this year received repairs, or alterations, in the progress of which it could not be used, and an offer of their house by the German people, in the Lower Village, was accepted.   There is also a record of a meeting held on the 22d of February, 1854, with Rev. J. G. Johnson for chairman, and Daniel A. Cock for secretary, at which it was resolved to reconstruct the interior of the edifice ; and we think it was done, at an expense of something over twelve hundred dollars. The old stone edifice gave place, in 1871, to the present handsome and commodious Gothic wooden structure, erected under the supervision of a building committee composed of Edwin Knickerbocker, Arthur Nelson, John Losee, James R. Kerley, William R. Moore and Peter Feroe ; Edwin Knickerbocker, chairman ; Arthur Nelson, Treasurer.   This committee contracted with Milton Cramer to erect the building for thirteen thousand one hundred dollars ; but we learn from the treasurer that extra work brought up the cost to fully fourteen thousand dollars.   The corner-stone was laid on the 12th of September, 1871, and the house dedicated on the 15th of May, 1872.   It includes ample Sunday School rooms, on the same floor with the audience room.   Its pews are spacious and without doors ; and there is an aspect about all its appointments which says to the sojourner, and all the neighborhood, " come in and feel yourselves entirely at home with us."   The interior is greatly enlivened and beautified by three memorial windows of stained glass, all on the eastern side, and therefore all in the morning sun.   The first is to the memory of Harmanus Hoffman and his wife, Catharina Verplank, and was a gift from their son, Philip Verplank Hoffman, of New York City.   Harmanus Hoffman was an elder of the church in 1789.   A lady who attended the district school of Red Hook with the son, says, " he was very full of life, and very full of pranks."   The second is to the memory of Rev. J. G. Johnson, and was put up in its place by the church.   It represents a shepherd with his crook, and a lamb lying at his feet—an appropriate design, and a beautiful window.   The third is to the memory of Ebenezer Adams, whom we remember as a veteran of the revolution, and was a gift to the church from his daughter, Ruth.   He was often an elder of the church. He died on the 31st of January, 1846, aged ninety-four years.

There is but a step from the door of the parsonage to the door of the church. The adjacent cemetery is spacious and well ordered, and crowded with slabs and monuments to the memory of the sturdy people who founded the town, and sub-dued the wilderness of Red Hook. The church is located in a quiet village, is the sole occupant of a large territory, and hence the Sabbath-home of a community of people unchafed and unsoured by sectarian rivalries ; and who, while they have a proper respect for themselves, entertain a good opinion of, and are prepared for kind offices toward each other.

CHAPTER XX.

THE RHINEBECK METHODIST CHURCH.

The Methodist Church came into Rhinebeck with the Rev. Freeborn Garrettson, about 1793. Dr. Thomas Tillottson, of Maryland, a surgeon in the Revolutionary army, and a promin-ent man in the politics of the state of New York after the war, married Margaret, the second daughter of Judge Robert R. Livingston and Margaret Beekman, and settled on an estate purchased from the Van Ettens, on the Neck, or south end of the patent of Arie Roosa and company, the Van Ettens being heirs of the Roosas. The Rev. Freeborn Garrettson, also a Marylander, and known to Dr. Tillottson at home, was invited by the latter to pay him a visit at his Rhinebeck mansion. He accepted the invitation, and tarried with him for several weeks, preaching the doctrines of the Methodists to the people of the neighborhood. In what house or in what locality, we are not told. We are told, however, that he met Catharine Livingston, the sister of Mrs. Tillottson, at the residence of the latter ; that a friendship grew up between them which ended in marriage in 1793 ; and that the couple took up their residence soon after, on a portion of an estate the fee of which fell to the share of the wife in the division of the lands of her grandfather, Henry Beekman, between the children of his daughter and only child Margaret, known to the past generation of the people of Rhine-beck as Madam Livingston.

A map of the town of Rhinebeck, made in 1797, shows a Methodist church on a hill facing the road to Milan, a short dis_ tance beyond the house recently erected by Mr Edwin Knick_ erbocker.* The residence of the Garrettsons was in the imme_ diate vicinity of this church, a little to the southeast, in a stone house built in 1772 by Thomas Canner, for a man of the name of Hagadorn. At what date this church was built, and with what funds, there is no person or document to tell us; that it was there because the Garrettsons were there, there is nobody to doubt.

In 1799 the Garrettsons exchanged this farm with the Van Wagenens, on the patent of Arie Roosa & Co., they owning these lands as the descendants of Gerrit Artsen, one of the part- ners to the grant. The Van Wagenens moved into the farm house on the Hagadorn farm, the Garrettsons retaining the main residence while they built their mansion on the premises acquired from the Van Wagenens. This exchange of lands brought the Garrettsons into the immediate neighborhood of the Tillottsons, and gave them an extended and very handsome river-view from their residence. They moved into their new house in October, 1799, and their estate in time received the name of Wildercliff.

The first knowledge we get of the presence of the Metho- . dists in the village of Rhinebeck is contained in a deed from Mrs. Janet Montgomery to Rev. Freeborn Garrettson, Robert Sands, Simon Johnson Myers, Charles Doyl, and Daniel McCar- ty, trustees of the Methodist Episcopal Church at Rhinebeck Flatts, dated August the 1st, 1801, for one rood and six perches of land, bounded as follows: " Beginning at the northwest cor- ner of a lot leased by the said Janet Montgomery to the said Daniel McCarty, and now in the tenure and occupation of Ro- bert Scott, and runs from thence along the bounds of said lot north, eighty-nine degrees east, one chain and eighty-nine links to a stake; thence north, one degree west, one chain and fifty links to a stake; thence south eighty-nine degrees west, one chain and ninety-six links; thence, with a straight line, to the place of beginning, containing one rood and six perches of land."   ·

This lot is now owned and occupied by John E. Traver in Center street. A venerable lady, now in the 89th year of her age, a daughter of Robert Scott, who grew from childhood to womanhood in the immediate vicinity of this lot, remarkably preserved in body, mind and memory for her years, informs us that the Methodist Church on the road to Milan, three miles east of the village, "near Tommy Larwood's," was taken down, brought to the village and rebuilt on this lot by Daniel McCarty; and, to the best of her memory, in the year when the lot was given. The parsonage, the residence now occupied by Mr. Traver, she thinks, was built two or three years later. Among the preachers whose goings to and fro brought them to Rhinebeck, she remembers to have heard Lorenzo Dow, "Billy" Hibbard, Ensign, Foster and others, in this church. Daniel McCarty, she says, who ran the lower grist mill, and lived in the old stone house, and afterwards moved to the Schell place, now occupied and owned by Mr. Luther, was the most ardent, active and influential Methodist in the town in his day, the preachers making a home of his house when they reached the Flatts, before the parsonage was built, and he always working for the church. Some of us remember him as a revolutionary veteran.

The lot on which the present church edifice stands was also a gift from Mrs. Janet Montgomery. The deed was for half an acre of ground "on the north side of the road commonly called Ulster and Delaware Turnpike," and is a conveyance in trust from Janet Montgomery, of Red Hook, to Mary Garrettson, of Rhinebeck, on the express condition "that she shall not at any time hereafter assign her right or trust to any but such persons as may be appointed trustees of the Rhinebeck Methodist Episcopal Church by the members thereof;" and that neither she, or her assigns, "shall, at any time, build on the premises more than a house of worship, with the necessary appurtenances, for the use of the said Methodist Episcopal Church." This deed bears date, March the 3d, 1822. From this date on the history of the church is contained in the records, which are very full, and were very carefully and intelligently kept by Freeborn Garrettson, Esq., Rev. Stephen Schuyler, Dr. William Cross, and other competent clerks. The following, pertaining to the new church and premises, is transcribed from the records, and, as the reader will discover, is the language of Freeborn Garrettson, Esq.:—" At a meeting of the Methodist society on Rhinebeck Flatts, convened at the Rev. Jesse Hunt's, January, 1822, for the purpose of taking into consideration the expediency of erecting a Methodist chapel at said Rhinebeck Flatts, and for the further purpose of choosing nine trustees for the same ; Whereupon, the Rev. Freeborn Garrettson was called to the chair, and Freeborn Garrettson, Jr., appointed secretary. The business of the meeting being opened, and the deed of the old chapel at said Rhinebeck Flatts being read, proceeded to the choice of trustees. The Rev. Jesse Hunt, being the preacher in charge, it was accordingly his prerogative, agreeably to discipline, to nominate the same. He, therefore, nominated the following persons, who were duly appointed, viz : Rev. Freeborn Garrettson, Robert Sands, William Cross, Sen'r, James Raisbeck, William C. Freeman, Freeborn Garrettson, Jr., Samuel Bell, Jeffery H. Champlin, and Nicholas Drury."

" The subject of the new church was then taken up, and it was unanimously agreed that it was necessary to go on with its erection, provided a suitable site could be obtained, and funds procured. The trustees were, therefore, instructed to consider the matter, and make their report as soon as possible ; and also to consider of what materials the building should be composed."

" It was agreed that two persons be appointed to superintend the building, and for said two persons to be under the direction of the trustees. Freeborn Garrettson, Jr., and William C. Freeman were accordingly appointed, and were instructed to present their account for services to the trustees, to be audited by them."

" It was agreed that the chairman appoint persons to go around to solicit subscriptions to the building. The Rev. Jesse Hunt, Freeborn Garrettson, Jr., and William C. Freeman, were also appointed treasurers. Adjourned to meet again on the 23d of January, 1822."

At this adjourned meeting the Rev. Freeborn Garrettson was appointed president of the board of trustees, and Freeborn Garrettson, Jr., chosen secretary ; when the president stated that Mrs. Janet Montgomery had presented the society with half an acre of ground, in a conspicuous place in the village fronting on the turnpike; and named other successes in the way of subscriptions. It was then unanimously agreed that the church be built, and built of stone, of the size of forty-five feet by fifty-five, from outside to outside; and that the Rev. Freeborn Garrettson, Rev. Jesse Hunt, Freeborn Garrettson, Jr., William E. Freeman, and Jeffery H. Champlin be a committee to manage the building, and that Freeborn Garrettson, Jr., be considered as the centre of that committee, and the general superintendent thereof. "After agreeing that the building be forwarded with as much expedition as possible, this meeting adjourned."

The corner-stone of the building was laid by the Rev. Freeborn Garrettson, on the 1st day of May, 1822, and the building was completed on the 6th day of October following. Freeborn Garrettson, Jr., the superintendent of the building, records that the thanks of the society are due to Thomas Sanford, the master mason, and Henry C. Teal, the master carpenter, for diligence and skill in the execution of their tasks; that no accident happened about the building; that not a drop of spirituous liquors was drank during its erection; that the carpenters, masons and laborers all acquitted themselves well; that all were peaceable, industrious and respectful; that never was a building raised with more harmony and good feeling. He gives special credit to John King, a colored man, for diligence and industry; and thanks the neighbors for the willingness with which they assisted with their teams in collecting the materials for the building. And then he mentions what he calls "a remarkable circumstance," as follows:

A well was dug for "the accommodation of the building," for the first step. "It afforded a full supply of water for all the purposes of making mortar, and every other use necessary as long as it was wanted; and not many days after we ceased to use it, the well became dry."* Another circumstance in the

*There is a tradition among the old people that the Rev. Freeborn Garrettson locked his well-curb against the workmen in the Fox Hollow factory, and the children from the neighboring school, who were in the habit of resorting to the well for water, and was astonished to discover, soon after, that the well refused to hold water

digging of the well is also deemed worthy of note. " After excavating the earth a short distance, we presently discovered an excellent vein of loam; and in going a little deeper found another of sand, and in still going a little deeper found another of gravel, which answered all the purposes for erecting the stone building, in making mortar for the wall, for the plastering, and for the rough casting of the building, upon the outside. This was fortunate for us, which saved us much trouble and expense."

The cost of the building was $3,559.88. The subscriptions amounted to $3,234, leaving the committee in debt, $325.88. This was assumed, and finally presented to the church, by the Rev. Freeborn Garrettson.

There were one hundred and twenty-six subscriptions to the building fund. Mrs. Catherine Garrettson gave $800; Mrs. Catherine Suckley, $500; Miss Mary Garrettson, $100; Rev. Freeborn Garrettson, in money, timber and labor, $300; Freeborn Garrettson, Jr., superintendent, $300; Mr. George Suckley, Mr. John L. Suckley, Mr. Rutsen Suckley, Mr. Thomas H. Suckley, Miss Mary Suckley, Miss Sarah S. Suckley, Miss Catherine Suckley, $100; Colonel Henry B. Livingston gave 480 loads of stone in the quarry; Edward P. Livingston gave $50; Robert L. Livingston, $50; Thomas Tillottson, $40; Mrs. Thompson, $50; Mrs. General Armstrong, $20; Mrs. Margaret Astor, $20; Coert DuBois, $25. Everybody in the village who could afford it gave something, from twenty dollars down to one dollar each. Mr. Zebulon Hibbard gave the inscription stones; Mr. Brewer, of Kingston, the keystones to the doors and windows in front of the building; Mr. Rutsen Suckley gave two of the Birmingham lamps; Miss Catherine G. Suckley presented the sacramental cups; William Cross and Robert Dixon, gave the mahogany table within the altar; and John E. Brooks made and presented the book board.

.At a meeting of the trustees, held on the 8th of December, 1823, at the parsonage house, then occupied by James Young, 'the ruling preacher in charge on the circuit," James Raisbeck

for his own family. Whether he thereupon removed the lock and recovered the water tradition has not informed us.

and John E. Brooks were appointed a committee to take charge of the "new cemetery." It was agreed that all such as belong to the Methodist Church at Rhinebeck and its vicinity, and all such as are in the habit of attending worship in Mission Chapel, and contributing to the support of the gospel in said chapel, shall be privileged to inter their dead in said burying ground " under the direction of the committee.

The Rev. Freeborn Garrettson entered the ministry in 1775, and, we are told, was appointed presiding elder over the district extending from Long Island to Lake Champlain, in 1788. In 1827, while at the house of a friend in the city of New York, he was taken suddenly ill and soon died, in the 76th year of his age and the 52d of his ministry.

The church was incorporated with Freeborn Garrettson, the nephew, William Cross, Nicholas Drury, Jeffery H. Champlin, and William Mink, as trustees, on the 2d day of June, 1829, and the certificate thereof recorded on the 11th day of the same month, in Liber No. 1 of records of church incorporations, on pages 97 and 98, Clerk's Office, Dutchess County.

A deed for one rood and thirteen perches of land for a parsonage lot in the rear of the church lot, was presented to the church by Hon. Edward Livingston, on the 12th of November, 1829, (all the village lands having come into his possession by the will of his sister, Janet Montgomery, which was admitted to probate and recorded by James Hooker, Surrogate of Dutchess County, on the 28th of April, 1827.) A new parsonage was built on this lot in the same year, at a cost of $1,305.79. The subscriptions to meet this expenditure amounted to $664. Of this amount Mrs. Catherine Garrettson gave $300; Freeborn Garrettson, $75; William B. Platt, $15; Rev. George W. Bethune, $10; David Rowley, $10; Cornelia Bayard, of Philadelphia, $10; and fifty-five others in proportion to their means, and their interest in the cause of the Methodist Church.

On the 30th of June, 1832, Mrs. Catherine Garrettson presented the church with half an acre of ground for the burying ground south of the village, on the conditions that the church surround it with a good fence, and permit no more interments in the ground attached to the church. The deed for this ground bears date, March the 27th, 1835.

A deed for half an acre of ground adjoining the parsonage lot was presented to the church by Mrs. Louisa Livingston, widow of the Hon. Edward Livingston, on the 7th of November, 1838. (She came into the possession of all the worldly estate of her husband by his will, dated at Paris, on the 7th day of March, 1835, and admitted to probate by James Hooker. surrogate of Dutchess County, on the 23d day of July, 1836.)

In 1834 the church found itself in debt in the sum of $954, and appealed to the court for leave to sell the old parsonage and lot, the proceeds to be applied in payment thereof. An order permitting the sale was obtained by John Armstrong, Esq., on the 1st of October, 1834, a strip on the north of the lot, thirty-two feet front and rear, on which there was a "new school house," to be reserved. The sale was not immediately effected, and the premises continued in the possession of Harvey Seymour as tenant. On the 12th of November, 1838, it was resolved to sell the premises, with the reservation on the north, to Robt. T. Seymour, for $600. Failing in this, it was rented to Mr. Seymour for another year, at $50, and in 1839 sold to Rev. Benjamin Griffin, presiding elder of the Methodist church at the time for the Rhinebeck district, at $500, he to pay the expense of a second application to the court, and fence the lot reserved for the school house. Our recollection is that a classical school—the beginning of the Rhinebeck Academy—was taught in this house by the Rev. Samuel Bell, a Methodist clergyman from the east.

THE RHINEBECK ACADEMY.

The credit for building up the Academy in Rhinebeck is certainly due to the Methodists, and very largely to Dominie Griffin. Bell, Marcy, Park, Comfort, Powers, Stocking and Schuyler, were all Methodists. When the Rev. Charles A. Smith was the Lutheran preacher in the village, he brought a Lutheran from Gettysburg to take charge of it, in the person of the Rev. Henry Schmidt, an accomplished scholar and gentleman, who, however, soon left the post.

The school house on the old church lot was the property of Miss Mary Garrettson, probably because it had been built with her money. Superseded by the academy, in the building of which she had taken an active interest, she offered it to the Methodist church, with a lot fifteen feet wide on the west of the Methodist church lot, in 1842, to be fitted up exclusively for religious meetings and purposes. The removal was effected and the old lot sold to Rev. Benjamin Griffin also, then of New York, for five dollars per foot, in 1843.

In 1848 the church found itself in debt in the sum of $1,005, and on the 1st of May in this year, Mr. Rutsen Suckley placed $1,000 at the disposal of the trustees with which to pay it, and bound them not to run in debt again. On the 12th of March, in this same year, Miss Mary Garrettson transferred her trust of the church lot to the trustees of the church, having held it in her hands as sole trustee for the period of twenty-six years.

On the 14th of June, 1849, Mrs. Catharine Garrettson, widow of the Rev. Freeborn Garrettson, died very suddenly, at Montgomery Place, the residence of her sister-in-law, Louisa, the widow of Hon. Edward Livingston. Born on the 13th of July, 1752, she was in the forty-first year of her age when she married, and the ninety-seventh when she died. She was calm and dignified in her manner, tall and stately in her person. Kindly disposed toward all who met her, she was as generally loved as she was respected.

In 1851 the portico and steeple were added to the church edifice, at an expense of $1,100. A bell being desired for the steeple, the Rev. L. W. Peck, the minister in charge, was authorized to write to Mr. Suckley for leave to run in debt $200 in order that they might procure one. He declined the request, but sent a subscription of $50 toward the amount needed. The record says they thanked him for his liberal subscription, and examined their financial condition, " which they found so favorable that the bell was immediately purchased."

In 1853 the church received a donation of five acres of land in the Bucobush (Beech-woods) from Miss Margaret B. Livingston, which was sold for $70 per acre, and the proceeds applied to the payment of church debts.

In 1854 the church found itself in debt again, and obtained an order from the court to sell the lot purchased from Gilbert Akerly, on the 1st of May, 1845, the proceeds to be applied to the payment thereof. It was thus sold on the 5th of December, 1854, to Miss Mary Garrettson for $400.

On the 19th of February, 1856, Miss Mary Garrettson made a gift to the church of five acres of land for an addition to the cemetery; and it was resolved that the cemetery thus enlarged should be styled the "Rhinebeck Cemetery of the Methodist Episcopal Church." On the 27th of August, 1853, she had given half an acre of ground for a cemetery for the people of color, access to which was had over the cemetery of the Reformed Church ground. By the addition of these five acres this cemetery is now within the limits of the Methodist ground, and accessible therefrom.

In 1863 the church edifice was greatly enlarged, internally reconstructed, and greatly improved, at an expense of six to seven thousand dollars. It is now a very commodious and tasteful structure.

In 1868 the church received a gift from Miss Mary Garrettson of the Akerly lot, and built the present handsome and commodious Sunday school and lecture room upon it.

In 1871 the parsonage was reconstructed and enlarged, and is now, with its handsome situation, a very desirable residence.

With its enlarged premises and improved buildings the Methodist church property is now one of the most attractive features in our beautiful village; and the picture of Rhinebeck, which omitted it, would not do us justice.*

*In a book entitled "Historical Recollections of the state of New York," published in 1842, we get pictures of prominent parts of inland cities and villages. In Dutchess County we have fine views of Matteawan and other places in Fishkill; and of Poughkeepsie we have views, in and about the city, that do justice to the place. Of Rhinebeck we get what the author calls an "Eastern View of the Methodist Church and the academy, in the central part of the village of Rhinebeck." Now, every child in our village at that time knew that this was not the "central part of the village of Rhinebeck." The Methodist church was a stone and substantial, but a small and a very plain building. It had not the pillars in front, or the addition in the rear which give it its present respectable appearance; and the academy was an insignificant affair compared with what it is now in the stately structure of the De Garmo Institute. The view and the history are in no sense an adequate advertisement of our old and beautiful Rhinebeck Flatts. The view should have been from the south, and included the old Beekman mill, and the old Dutch Reformed Church, a substantial brick and stone building, a handsome structure, and twice as large as the Methodist edifice. These two buildings were the nucleus of the village; and at the date of this history the centre of the village was at the crossing of Market and Montgomery streets, where it is now, and will always remain. And the history ought to have been of the old church, and of the old Kingston preachers from whom it received its life; and of Mrs. Montgomery, who owned all our real estate before we became a village, and did all she could to help us to become one.

Mr Rutsen Suckley, whose liberality and devotion so often came to the relief of the trustees when they found themselves in need, and who was held in very high esteem by the people of Rhinebeck generally, died in the city of New York on the 22d, and was buried from this church on the 24th of June, 1875. A funeral discourse, bearing deserved testimony to his worth, was preached by the Rev. Dr. Holdich, of the Methodist church. The large and beautiful organ was put into the gallery in the fall of 1876, at an expense of $2,500, and was a memorial gift from Mr. Thomas Suckley for his brother Rutsen.

Miss Mary R. Garrettson, the daughter and only child of the Rev. Freeborn Garrettson and his wife, Catherine Living. ston, died March 6, 1879. Born on the 8th of September, 1794, she was in the 85th year of her age. She had been a constant and generous supporter of her church, and the large audience at her funeral obsequies attested that her loss was deeply and widely felt by her people.

The position, character, piety and wealth of Mrs. Catharine Garrettson gave great prominence in the denomination to the Rhinebeck Methodist church. If she had not had her residence among us, we should probably never have heard sermons in a Rhinebeck pulpit from President Nott, of Union College ; Dr. Kirk, of Boston ; from Maffet, Summerfield, Derbin, Olin, Holdich, Pitman and Foss of the Methodist Church ; nor found among the ministers stationed here the names of Remington*, Craigh, Mercien, Sing, Kettell, Hunt, Otheman, Wheatly and Harrower. While we have found the church remarkable for the frequency with which it found itself in debt, we have found it equally remarkable for the facility and promptitude with which it found the way out of it. We presume that to-day it finds itself competent to open its doors and its pews to the people at quite as moderate a price as any other in the village.

*Stephen Remington became a Baptist shortly after he left Rhinebeck. He died in Lowell, Massachusetts, a few years since, and, we are told, had a record of three thousand baptisms as a Baptist minister.

CHAPTER XXI.

THE RHINEBECK BAPTIST CHURCH.

The Baptist church was brought into Rhinebeck by Robert Scott. He was an Englishman. His family, we are told, were Episcopalians, and he was brought up in the faith of the English church. He received a classical education, but learned the trade of a cabinet maker in his native country. He became a Wesleyan at an early age, and traveled about preaching as a Wesleyan minister in his own country. In the progress of his ministrations he became a Baptist in his opinions, joined the Baptist communion, and settled down to his trade. He came to America with his family, in company with the Vassars and Slaters, and arrived in the city of New York on the 6th of October, 1794. Here he went to work for Gen. Morgan Lewis, in Leonard street, as a carpenter. On the persuasion of Madam (Margaret Beekman) Livingston, he moved to Rhinebeck with his family, and opened a school in 1796. Mr. Slater had bought Daniel McCarty's lease of the lot and house in South street, known as the "Scott premises," and opened a store. After a little while Robert Scott bought him out, lot, house and store, and continued the business of a merchant for four years, when he gave it up, and opened a boarding school, and followed the occupation of a teacher and surveyor for the balance of his life. He had for pupils James Stokes, who was a member of the firm ot Phelps, Dodge & Co., and is now of the firm of Phelps, Stokes & Co., bankers. Henry Stokes, president of the Manhattan Life Insurance Company, was a pupil in his school nine years. B. Stokes, who was killed by the falling of the store of Phelps, Dodge & Co., in Cliff Street ; and several of the Colgate family, among them Robert Colgate, president of the Atlantic White Lead Works, were pupils in his school. Thomas Stokes, of whom a memorial book has been published, was one of his last pupils. "His ministerial life," we are told, "never ceased from eighteen years of age ; where a door was opened there he went, whether a court house, dwelling house, or barn." And we are informed he published the following works: " Antidote to Deism ;" " Chronology from the Creation to the year 1810 ;" " A Treatise on Our Blessed Lord's Return to this Earth ;" and last, " His Own Funeral Sermon."

Having said this much by way of introduction, we will let the record, made by Father Scott himself, tell us of the beginning of the Baptist Church in Rhinebeck.

"This certifieth that on the Lord's day, June 2, 1821, Elder Freeman Hopkins preached at Rhinebeck Flatts, and after examination upon their profession of faith in the Lord Jesus Christ, baptized the following persons: John Reed, William Styles, Calvin O'Harra, Wadsworth Brooks, Jacob Dedrick, Elizabeth Thompson, Ann Logan, Catharine Thompson, Elizabeth Ann Thompson, and Caty Myers; and that the said persons, with Robert Scott, James Canfield, Ann Cook, Elizabeth Scott, Mary Scott, Jane Scott, James Styles, Jr., and Sarah Styles, agreed to enter into a covenant to walk in fellowship as a church of the Lord Jesus Christ."

Letters were, at the request of these people, sent to the churches in North East and Sandisfield, requesting them to send delegates to sit in council with them on Wednesday, July 4, 1821. These churches sent their delegates, and on the evening of the day appointed, a council was formed, the delegates present being as follows: From the church in North East, Elders Freeman Hopkins and Buttolph; brethren, Filo M. Winchell and Nicholas Vasburg. From the church in Sandisfield, Elder, Jesse Hartwell; brethren, Jonathan Smith, Sylvester Doud and Asahel Doud. These delegates, with the brethren dwelling in Rhinebeck, constituted the council. Elder Jesse Hartwell was chosen moderator, and Elder John Hopkins, clerk; " when the moderator, in behalf of the council, extended to the people of the Rhinebeck organization the right hand of fellowship as a sister church." And thus the Rhinebeck Baptist Church came into being on the 4th of July, 1821.

Having heard Robert Scott on his experience and call to the work of the ministry, and on his views of doctrine, at the request of the church the council voted to ordain him. Elder Jesse Hartwell was selected to preach the sermon ; Elder John

Buttolph to make the consecrating prayer; Elders Hopkins, Buttolph and Hartwell to lay on hands; Elder Hartwell to give the charge; Elder Buttolph to give the right hand of fel-lowship; and Elder Hopkins to make the concluding prayer. At ten o'clock on the morning of the next day the church met and carried out this programme, in the presence of the people. And thus Robert Scott, at the age of sixty years, was ordained to the work of the Gospel ministry, and set over the infant Bap-tist Church of Rhinebeck as a pastor. There was no Baptist house of worship, and these services were conducted at the house of Elder Scott.

The book of records before us sets forth quite elaborately the creed to which these people subscribed on entering this church. It sets forth that it is the duty of baptized be-lievers to unite together in fellowship, to walk in the command-ments and ordinances of the Lord; and that where this is done there is a Christian church, competent to elect its own officers, and call upon them to do their duty; that the Holy Scriptures are a sufficient, and the only rule of faith and practice; that bap-tism is the immersion of the whole body in water, that it may represent a burial and resurrection, and that nothing else is baptism; and that "it is the duty of believers to break bread together often;" and in 1831 the church resolved to do this "every Lord's day;" and it was so done for the space, we think, of ten years thereafter.

At a church meeting held on the 29th of July, 1821, the the record says: "Brethren Stokes and Colgate, of York, were with us." At the monthly meeting held September 30, 1821, it was asked whether the church would proceed to ordain dea-cons; but, upon consideration, it was concluded, that, as in the primitive church none were appointed until needed, we need not do it until they are wanted."

The church at this early day had no local habitation. It assembled sometimes in one place and sometimes in another; and sometimes in Kingston. It met in Kingston on the 16th of June, 1822, and again on the 8th of September, when Ann Voorhis and Eliza Showers were baptized in the Rondout Creek; and the day was concluded by public worship in the

Court house. On the 23d of February and the 31st of August, 1823, the church met at Kingston again. On the 30th of June, 1825, James Canfield was set apart for the office of deacon by the imposition of hands. At a meeting held on the 28th of December 1823, it was made known that Janet Montgomery had given a lot of land to the Baptist chuich, and James Canfield and Robert Scott were appointed a committee to solicit assistance, and oversee the building of a "small, convenient house for the use of the church for public worship." At a meeting held on the 31st of October, 1824, it was recorded that the building of a house for public worship had commenced; that it had been inclosed and covered; that it was 30 feet wide. 34 feet long, and 18 feet high from the ground. At a meeting held on the 29th of May, 1825, it was agreed to defer the next meeting "until the first Lord's day in July, as it was expected the meeting house would be done by that time." The house being ready, public worship was held therein for the first time on the 3d of July, 1825. The record is that "Brother Scott preached at ten and broke bread; that Brother Babcock preached at two, and after he had preached, bread was again broken." On November 26, 1825, the record says, "as there was no prospect of getting stoves for the meeting house this fall, it was agreed to hold our meetings in the school house during the winter." On the 20th of August, 1826, the church met at Kingston again; and on the 1st of October, 1827, James J. and Robert Styles, from Kingston, and Eliza Styles were baptized in Rhinebeck, and received into church fellowship; and on the 28th of October, 1827, William J. Styles was ordained a deacon by the imposition of hands, to assist Deacon Canfield. On August 24, 1828, the record says, "Brother Thompson from New York, formerly pastor of the Old General Baptist Church in the city of Norwich, in England, has visited us, and preached amongst us with universal approbation."

At the yearly meeting on the 4th of July, 1830, the record says, "since the constituting of the church, nine years ago, forty-two have been baptized, two have died, five have been excluded, three dismissed to join other churches, and three moved to a distance from us, but had no dismission, so that there are left" thirty-six members. Of this number ten were Styleses, as follows ; James Styles, Sr., James Styles, Jr., William J. Styles, deacon ; James J. Styles, Robert Styles, Sarah Styles, Sarah Ann Styles, Jane Styles, Eliza W. Styles, Julia Styles.

On the 15th of August, 1831, Deacon James Canfield died, and on the 26th of May, 1831, James Styles, Jr., of Kingston, was appointed trustee in his place ; and on the 12th of May, 1832, George Snyder was appointed a deacon in his place.

In June, 1833, innovations were distracting the church and Rev. Robert Scott records an address to the brethren, from which we extract the opening paragraph as follows : " To the church of baptized believers at Rhinebeck Flatts : Brethren, I have for a long time past perceived that I should in the end be obliged to bear testimony against the innovations introduced amongst us, and thereby, perhaps, sacrifice the friendship of some, if not of you all ; or else, for peace sake, sacrifice the truth." He died on the 24th of September, 1834, in the seventy-fourth year of his age.

At the death of Father Scott, in 1834, the innovators against whom he had so earnestly protested, obtained full control of the church. Our recollection is that about 1840 it was generally understood that the people who constituted the Rhinebeck Baptist Society had become Campbellites and called themselves " Disciples." The book of records before us says that on the 28th of September, 1835, it was unanimously agreed that John Black should be an elder and a bishop among them.

At a meeting held at Sister Scott's, on the 15th of August, 1842, Elder Isaac Bevan, a Regular Baptist minister, came into view for the first time. An election of trustees proposed was, on his motion, postponed for want of legal notice. Due legal notice having been given, on the 8th of October, 1842, John Reed, George Snyder and Walter Sitzer were duly elected trustees, to serve until the 4th of July, 1843 ; and it was agreed that from henceforth there should be a meeting of the church held on the last Friday of every month. At the next meeting Rev. Isaac Bevan, his wife, Mary, and her sister, Hannah Lewis, were admitted to membership in the church, and by a unanimous vote Dominie Bevan was chosen to preside over its meetings until the end of the year, with John Reed, who, it seems, was the church's presiding elder by a previous vote. According to our recollection, the work was soon after left wholly in Dominie Bevan's hands. He was an earnest, indefatigable worker, and it soon became widely known that there was a Baptist church in Rhinebeck, with a strong and trustworthy man at its head. At a meeting held on the 30th of August, 1844, he asked the church to vote whether they would join the Dutchess County Association. The vote was taken, and resulted in a tie. But the strength of the Regulars, thus evinced, disheartened the Disciples, and a number of them left the church, and thus gave the vote to the Regulars at the next meeting. At a meeting held on the 5th of January, 1846, it was decided by the church that they would "remain" in the association; that they adopted the creed in the church book, recorded by Robert Scott; and that they would, in the future, break bread on the first Lord's day in every month only. And this attitude of the church on these questions is its position to-day, except that it is now in the Hudson River Central, instead of the Dutchess County Association.

Rev. Isaac Bevan continued in the pastorate until January, 1848. He added twenty members to the church by baptism, and built up the Baptist Church at Tivoli, in Red Hook, at the same time.

Terry Bradley, from Wilmington, in the State of Delaware, was Isaac Bevan's successor. He came to Rhinebeck from the University at Hamilton, and was ordained to the work of the ministry here, on the 15th of June, 1849, by a council of which Dr. William R. Williams, of New York, was moderator, and Thomas Reed, clerk. He lost his health, and resigned his call on the 7th of April, 1850.

Dr. James Lillie, having become a Baptist, and entering the service of the American Bible Union as a translator, took up his residence in Rhinebeck. He joined the church here on the 19th of June, 1852, his wife joining at the same time. He served it as pastor for a short time, and gave his hearers the benefit of his studies of the Hebrew and Greek texts of the

Scriptures.   His last sermon, on the meaning of the word " hell "
in the Old and New Testaments, was preached to a crowded
house in the Dutch Reformed Church, on invitation of the
pastor.

Rev. Samuel W. Culver succeeded Dr. Lillie, coming into
the pastorate in 1854, and going out on the 1st of January,
1857.   The church received the recess, new seats, new windows,
and the corniced and paneled ceiling during his pastorate, the
expense being mainly borne by the Hon. William Kelly, who
was a member of the building committee.

Rev. M. R. Fory, for a number of years the conductor of
a classical school in North Carolina, and at the North on account of the extreme suspicion entertained by Southern men of
Northern teachers, at this time, preached in this church for
several months during the year 1858, and delivered an illustra-
ted and very interesting course of lectures on Astronomy in the
church during the winter of this year.

William I. Gill came to Rhinebeck from the University at
Rochester.   He was ordained here on the 2d of September,
1858, by a council of which Dr. John C. Harrison, of Kingston,
was moderator, and W. Sherwood, clerk.   He came on the 15th
of August, 1858, and left on the 15th of October, 1859.

After this date the book contains no records for several
years, except the yearly election of a trustee.   We, however,
remember that in these years the church was ably supplied at
different periods by the Rev. J. N. Smith, a missionary of the
Hudson River Central Association, and Messrs. Harriman and
Coit, from the Rochester University.   The Baptistry and dress-
ing rooms were built in 1867, under the direction and at the
expense of the Hon. William Kelly.

Rev. A. M. Prentice, a student in the Seminary at Hamilton, was called to the pastorate, and ordained by a council convened in the church on the 9th of September, 1869, of which Rev.
W. H. Wines, of Poughkeepsie, was moderator, and H. C. Long-
year, of Saugerties, clerk.   The council was a noted one for the
prominence and ability of many of the preachers present.   The
ordaining prayer was delivered by the Rev. James Cooper, of
Rondout ; charge to the candidate by Rev. George W. Eaton,

D. D., LL. D., president of the Hamilton Seminary; hand of fellowship by Rev. W. H. Wines; charge to the church by Z. Grenell, Jr., of Kingston. Dominie Prentice served the church until the 1st of January, 1874, when he took the pastorate of the Baptist Church at Brockport, N. Y. He baptized twenty-nine persons, and added thirty-five to the membership of the church.

Benjamin Franklin Leipsner succeeded Dominie Prentice. He preached his first sermon on the 26th of July, 1874, and his last on the 13th of June, 1875. He was a graduate of the college at Hamilton, but did not enter the seminary. He was ordained at Newburgh, on the 4th of November, 1874. He added eighteen to the membership of the church by baptism.

Rev. George W. Barnes was Mr. Leipsner's successor. He commenced his pastorate on the 11th of October, 1875, and ended it on the 1st of May, 1880. He added fourteen to the church by baptism.

When we say that Dr. Richard Fuller, of Baltimore, Dr. William R. Williams, of New York, Dr. Martin B. Anderson, president of the University of Rochester, and Dr. Kendrick, professor of Greek in the same, have preached from the pulpit of this little church, it will not be doubted that those who worship there have heard as good sermons as were ever preached in the village of Rhinebeck.

THE CHURCH LOT.

The original church lot was fifty-one feet wide and one hundred and eighty deep. It was a gift from Mrs. Janet Montgomery, in 1823. The deed for it was given after her death, by Edward Livingston, her brother and heir, on the 25th day of July, 1829, in fulfilment of her intentions, It was given to Scott, Reed and Canfield, and their successors in office, as trustees, forever. In 1869, at the widening of Livingston street, the Hon. William Kelly purchased what was left of the corner lots, and added it, a gift, to the church lot. It was thus increased to eighty-nine feet front, and made a corner lot. At the corner of Montgomery and Livingston streets, it is the most eligibly situated church lot in the village ; and the Baptist people here are looking forward to the time when they will have a house worthy of their lot.   They are out of debt, their seats are free, and the minister's salary is promptly paid.

CHAPTER XXII.

THE VILLAGE LUTHERAN CHURCH.

The Third Evangelical Lutheran Church of Rhinebeck came into being so recently and so naturally, that there is very little in its history that will be new or interesting to our readers.   It was founded by the Rev. Charles A. Smith, who came into Rhinebeck the successor of the Rev. Augustus T. Geissenhainer in the pastorate of the Wurtemburg Lutheran Church.   This church had no parsonage at this date, and, as his predecessors, William J. Eyer and Augustus T. Geissenhainer, had done before him, he took up hes residence in the village of Rhinebeck, four miles from the Wurtemburg house of worship.   His first residence here was in the house in Livingston street now owned and occupied by the Widow Quick.   He preached in the Wurtemburgh church in the morning, and in the Baptist Church in the village in the evening.   An intelligent and attractive preach_er, this church soon became too small for his audiences.   Many of his hearers were village people belonging to different churches and no churches; but the large majority were Lutherans, and many of these were from the country, and manifested a preference for a village Lutheran Church.   And out of these facts arose the effort which resulted in the organization of the Third Evangelical Lutheran Church, and the erection of their house of worship in our village.

This house was built in the summer of 1842 by a building committee of which the Rev. Charles A. Smith and John Benner were the working members.   The lot on which it stands was the gift of John T. Schryver, who came in possession of the lands on Livingston street as a member of the Rhinebeck Improvement Company, who had bought of the Hon. Edward Livingston all the lands on the Flatts of which he had become the owner as the heir of his sister, Janet Montgomery.   The house was built at the head of and in the track of Centre street, because Mr. Schryver would give the land just there and no where else.

The house was built at a cost of five thousand five hundred dollars, and when completed, was, by common consent, the handsomest church edifice, in its interior finish and style, in the town. The pulpit, especially, was not only a new thing with us, but a very chaste and elegant thing of its kind ; and it sealed the doom of all the old pulpits in the town. The first to be inspired with the spirit of improvement by it, was our venerable Dutch Reformed Church. In a very few years after, its staid and steady and very respectable membership resolved to reconstruct the interior of their house. They built a recess and pulpit after the Lutheran model, and as nearly like it as possible, without being exactly the same.

The Bronson house in Livingston street was built by Lewis Marquet for the Lutheran parsonage. The joiner work in this, was done by James Latson, an ingenious young Rhinebeck carpenter, and the mason work by John E. Giles, the miser, and religious impostor and beggar, who was found dead in an outhouse at Niskaunah, in 1880, with nineteen thousand dollars in government bonds, and five thousand dollars in cash on his person. When the house was completed, and the time had arrived for the Lutheran people to buy, the price asked by Mr. Marquet was higher than the church were willing to pay, and they bought a lot of John T. Schryver, and built upon it the house which is now the parsonage. The Marquet house was occupied by Dominie Smith, as a tenant, for a year or two before this was accomplished.

The Rev. Charles A. Smith continued to minister to both the Wurtemburgh and the village church until 1849, when he took charge exclusively of the village church. We think he continued in this until 1851, when he accepted a call to a Lutheran church in Easton, Pennsylvania. He was followed in the pastorate of the Rhinebeck church by the Rev. John McKron, of Maryland, for two or three years. He was a highly tropical, and thus to many people, an eloquent preacher. He was succeeded by the Rev. J. W. Hasler, of whom we have no recollection. He was followed by Rev. Jacob Heck, whom we frequently met in Platt & Nelson's office, and whom we remember as an affable and intelligent young preacher. He was succeeded by Ernest Lubekert, who, we think, had been a music teacher, had become a good preacher, and was pretty high-church in his notions.   He was succeeded by the Rev. William H. Lukenbach, a very good preacher.   He was succeeded by the Rev. Reuben Hill, whom we remember as an intelligent man, and a preacher of more than ordinary ability.   He was succeeded by the Rev. Henry L. Zeigenfuss, who left the Lutherans for the Episcopalians, after a very short Lutheran pastorate, and is now the pastor of a strong Episcopal church in the city of Poughkeepsie.   And Dominie Zeigenfuss was succeeded by the Rev. William D. Strobel, who came into the pastorate in 1873, and is the present incumbent.   In the summer of 1876 he had important alterations and repairs made in the interior of the church edifice.   He had the platform of the pulpit brought down to a level with his people ; the pew doors removed, and the pews widened ; new windows, a new desk, and a new alter-rail constructed ; and the whole interior of the building newly painted and handsomely frescoed.   This work was done at a large expense, under the Doctor's supervision, and does credit to all concerned.

We have written this sketch of the Lutheran Church in our village from memory, having had no documents to consult ; and we have no doubt that many of our readers will recall facts that we have forgotten, or never knew.   And we shall close what we have to say with a few matters of opinion.

When sickness or death strikes a Rhinebeck family ; when drunkenness or any other misfortune assails it, no man among us is more readily consulted, or more promptly and cheerfully lends his sympathy and assistance, than Dr. Strobel.   People do not stop to ask, " Is he of our church? Is he a Free Mason, Odd Fellow, or Son of Temperance?"   He is a Christian minister, and the people recognize that he is such by divine right, with all his credentials properly authenticated.   There is not a drunkard in the town who would not sooner be caught reeling, or be lifted out of the gutter by any other man in the town than by Dr. Strobel.   The respect with which the masses regard a man's opinions, and the duties of his position, is always the measure of his influence for good in a community.   When the drunkard taunts him with the extravagance of his opinions, and is not ashamed to reel, or drop into the gutter in his presence, he ought to be satisfied that his mission is not that of a temperance lecturer, or that there is something wrong in his tactics. It avails nothing that a man stands well with sober people, and meets them in the lodge room of the Good Templars. He must stand well with the drunkard, and be able to "sup with publicans and sinners," without taking harm, when virtue will certainly pass out of him, and good be done to others.

CHAPTER XXIII.

THE RHINEBECK EPISCOPAL CHURCH.

FOR many years prior to the establishment of the Episcopal Church in the village of Rhinebeck, Episcopal services were held at intervals in different places. The first Episcopal service held here was by the Rev. Mr. Johnson, of Kingston, who, by courtesy of the Methodist Church people, held service in their edifice once a month. Subsequently, services were held in the " Baker Building" by Rev. Sheldon Davis, Rev. Mr. Wyatt, Rev. Dr. Sherwood, Rev. Dr. Montgomery, and Rev. J. C. Talbot, the present bishop of Indiana. In the year 1852, Rev. Richard S. Adams became a resident in Rhinebeck, and took the following measures to organize an Episcopal church in this village.

ORGANIZATION OF THE CHURCH.

" WHEREAS, It is the desire and intention of the parties whose names are hereunto affixed to establish a Protestant Episcopal parish in the village of Rhinebeck, under pastoral care of the Rev. Richard S. Adams, a minister of the Protestant Episcopal Church of the United States, and to incorporate the same according to the statute in such case made;

" Now, therefore, the said parties by this instrument, declare that they attach themselves to the Protestant Episcopal Church; and the said Richard S. Adams, also, hereby declares that he receives and recognizes the said parties as belonging to said church.

" Given under our hands this eleventh day of August, in the year one thousand eight hundred and fifty-two.

" JAS. M. PENDLETON,   A. WAGER,
   GOUVERNUER TILLOTSON,   E. PLATT,
   T. GILLENDER,   JULIUS BELLARD,
   G. W. CLARKE,   M. E. A. GEER,
   ISAAC F. VAN VLIET,   R. S. ADAMS,
            WILLIAM BETTERTON.

" NOTICE.—The persons belonging to the Episcopal Church congregation will meet in this room in the Baker building on Wednesday, the 18th instant, for the purpose of incorporating themselves, and of electing two wardens and eight vestrymen.

                                        " R. S. ADAMS.

" Rhinebeck, August 8, 1852.

" Dutchess County, ss.: R. S. Adams, being duly sworn, says that the above notice was publicly read by him in the time of morning service, on Sunday, the 8th day of August, and on Sunday the 15th day of August, in the year 1852, to the congregation worshipping in the ' Baker building,' in the village of Rhinebeck, according to the rites of the Protestant Episcopal Church.

                                        R. S. ADAMS.

" Sworn before me this 18th }
    day of August, 1852.   }

                        TUNIS WORTMAN,
                          Justice of the Peace."

                    " RHINEBECK, Dutchess County, }
                            August 18th, 1852.   }

" On this day the following persons of full age, belonging to the church and congregation, worshipping in a building called the ' Baker building,' in the said town, in which divine service is celebrated according to the rites of the Protestant Episcopal Church, in the State of New York, met together at their said place of worship, pursuant to notice duly given, in the time of morning service, on the two Sundays previous thereto, for the purpose of incorporating themselves as a religious society, under the acts of the Legislature of the State of New York:

" Rev. Richard S. Adams, George W. Clarke, Isaac F. Van Vliet, Theophilus Gillender, Julius Bellard, William Betterton, and Marshall E. A. Geer.

" The Rev. Richard S. Adams being the minister of said church and congregation, was called to the chair, and Theophilus Gillender was appointed secretary. The notice of the said meeting was then read. It was then, on motion,

" *Resolved*, That the persons here present do proceed to incorporate themselves as a religious society in communion with the Protestant Episcopal Church in the United States of America, and that the said church and congregation be known in law by the name and title of " The rector, wardens, and vestrymen of the Church of the Messiah in the town of Rhinebeck, in the county of Dutchess.

" The said meeting then proceeded, on motion, to choose two church wardens and eight vestrymen of the said church, when the following persons were duly elected : Eliphalet Platt and Isaac F. Van Vliet, church wardens; James M. Pendleton Gouverneur Tillottson, George W. Clark, Ambrose Wager, Julius Bellard, Isaac F. Russell, George Lorillard, and Marshall E. A. Geer, vestrymen. A certificate of incorporation having been proposed, was presented, containing the above proceedings, which was signed by the chairman of. this meeting, and by Isaac F. Van Vliet and George W. Clark, and was witnessed by William Betterton and John R. Rynders ; and the said William Betterton was requested to prove the due execution of the same, and cause it to be recorded by the county clerk.

R. S. ADAMS,   I. F. VAN VLIET,
Chairman,   G. W. CLARKE,
THEOS. GILLENDER, Secretary."

" CERTIFICATE OF INCORPORATION.

" *To all whom these presents may concern :*

" We, whose names and seals are affixed to this instrument, do hereby certify that on the 18th day of August, in the year 1852, the male persons of full age, worshipping in a building called the " Baker Building," in which divine worship is celebrated, according to the rites of the Protestant Episcopal Church,

in the State of New York, and in pursuance of notice duly
given to the said congregation in the time of morning service
on two Sundays previous to such meeting, that the persons belonging to said congregation would meet at the time and place
aforesaid, for the purpose of incorporating themselves, and of
electing two church wardens and eight vestrymen ; and we further certify that the Rev R. S. Adams, minister of said congregation, presided at the said meeting ; and we further certify
that at the said meeting, Eliphalet Platt and Isaac F. Van Vliet
were duly elected church wardens of the said congregation and
church : and James M. Pendleton, Gouverneur Tillottson,
George W. Clarke, Ambrose Wager, Julius Bellard, Isaac F.
Russell, George Lorillard, and Marshal E. A. Geer were duly
elected vestrymen. That Monday, in Easter week, was, by the
said meeting, fixed upon as the day on which the said offices of
church wardens and vestrymen should annually thereafter cease,
and their successors in office be chosen ; and that the said meeting determined and declared that the said church and congregation should be known in law by the name of " The rector,
church wardens, aud vestrymen of the Church of the Messiah,
in the town of Rhinebeck, in the county of Dutchess.

" In testimony whereof, we, the said Richard S. Adams, who
presided at the said election of wardens and vestrymen, and
Isaac F. Van Vliet and George W. Clarke, who were present
and witnessed the proceedings aforesaid, have hereunto subscribed our names, and affixed our seals, this 18th day of August, in the year of our Lord one thousand eight hundred and
fifty-two.

" Signed and sealed in }   R. S. ADAMS,
   presence of   }   I. F. VAN VLIET,
        " WM. BFTTERTON,   GEO. W. CLARKE.
       JOHN R. RYNDERS."

The above certificate was duly recorded in the clerk's office
of the county of Dutchess.

The interesting ceremony of laying the corner stone of the
Protestant Episcopal Church in this village, took place
on Thursday last (Sept. 16, 1852), in the presence of a large
assemblage. Services were held at the " Baker Building," at

THE RHINEBECK EPISCOPAL CHURCH

half past two o'clock P. M., the following named clergy being in attendance :

"The Rector of the Parish, Rev. Reuben Sherwood, Rev. George B. Andrews, Rev. William B. Thomas, Rev. Samuel Buel, Rev. William Watson, Rev. Sheldon Davis, Rev. George Waters, Rev. Jonathan Coe, of the Diocese of New York, Rev. J. C. Talbot, of the Diocese of Kentucky."

After the usual solemnities had been performed, Rev. Mr. Coe read a paper bearing the following inscription, a duplicate of which is deposited in a tin box in the corner stone :

"The Parish of the Church of the Messiah was organized August 18th, 1852. The Corner Stone was laid by the Rev. Reuben Sherwood, D. D., rector of St. James' Church, Hyde Park, on Thursday, September 16th, 1852. Rev. Richard S. Adams, Rector."

"Eliphalet Platt, M. D., Isaac F. Van Vliet, M. D., wardens."

"James M. Pendleton, Gouverneur Tillottson, George W. Clarke, Ambrose Wager, Julius Bellard, Isaac F. Russell, George Lorrillard, M. D., Marshal E. A. Geer, vestrymen."

There are likewise deposited in the stone the names of the village trustees, the names of the building committee, Theophilus Gillender and Gouverneur Tillottson, the name of the donor of the lot of ground (Rutsen Suckley, Esq.), on which the edifice is to stand, the names of the master carpenter and mason ; also a Bible and a prayerbook, a church almanac, a number of the Churchman, a number of the Gospel Messenger, a number of the Rhinebeck Mechanic and Gazette, and a number of the Rhinebeck Gazette and Dutchess County Advertiser.

The corner stone was then laid by Rev. Reuben Sherwood, D. D., of St. James' Church, Hyde Park ; after which an address was delivered by the rector of the parish, and listened to with marked attention by the large audience.

The church was consecrated on the sixth day of October, 1855, by the Right Rev. Horatio Potter, D. D., provisional bishop of the diocese.

The Rev. Richard S. Adams was the first pastor. He was elected on the 18th of December, 1852, and resigned on the

24th of December, 1853, thus serving the church as pastor for one year.

The Rev. George Herbert Walsh succeeded Mr. Adams. He was elected on the 1st of June, 1854, and resigned on the 18th of June, 1866, having thus served the church for twelve years.   He was highly esteemed as a member of our commnnity, and while he retained the esteem and affection of all his people to the last, he carried away with him the best wishes of all among us who had made his acquaintance.   The lecture room and the chapel at Rhinecliff were built, and the rectory purchased during Mr. Walsh's pastorate.

The Rev. A. F. Olmsted succeeded Mr. Walsh.   He was elected rector on the 29th of September, 1866, and entered on his duties on the 1st of November, 1866, is the present incumbent, and thus in the fourteenth year of his pastorate.

The Episcopalians of Rhinebeck, as they are almost everywhere else in America, are an intelligent, self-reliant people, and manifest their zeal as Christians in a manner peculiar to themselves.   Goodness with them is not so much a matter of going to church and to meeting to exhort and probe each other for spiritual manifestations, as it is deeds of actual and practical benevolence.   Mr. Olmsted's congregations are full in summer, but not large in winter.   He is a preacher of thorough education, great learning, logical acumen and large charity.

The people in our little village of five churches are more disposed to agree to differ than they were in times past, and the presence in our midst of Dominie Olmsted has contributed largely to this result.   A union among men of diverse opinions is far more difficult, and requires much more culture and grace than a union among those whose opinions are the same.   The sentiment, " No church but ours—our church or none," when held by two sects in close proximity to each other, presages unneighborly relations and impending war.   Whereas, when they have been brought to see that " the truth is not all with us, but shared by our neighbors," harmony at once sets in.   God is honored in the evidence of human exaltation when men of different religious opinions have become able " to agree to differ."

The following persons are the present officers of the church :

Theophilus Gillender and James M. DeGarmo, wardens; Ambrose Wager, R. P. Huntington, Edward Jones, D. F. Sipperly, F. H. Roof, James C. McCarty, and John O'Brien, vestrymen.

The following persons have been large contributors to the establishment and the support of the church: Mrs. Mary R. Miller, Mrs. Franklin Delano, Miss Elizabeth Jones, Mr. Horatio Miller, Mr. Edward Jones, Mr. William Astor, and Mr. Lewis Livingston.

Since the organization of the church there have been two hundred and thirty-six baptisms and one hundred and twenty-seven confirmations.

During the past year the church has been thoroughly repaired and painted, handsomely decorated in the interior, and received four large and costly oil paintings, by celebrated artists, from Rome—a gift from Mrs. Francis H. Delano.

CHAPTER XXIV.

RHINEBECK ROMAN CATHOLIC CHURCH.

THE Roman Catholic Church was brought into the town of Rhinebeck by Rev. Michael Scully, in 1862. He preached in the hall of the Starr Institute during this year. A lot was purchased, and steps taken to build a church in the village of Rhinebeck, on the northwest corner of Livingston and Mulberry streets. This lot was sold, and finally became the property of Henry Latson, who is the present owner and occupant. In 1763 George Rogers, of Tivoli, bought of Charles H. Russell six acres of land at Rhinecliff, for $4,000, and deeded them over to Rev. Michael Scully, the parish priest, for a church lot and cemetery. St. Joseph's Church, at Rhinecliff, was erected on this lot, under the direction of Father Scully, in 1864, with George Veitch as architect, and John Bird as master mason.

CHAPTER XXV.

RHINEBECK FLATTS.

WILLIAM TRAPHAGEN was the first owner of lands on Beekman's Rhinebeck patent, and of a tract comprising several hundred acres, and including a part of the Flatts. On the 4th of June, 1706, he called himself a wheelwright in Kingston, and sold to Jacob Kip twenty-four acres of land, " situate, lying and being in Dutchess county, to ye west of a hill, beginning at a white oak tree marked with three notches and a cross, along ye bounds of Col. Beekman's lands to a run of water on ye west side, and along ye said run of water * * * to a bend in said kill," etc. On the 17th day of February, 1710-11, he sold to Arie Hendricks one hundred and twenty-eight and a half acres of land, beginning at a plain of the said Col. Henry Beekman on the east side of a small run of water, by some people called Kip's kill, parting it from the lands of Hendrick Kip, Jacob Kip and Gerrit Aartsen, extending south to the kill named Landsman's kill, where both do meet and join together in one, making a point; and on the east side all along and through the land of the said William Traphagen.

On the 27th of April, 1736, William Traphagen made a will in which he directed that all his landed estate should be equally divided among his three children, Arent and William Traphagen, and Geesje, his daughter, wife of Isaac Kool. On the 25th of June, 1741, Arent and William deeded to Geesje her share of this land in four lots ; one called her " home lot," containing thirty-five acres, three roods and thirty perches ; the second, " lot No. 2," containing twenty-two acres, three roods and sixteen perches ; the other, a " meadow lot " containing five acres, two roods and twenty perches ; the other, " two acres of upland or woodland, which remains undivided ; containing altogether about sixty-six acres of land. Out of the home lot was reserved " to the said William and Arent Traphagen two-thirds of the old dwelling house which now stands on the said lot."

This old dwelling house was doubtless the old stone house in West Market street, called the " old states prison." This was also pretty certainly the residence of William Traphagen, when he joined Lawrence Osterhout and Jacob Kip in the request for the land of the Reformed Dutch Church, in 1730, and was thus one of the first substantial houses built in this town.

On the 26th of September, 1769, Isaac Cole, yeoman, and Simon Cole, merchant, conveyed this land to Dr. Hans Kierstead, of Kingston, Ulster County, and about the same time Everardus Bogardus became the owner of Arent Traphagen's home and wood lot. In 1774, Evarardus Bogardus and Dr. Hans Kiersted adjusted their boundaries by mutual conveyances. In the conveyance of Bogardus to Kiersted we are told that the lands of both are " situated in Rhinebeck precinct, on the west side of the post road," and the division line agreed upon commences " upon the south side of the road leading from the post road to Kip's ferry, and on the east side of the lane leading from the ferry road to Kiersted's house."

THE RHINEBECK HOTEL.

It thus appears that William Traphagen's lands were purchased from Henry Beekman, the father, before 1706 ; that they reached from the Rhinebeck kill to the post road ; and from the junction of Landsman's and Rhinebeck kills in the sawmill pond north to the north bounds of the land sold by him to Jacob Kip in 1706 ; that the hotel corner fell to Arent Traphagen at the death of his father ; that at his own death, about 1769, it was conveyed by his heirs to Everardus Bogardus, who was a merchant here and probably an inn keeper also, from 1769 to the close of the century. In 1802 the property was in the possession of Benjamin Bogardus, and on the 7th of October, in this year, was conveyed by him to Asa Potter, who, according to the Institute map, was an inn keeper in a house in the vicinity of the present residence of Mrs. W. B. Platt. Asa Potter died on the 9th of October, 1805. On the 25th of November, 1807, Philip J. Schuyler, as administrator of Asa Potter, sold the property to Elisha R. Potter, of Kingston, Rhode Island. On the 11th of November, 1834, Elisha R. Potter sold it to Richard Schell. On the 1st of May, 1837, Richard Schell sold it to Johnathan Wilson. On the 7th of September, 1839, David

Seymour, master in chancery, sold it to Elisha R. Potter, son of Elisha R. On the 1st of May, 1848, Elisha R. Potter sold it to Garret Van Keuren, Henry DeLamater and William B. Platt. From 1802, when this property passed out of the possession of the Bogarduses, to the purchase by Van Keuren, DeLamater and Platt, in 1848, it seems to have been in the possession, or under the lien of the Potters. William Jacques, by whose name the house was known during most of the period between 1805 and 1848, appears in our old town records as early as 1794. He died on the 9th of October, 1835, aged 67 years; and the house ceased to be Jacques' hotel in 1837. It was rebuilt a few years since, and greatly enlarged, and is now kept by the Tremper Brothers, a first-class hotel.

RHINEBECK VILLAGE.

A map of Rhinebeck Flatts, laid out in village lots, was made by John Cox, Jr., as early as 1792. We have not seen the original map, and do not know where to look for it, except among the papers of the late Edward Livingston. We have seen references to it in old deeds. In an old deed in the possession of Jacob L. Tremper, we are told that on the 20th of March, 1799, Nathan Brownson and his wife sold to William Tremper, "all that certain lot of land situated, lying and being in the town of Rhinebeck, at the Flatts, and distinguished in a map thereof, made by John Cox, as lot No. 11, beginning at the southwest corner of Butler and Bartholomew's lot, known as No. 9." This lot was bounded on one side by the post road, and contained one acre of land. In a deed to Wiiliam Carroll for the Mathias lot on the west side of the post road, we are told that it was conveyed by Margaret Livingston to Abraham Adriance, and by said Adriance to Henry DeBaise, and known as lot No. 4 in a survey made by John Cox, Jr.

We have a copy of a part of this map, covering the land laid out on the east side of the post road, which shows that East Market street was laid out as early as 1792, as far as the church lands, now Mulberry street. In 1801, the commissioners of highways carried this street through the church lands as a public road, commencing at Pultz's corner, which was then in the possesion of Abram Brinckerhoff. In 1802, it became the Ulster and Saulsbury turnpike. Before this date we can find no evidence that there was a single building on East Market street. The village seems to have been laid out in acre lots. The southeast corner lot extended south to the church lot, and the same distance east, being an exact square, and was purchased by Coert and Henry DuBois. The next lot east, also a square, was purchased by a Mr. Jones, probably Gen. Montgomery's nephew. The next lot east was purchased by Philip Bogardus, probably son of Everardus. The northeast corner, also a square acre, was purchased by John T. Schryver and Tunis Conklin. The next square east, by Asa Potter; and the square next east to his, by Frederick Kline. North, the lots had the depth of two squares, and the width of half a square. The lot next east to Schryver and Conklin's corner was purchased by Gen. Armstrong. The old building on the corner was built and used for a store and post office before 1800, and possibly many years before. The old house rebuilt by Dr. Van Vliet was the residence of Asa Potter at an early date, and probably built by him. It was, at one time, the residence of Coert DuBois, and at another, of Henry F. Talmage. The residence of Jacob Schaad was on the lot of Frederick Kline, occupied by him at an early date, and probably built by him. The purchasers of these acre lots subdivided them, and sold to other parties. On the 23d of November, 1807, Elisha R., son of Asa Potter, sold his lot to Peter Brown and Christian Schell, then in the occupation of Schryver and Conklin, and bounded westerly by Spaulding, and northerly by Gen. Armstrong. These lots have had many owners. Whether Coert and Henry DuBois built the first store on their corner or not, we have not learned. They were merchants there at an early date, and had, for successors, John Fowks, Christian Schell, John Davis, Henry and James Hoag, George Schryver, John Benner, Moses Ring, George Fellows and George Storm. John Benner rebuilt the corner, and rented the second story to John Armstrong, Esq., for a law office. John T. Schryver, William Teller, Benjamin Schultz, Henry DeLamater, Freeman Jennings, William Bates, Simon Welch and John M. Sandford were merchants on the northeast corner. At the hotel corner,

Henry F. Talmage, Smith Dunning, John C. Ostrom, Isaac F. Russell, William Bates and George Bard sold dry goods, groceries and hardware at different times.   Platt's corner was purchased by Christian Schell, and the present stone edifice erected thereon by him.   We cannot learn from whom he made this purchase.   Our old people tell us that this was an open field before this date.

It was conveyed to William B. Platt by. Richard Schell in 1835, and is still in the possession of his family.   We think the store adjoining on the west, on the same premises, was the millinery shop of Margaret A. Elmendorf and Gertrude Buckland when we first knew it.   The next building west was the well-known storehouse of William S. Cowles & Co., for many years. The first proprietor of whom we get knowledge was James Teller, whose executors conveyed it to Thomas and Albert Traver. It is now in the possession of our worthy townsman, Martin Diechelman, and in the occupation of David E. Ackert, mercantile successor to the Cowles Brothers.

THE VILLAGE INCORPORATED.

The act for the incorporation of the village of Rhinebeck was passed on the twenty-third of April, 1834.   The first election under it was held on the twenty-sixth of May, 1834, and the officers elected were as follows: *Trustees*, Eliphalet Platt, Peter Pultz, John Drury, John I. Smith, John T. Schryver, Jacob Heermance, John Jennings.   *Assessors*, John A. Drum, Theophilus Nelson, Stephen McCarty.   *Treasurer*, Nicholas Drury.   On the seventeenth of June following, John T. Schryver was elected president of the board of trustees, and Nicholas V. Schryver, secretary.   The president appointed John Drury, John Jennings, and Peter Pultz, a committee to ascertain and report the extent of side-walks necessary to be flagged; John I. Smith, John Drury and John Jennings, a committee on fire, and Eliphalet Platt, John Drury and Jacob Heermance, a committee on nuisances.

The part of the town of Rhinebeck included within the limits of the corporation was as follows: " Beginning at the northwest corner of the late Andrew Teal's land, it being also

the southwest corner of Zachariah Traver's farm, at the old lot
line between the Rutsen and Beekman patents ; and running
thence south three degrees east, thirty-five chains, to Landsman's kill or creek ; thence along the south side thereof, as it
winds and turns, to a stone set by a rock, the stone being marked C ; thence north, twenty-four degrees west, twenty-four
chains fifty links, to the corner of John Teller's field on the line
between his lands and those of the late Henry B. Livingston,
at the south side of Ulster and Delaware turnpike ; thence
north, twenty-six degrees thirty minutes east, along their line
to Edward Livingston's land ; then across his land in the same
direction to a stone, twenty links southwest of an apple tree
marked ; the whole line measuring thirty-six chains fifty-seven
links ; thence across the south end of Jeffry H. Champlin's land
north eighty degrees east, eleven chains, sixty-six links, to his
southeast corner by the west side of the post road ; thence south
fifty degrees east forty-five chains to the place of beginning ;"
the territory embraced within these limits " to be known and
distinguished as the village of Rhinebeck." By an act of the
Ligislature passed in the year 1867, the limits of the village
were greatly extended, with the motive of those who petitioned
for it, to increase its taxable property. The farmers to be included by this enlargement generally protested against it, and
John J. Hager had influence enough with the trustees and Legislature to have his farm left out.

CHAPTER XXVI.

PUBLIC INSTITUTIONS AND BUSINESS.

THE STARR INSTITUTE.

THE Starr Institute is a gift to the people from Mrs. Mary R. Miller, a granddaughter of General Philip Schuyler, of Revolutionary fame, in memory of her husband, the Hon. William Starr Miller, who died in the city of New York in 1854. The Institute building is a commodious and substantial structure, perfectly adapted to its purpose. It contains a spacious free public reading room on the right ; a circulating library and ladies' reception room on the left ; a large and handsome lecture hall in the rear ; and a kitchen and dining hall in the basement. The second story consists of one room, which is given to a Standard Library. The price of membership is fifty cents per year, which entitles the holder to draw books from the Circulating Library, and to consult at his leisure those in the Standard Library. A small rent is charged for the use of the Lecture Hall. The Reading Room is stocked with the New York, Albany and Poughkeepsie daily papers, and other reading matter, and is free to all. The Institute was incorporated in 1862, and the building completed in the same year.

THE DE GARMO CLASSICAL INSTITUTE.

This educational institution had its birth in the Rhinebeck Academy, established in the year 1840. It maintained its existence as an Academy, under different teachers, until 1860, when it became the property, by purchase, of Professor James M. De Garmo, and has since been conducted under his name. He erected the present large and handsome structure in 1871. It is a prosperous school, and has everywhere an excellent reputation.

UNION FREE SCHOOL.

.The lands for this School were procured and the building erected in 1869. The districts were united and the school made free several years earlier. The number of children in the district, between the ages of five and twenty-one, is 655. The full valuation of property in the district is $1,162,789. The tax collected in this year for the support of the school, was $2,110.

THE RHINEBECK BANK.

The Bank of Rhinebeck was established in 1853. The subscriptions to the stock were procured in the previous year by Theophilus Gillender, Esq., on a paper, the heading to which was drawn up by Gouverneur Tillottson, Esq., who came into the practice of the law here on the death of John Armstrong. The Bank was commenced on a capital of one hundred and fifty thousand dollars. It has since been raised to one hundred and seventy-five thousand dollars. Its first officers were: Henry De Lamater, President; Wm. B. Platt, Vice-President; De Witt C. Marshall, Cashier. It has been well managed, and a prosperous institution from the commencement.

THE RHINEBECK SAVINGS BANK.

For the establishment of this institution the public are also indebted to the enterprise of Theophilus Gillender, Esq., who was its first Secretary and Treasurer. It was organized in 1862. Its deposits are now $248,150, and its present officers are: Joshua C. Bowne, President; Simon Welch, Secretary and Treasurer.

RHINEBECK HALL.

In 1872 the people of Rhinebeck, at a special election, voted (238 to 128) to build a Town Hall. Virgil C. Traver, Esq., was supervisor of the town in this year, and, his term of office about to expire, the town auditors, on February 15, 1873, appointed him to superintend the construction of the building until completed. It was finished in this year, at a cost of $20,-500. The money was procured on the bonds of the town, all of which, excepting four thousand dollars, have been redeemed. The mason work was done by Jas. D. Hogan and Rensselaer Worden, and the carpenter work by Henry Latson, all Rhinebeck mechanics. It is a very handsome and a very substantial building, answers all the purposes of its construction, and is nearly self-supporting.

CHAPTER XXVII.

THE BENNER FAMILY.

WE find among the earliest settlers of Rhinebeck a branch of the Benner family, of which the descendants in this county are somewhat limited. Yet the name and family are largely represented in the United States, especially in the States of Maine, Pennsylvania and Virginia. It is perhaps one of the largest German families; and in the early Baronial times had a remarkable history. The ancestors are described as being of great size and muscular strength; and many of them were distinguished as bold and gallant knights in the days of chivalry. The following is an abstract from a work on chivalry and the armorial bearings of families in central Europe, in the library of Vienna, in Austria:

The Benner family is a very old and widely extended one in Upper Bavaria and along the Rhine; and among the many distinguished men from this family, the first mentioned was a knight by the name of Oluf, who is described as living on the Benner estate, in Upper Bavaria; and his name is preserved in a chapel near by, called "Chapel of Oluf der Benner," on account of the munificent gift which he made for its erection, in the year 1053.

Gurth der Benner, while stiil a youth, joined the army of the Crusaders under Godfried de Bouillon, in the year 1079, and on the approach to Antioch, in the early dawn, when the morning stars were waning, he encountered and slew a knight of the enemy, who is said to have been of great size and strength; and for which heroic deed he was at Antioch made and called " Knight of the Morning Star," and ever after wore a star in the centre of his shield. He returned safely, and settled on the banks of the Rhine; and from him the family was there widely extended.

Odo der Benner was a lineal descendant of the distinguished knight; and as a knight himself was engaged in the tournament held at Maintz, in the year 1263, and was awarded the first prize for his bold and dextrous exploits on that occasion.

Waldemar der Benner, in the year 1322, was one of the leaders of the Rebellion which was formed on the Rhine against King Ludwig, and so distinguished himself at the battle of Muhldorf that he afterwards received from the government not only its highest honors but a large tract of land, extending towards Bergennes, as the reward of his gallantry. Waldemar at his death divided this large estate between his four sons and the Cloister of Holy Laurentius, at Colle.

From this time onward the wealth and fame of the Benner family began to decline, and four of the above named five sons entered the Venetian army, and but one of them returned. This was Wernker der Benner. He returned to his home, sold what remained to him of his father's estate, and in the year 1362 entered the Cloister of Saint Laurentius, to which his father had been such a liberal benefactor. How long he remained in the Cloister does not appear, but he left one son, Dietselm der Benner, who appears to have returned to and cultivated the land of his ancestors.

Ulrich der Benner was a son of Deitselm, and in 1387, we are told, he went to Hohlstein and greatly improved his social and pecuniary condition. But at the same time it is said his descendants became numerous and poor, and were obliged to pursue the ordinary avocations of life for their support.

Eustachias der Benner is the next name in the consecutive history of the family. In the year 1435 he is mentioned as a Stadtholder of one of the provinces, and, it is said, he held the office many years on account of the faithful and upright manner in which he discharged his duties.

After this, in 1520, the Bavarian wars set in, and the family became very much scattered, and for a time lost to history.

Dietrich der Benner is the last named in history who bore the armor of a knight, and claimed to belong to the Royal lineage. He lived on a small estate in Bavaria, and on small means, but still maintained the dignity and character of Royalty until 1628, when he was appointed a Field Marshal of a division of the Bavarian army, and so ably discharged his duties that he became very distinguished, and received an addition to his estate. On his shield he bore a rampant unicorn, on a ground of green and gold.

This Dietrich der Benner was a Protestant from Protestant Bavaria, and was no doubt the General Benner who figured so conspicuously in the History of the Huguenots. It is said that all the Benners were notably Protestants.

About this time the name of this great family began to be indifferently written Bender, or Benner, in different localities. And it is supposed that the former authography arose from the fact that large numbers of them located in different towns and cities, and engaged in the same mechanical work, which required binding, or tying together, such as book-binders and coopers; and from this circumstance they were as a family or class called Binders, or Benders. In the same way the aristocratic Dutch of our own State, particularly at Albany, who had individual names, were yet as a class called Knickerbockers, from the circumstance of having nearly all been employed in the making and baking marbles for the children. The name is derived from Knicker, a marble, and Bakker, a Baker. Knickerbakker, from which the transition to Knickerbocker was easy.

In the records of the German Reformed Church here, Rev. Johan Casper Rubel always wrote the name, Benner; while Rev. Gerhard Daniel Cock, who came after him, always wrote it Bender.

The first family of the name in the town of Rhinebeck, of which we have any tradition, was that of Valentyn Bender and Margaret, his wife, who, with their two sons, Johannes and Henrich, came to Rhinebeck from Upper Bavaria, in the beginning of the 18th century. He obtained of Col. Henry Beekman the usual life-lease of a farm on the Hudson River, about three miles north of Rhinebeck Landing, being the same farm afterwards long the residence of Gen. Armstrong, and now owned by the heirs of his son-in-law, Wm. B. Astor. The site selected by Bender was too fine to leave him long at rest. Col. Beekman and his family soon discovered that this was the finest situation on the banks of the river, and wished to possess it again without delay. He, therefore, proposed an exchange, and offered for the surrender of the life-lease a like quantity of land in fee, in any part of his lands. This proposition was accepted by Valentyn Bender, and eagerly by his wife, who, by the tradition of all her descendants, was a somewhat remarkable woman, possessing an energetic character, and a keen eye to the future. Col. Beekman thereupon executed a deed for a piece of land situate about one mile sonthwest of Lower Red Hook village, which forms a part of the farm which became the Benner homestead, and which, from the time Valentyn Bender took possession, under his deed, until about four years since, was uninterruptedly owned and occupied by the Benner family. The deed from Henry Beekman bears date, January 25, 1721, and describes the lands as "certuating on a large plaine, being part of a tract of land formerly obtained from Coll. Peter Schuyler, on the east side of Hudson's river, in the above said County, lying northward from ye town of Rinbeek, and joins partly to ye southeast end of a meadow called Peek's Vly, and so northerly where it begaineth by a stony point, which is over against where a small rune of whater comes from Countryman's fountaine, and intersax with a small rune of whater that comes out of the aforesaid Peek's Vly." This is the only deed we have seen in which the land laid out for the High Dutchers, is called the "Town of Rhinebeck." It shows that Valentyn Bender was not one of the settlers for whom the land was laid out.

Valentyn Bender died soon after he took possession of this farm, and left him surviving his widow, Margriet, his two sons, Johannes and Henrich, and three daughters, Anna Maria, Catharina, and Margriet: It was now that his widow Margriet displayed her energy and perseverance. She managed the household and the farm ; brought up the children in habits of industry and frugality ; made large additions to her possessions; and, before her death, owned over three hundred acres of good land. She lived to see all her daughters well married, and, at the close of her life, divided her land between her two sons, giving to Johannes the old homestead, and to Henrich that portion of her acquired land which became the possession of Jacob Cholwell, is still owned by his heirs, and which was sold by Henrich some time after his mother's death.

Valentyn Bender certainly left two sons and two daughters, and there may have been a third son and daughter. The daughters of whom we have knowledge were : Anna Maria, who married Zacharias Schmidt, and Catharina, who married Henrich Tidter, whose families are recorded on another page.

Henrich, son of Valentyn Bender, married Catharine Betzer (now Pitcher), and had children as follows: Anna Margreda, baptized May 6, 1741, married Jan. 20, 1761, Zacharias Volandt ; Catharina, baptized Aug. 12, 1744, married Feb. 7, 1762, Frederick Streit, Jr.; Annatjin, baptized Jan. 27, 1752, married Oct. 10, 1774, Phillip Mohr ; Christina, married Dec. 16, 1770, Petrus Mohr ; Magdalena, baptized May 18, 1755 ; Henrich, baptized Sept. 10, 1758, married Catharina Pitcher, probably his cousin. There were other children in this family, probably born between 1744 and 1752, of whose baptism the book before us contains no record.

Johannes, son of Valentyn Bender, married Magdalena Streid (now Streit), and had children as follows : Hans Velden, in other words, Valentyn, the son of Hans, born Dec. 26, 1741, married, 1st, Alida Weitman, 2d, Lydia Feroe, widow, 1st of Conrad Lasher, 2d, of Benjamin Van Steenburgh ; Catharine, baptized Aug. 12, 1744 ; Henrich, baptized Aug. 16, 1751, married Marytjen Sagendorf; Johannes, baptized Oct. 1753 ; Jacobus, baptized Feb. 15, 1756 ; Anna Maria, baptized Aug. 13, 1758 ; Petrus, baptized Dec. 11, 1763, married Jenneken Waldorf ; Ludowick, baptized Jan. 29, 1766. There were other children in this family, also, of whom the book before us contains no records.

Henry Bender, Jr., and Catharina Pitcher, had children as follows : Catharine, baptized May 27, 1780, married, Nov. 8 1801, Garret Cock ; Henry, baptized June 29, 1783, married Jan. 1, 1805, his cousin, Anna Moore ; Maria, baptized Oct. 9, 1785, married, Jan. 8, 1804, John Knickerbocker ; Elizabeth, baptized Dec. 8, 1788, married Cyrus Burnap ; Christina, born May 11, 1799, married Capt. Samuel Nelson.

Hans Felten Bender and Alida Wietman had children, as follows : Hellena, born Dec. 19, 1775, married Capt. David Sipperly ; John, born Aug. 20, 1797, married, Sept. 8, 1808, Hannah Schryver ; Elizabeth, born Oct. 13, 1789, married Jacob Sipperly ; Jacob, born Sept. 27, 1791, married Dec. 25, 1810,

Margaret Feroe ; Wilhelmus, born March 2, 1794, married Hellena Ostrander; Amy, died young.

Peter Bender and Jenneken Waldorf had children, as follows : William and Maria, twins ; William married Elizabeth Feller ; Maria married George J. Pultz ; Lena, married Frederick Havenor ; Elizabeth, married Peter Hevenor ; Anna, married Phillip Fraleigh.

Of Hans Felton Benner's children we have the record of Jacob and his wife, Margaret Feroe. They had children, as follows : Lydia Maria, born December 8, 1811 ; Henry, born Feb. 19, 1815 ; Robert, born Feb. 1, 1818 ; Jacob Benner's wife, Margaret Feroe, died in 1824. He married, for a second wife, Helen Moore, by whom he had one child, a daughter, Margaret.

Jacob Benner was an industrious and successful farmer, and the last Benner owner and occupant of the homestead in Red Hook. He held several offices of public trust. He was Supervisor and Justice of the Peace in his town, and for several years Justice of the County Court of Sessions. He died, Nov. 5, 1869. The Hon. Augustus Martin married his daughter, Lydia Maria, for a first, and her half sister, Margaret, for a second wife. The latter survives her husband. His son, Henry, is now, and has for many years been a resident of the city of Newark, N. J. His son, Robert, is a practicing lawyer in the city of New York, and has for many years had his residence at Astoria, L. I. He married, Oct. 10, 1848, Miss Mary Van Antwerp Shaw, by whom he had sons, Franklin, Charles, and Willis, and a daughter, Mary. His wife dying, June 10, 1867; he married, for a second, Miss Helen Stanly Brown, Feb. 21, 1871.

UNKNOWN BENNERS.

We find among a number of Benners whose lineage we are not able to trace, a George Emerich Benner; a Frederick Benner, with Neeltje Heermance for a wife ; a Johannes Benner, with Catharine Enck for a wife ; a John Jacob Benner, with Margaritha Tidtmor for a wife ; and a Henrich Tidtmor, with an Elizabeth Benner for a wife. The last parties were the parents of John, Susanna and Daniel Tidtmor, persons who have descendants still living in Rhinebeck and Red Hook, and other places.

THE BERGH FAMILY.

Christian Bergh, the first, was the grandson of Chasper and the son of John Bergh. He was a resident of what is now the town of Rhinebeck in 1723. He was born in the month of May, in the year 1700. On the 7th of August, 1722, he married Anna Margretta Wolleben, who was one year and six months his senior. Hans Felten, Peter, and Peter Wolleben, Jr., were in Rhinebeck at the same time ; and we presume Anna Margretta was the daughter of one, and perhaps the sister of the others. They were doubtless among the Palatines brought over by Governor Hunter, and of the thirty-five families settled on the land laid out for the " High Dutchers" by Henry Beekman, the elder, and called " Rein Beek." One of them was the owner of a farm now included in the premises of Walter L. Ten Broeck, Esq., by a deed bearing date October 20th, 1718. Christian Bergh and Anna Margretta Wolleben had children, as follows ;

Anna Margretta, born December 13, 1725 ; Maria Barbara, born December 27, 1727 ; Cattarina, born January 26, 1729 ; Johannes, born November 15, 1731 ; Johan Petter, born November 20, 1733 ; Johan Marthin, born November 4, 1735 ; Anna Maria, born October 14, 1737 ; Adam, born August 16, 1740 ; Christian, born December 19, 1742.

Of these children, all born in Rhinebeck, we assume that Anna Margretta married Frederick Hillegas ; Maria Barbara, Martin Dob ; Catharina, Michael Brua ; Johannes, Elizabeth Weist ; Adam, Helletje Radcliff. Christian certainly married Catharina Van Benschoten.

Christian Bergh, the first, died August the 9th, 1780 ; his wife, Anna Margretta Wolleben, died December the 5th, 1782 ; they were both buried in Peter Fralick's burying yard. John Bergh, son of Christian, the first, died August 14, 1794, and was also buried in Peter Fralick's burying yard.

We have no knowledge of Peter Fralick's burying yard. It was somewhere in the precinct of Rhinebeck. Peter Fralick resided on the post road, between Beekman's mill at the Flatts, and Peter Schryver's, in 1753 ; and Christian Bergh, between

Peter Schryver's and the south end of the precinct. Mr. Edward Braman, a native of Staatsburgh, informs us that lots Nos. 1 and 10 of Pawling's purchase, or Staatsburgh, were the property of Major John Pawling, who built, in 1761, the stone house now standing. His initials and those of his first wife, Neeltje (Van Keuren,) are cut on a stone inserted in the wall of this house; and he finds that "Christian Bergh, in the same year Major Pawling built his house, 1761, bought of Gertruyd Coeymans, of the province of New Jersey, widow, lots 6 and 15; (239 and 256 acres,) in the Stattsburgh patent. This is about two miles south of Major Pawling's, and now closely adjoining the village of Staatsburgh. On this property he built a house of two stories, like most of the best houses of that day, of stone. A large stone in the east end, facing the road, bore an inscription upon two hearts joined, as follows:

"C B—A M B   A B—H B

"These are the initials of Christian Bergh and his wife, Anna Margaretta (Wolleben), and of his son, Adam, and his wife, Hilletje (Radcliff). This house stood until 1854, when its owner, Frederick Marshall, rebuilt, but preserved this stone, which may still be seen in the cellar wall of the new house, now the property of Mr. Richard Schouten. No doubt Christian Bergh died in this old house. The property remained in the family until 1789, when John Bergh and Elizabeth his wife released the same to Charles Shaw and others (mortgagees), who sold the south part, with the house, to Captain Jesse Eames, of Framingham, Mass., in 1790, and shortly after the north part to Captain Isaac Russell, of Sherborn, Mass."

CHRISTIAN THE SECOND.

Christian Bergh, the second, born December 19, 1742, married Catharina Van Benschoten, on the 11th of March, 1762. Tunis Van Benschoten, of Kingston, married Anna Sleight, of Rhinebeck, granddaughter of Kendrick Kip, on the 4th of December, 1737. Catharina was probably his daughter. Christian Bergh and Catharine Van Benschoten had children as follows:

Christian, born April 30, 1763, and baptized in the Witten-burgh church; Tunis, born July 2, 1765, and baptized in the Rhinebeck church; John, born December 14, 1766, and baptized in the Rhinebeck church; Elsye,* born February, 1769, and baptized at Rhinebeck church; Adam, born February 20, 1771, and baptized by Dominie Cuypers, of the Flatts church, at the house; Peter, born May 6, 1773, and baptized in the Flatts church; Anna Margreta, born April 20, 1775, and baptized at Rhine-beck church; Cattarina, born December 12, 1776, and baptized at Rhinebeck church;† David, born January 24, 1780, and bap-tized in New York; Jacob, born in New York, April 4, 1782, and baptized "at the Presbyterian Dutch meeting house in said place;" Cattarina, born October 1, 1788, and baptized at her father's house in Shelburn, Nova Scotia.

Of this family of eleven children, Christian, the third, born December 19, 1763, was the father of Henry Bergh, the presi-dent of the New York Society for the Prevention of Cruelty to Animals, and also of the late Edwin Bergh, of Staatsburgh. Cattarina died October 29, 1781, and was buried at Newtown; David died at New York, April 8, 1782, and was buried in the "High Dutch Presbyterian burying yard;" Jacob died August 21, 1783, and was buried "at the Presbyterian meeting house;" Adam died at sea, November 19, 1790, nine days out from Jamaica; his remains were committed to the sea; John was lost at sea, in a severe storm, on the 25th or 26th of November, 1793; Peter died January 16, 1805, and was buried at Batavia, in the Island of Java. He was master of the ship Frances Henrietta, of New York.

Christian Bergh, the second, Died October 20, 1803; his wife, Catharina Van Benschoten, December 11, 1831.

ADAM BERGH.

The name Radcliff is differently spelled by different per-sons, and often by the same person. The records of the Camp

---

* The record of this child's birthday we are told "was destroyed by the rebels in 1775."

† The Rhinebeck church always means the German Reformed Church at Pink's corner.

German Reformed Church tell us Joachim, the son of Joachim Radclift and Hellitje Hogeboom, was baptized by Dominie Casper Ludawick Schnorr, in 1748. Dominie Cock, in the Rhinebeck book of the German Reformed Church, spells the name at one time Redleft; at another, Redle; at another, Reddleft; and at another, Redlift. Major William, we think, always spelled his name Radclift. We assume that Adam Bergh was the son of Christian Bergh, the first, and his wife Hellitje Radclift, the daughter of Joachim Radclift and Hellitje Hogeboom, born March 31st, 1843, and married in 1762. They had children baptized in the Rhinebeck German Reformed Church, as follows:

Anna Margreta, January 26, 1763; sponsors, Christian Berg and Anna Margreta Wooleben. Joachim, November 6, 1764; sponsors, Corneles Redle and Helentie Hoogeboom. Helentien, September 7, 1766; sponsors, Johannes Redle and Neeltjen Schemehoorn. Neeltjen, November 8, 1772; sponsors, Rudolf V. Hoovenburg and Elizabeth Reddleft. Catharina, September 11, 1774; sponsors, Michel Brua and Catharina Berg. Christian, September 15, 1776; sponsors, Christian Berg and Anna Margreth Wolleben. Sarah, born July 17, 1778; sponsors, William Reddleft and Sarah Kip.

All we know of these children is that Joachim married Leah Radclifd (according to Dominie Scheaffer), and probably his own cousin. He was cousin to Christian Bergh, the third. Henry Burgh, the New York friend of the brute creation, and Mrs. Henry J. Kip, the mother of William Bergh Kip, were therefore second cousins.

ZACHARIAS SCHMIDT.

Zacharias Schmidt's name is the first to be found in the oldest church records in the town of Rhinebeck. But there is nothing to tell us that he had either father, mother, brother or sister, in this or any other country. He owned the farm, now the property of James Way, at a very early date, but was preceded in the ownership by Johannes Backus, whose deed was dated, October 20, 1718, and who was thus one of the " High

Dutchers" who founded Rhinebeck.   He was *Voor Leser* in the old German Reformed Church, and many of its records are in his handwriting.   He sold a lot of his land to Ryer Schermerhorn, in 1773.   We are told Ryer Schermerhorn built the house now known as " Shop's old store house," at the corner, north of Walter L. Ten Broeck's, on this land, and conducted a mercantile business therein during the Revolutionary war.   After Zacharias Schmidt's death his place was occupied for awhile by his son, Wilhelmus, and in 1798 was Moul's tavern.

Zacharias Schmidt's wife was Anna Maria Bender, now Benner.   They had children, as follows: Johannes, baptized April 5, 1830, married Feb. 3, 1761, Elizabeth Zipperlie; Henrich, baptized April 13, 1735, married Margaret Whiteman, Jan. 19, 1792.   (Think he is the Johannes Henrich Smit found at Niskata by Pierson, with a son Zacharias, by Margaret Whiteman, baptized May 15, 1763, "when he was six weeks old," and who married Margaret Peesinger for a second wife, October 8, 1765, by whom he had Andries, Elizabeth and Sabina.)   Catharine, baptized May 11, 1738, married Jan. 8, 1760, Johan George Schneider; Phillippus, baptized May 11, 1738, married Nov. 29, 1762, Elizabeth Hoff; Peter, baptized Aug. 13, 1741, married April 4, 1763, Elizabeth Berringer; Anna Margreda, baptized Sept. 30, 1744, married Jan. 23, 1763, Conrad Berringer; Anna Maria, baptized Jan. 9, 1753, married Nov. 7, 1773, Jeremias Welsch; Annatjen, married Cornelius Welsch, 2d, Christovel Weaver; Wilhelmus, married Anna Müller.

Johannes Schmidt and Elizabeth Zipperlie had children, as follows: Zacharias, baptized May 31, 1762, married Gretjen Holtzapple; Catharine, baptized Dec. 11, 1763, married Jacob Milhelm; Anna Maria, baptized 1767, married Johan Henrich Deves; Frederick, baptized May 12, 1771, married Catharine Strong; Philip, born June 27, 1773, married Dec. 4, 1796; Anna Coopernail, born October 26, 1778; Johannes, baptized Dec. 6, 1778, married Sarah Snell, born 1786.

Philip Smith and Anna Coopernail had children born, as follows: Sophia, March 3, 1798; Elizabeth, June 9, 1800; John, April 16, 1802; Catharine, October 29, 1803; Henry, September 6, 1805; Anna, December 29, 1808; Margaret, April 9,

1809; William, December 25, 1810; Philip, June 17, 1812; George, October 8, 1815; Edward M., March 29, 1817; Zachariah, March 5, 1819; Ebenezer, April 20, 1823. Philip, the father, died Dec. 13, 1851.

EVERARDUS BOGARDUS.

Everardus Bogardus' wife was Adriantjen Hoochtieling. At the baptism of their son, Wilhelmus, on the 25th of October, 1772, the sponsors were Wilhelmus Hoochtieling and his wife, Blendina Kierstead. The Bogarduses, Kiersteads, and Hoochtielings were thus probably related by intermarriages, and probably immigrated from Kingston to Rhinebeck about the same time. Everardus Bogardus died on the 9th of September, 1799, aged 61 years. He has a large tombstone, but a lonely grave, in the old cemetery of the Reformed Dutch Church.

DR. HANS KIERSTEAD.

Dr. Hans Kierstead was born in 1743. He came to Rhinebeck in 1769, and thus at the age of twenty-six years. He married Jane, the daughter of Anthony Hoffman and Catharine Van Gaasbeck, of Kingston. She was born in Kingston in 1744. Their daughter, Sally, was baptized by Dominie Cock, of the Rhinebeck German Reformed Church, on the 15th of August, 1773, the sponsors being David DeLamater and Sally Hoffman. Martin Heermance married Sally Kierstead on the 15th of June, 1789. Dr. Hans Kierstead's first residence was the old stone house which stood on the south of the Wager lot, was taken down by Martin L. Marquet some years since, and reached by the lane referred to in the deed from Everardus Bogardus. A record in Martin Heermance's family Bible says: "We moved into our new house, October 19, 1793." It is now known that this new house was the brick house now the resi dence of Eugene Wells, and sold to John I. Teller by Martin Heermance, in 1816. Dr. Hans Kierstead died September 29, 1811, aged sixty-eight years; his wife died January 18, 1808, aged sixty-four years; Martin Heermance died July 31, 1824, aged fifty-nine years; Martin Heermance's wife died July 18, 1838, aged sixty-five years.

HERMAN BROWN.

Herman Brown, the common ancester of the old and respectable family of Browns in the town, appears here at an early date. Herman Braun and Maria Magdalena Hoffman, supposed to have been his wife, stood sponsors at the baptism of Maria Magdalena, the daughter of Henrich Meyer and Elizabeth Monk, in 1738. This is a record in the old book of the German Reformed Church, at Pink's corner. It is held by the family that this Herman Brown had three children, of whom one was Bastian. Bastian Braun was married to Margaretha Schultz, the daughter of Christian Otto Schultz, on the 21st of February. 1767, by Dominie Cock, of the German Reformed Church. They had three children, as follows: Peter, born in 1770, died April 4, 1841; John, born in 1773, died March 2, 1824; Helen, died young. Bastian Braun died, and his widow married Richard Schell, born in Germany, in 1740. He and his wife, Margaretha Schultz Braun, had four children, as follows: Christian, William, Christina, and Catharine.

WILLIAM COOPERNAIL.

John Van Coppenol, from Remsen, farmer, with wife and two children, came to New Netherlands in the ship Faith, in 1659, and probably settled in the Mohawk Valley. The Hon. John Sanders, in his History of Schenectady, says Cornelius Antonisen Van Slyck married the daughter of a Mohawk chieftain, by whom he had several children; that the youngest daughter, Leah, married Class Willemse Van Coppernol, who died in 1692, leaving a son named William. I assume that Class Willemse was one of the children brought over by Jan Van Coppernol, in 1659; that his son, William, by Leah Van Slyck, his wife, was the William Coppernoll found a freeholder in Schenectady in 1720; that the William Coopernail who came among the Dietz's in what is now the town of Milan, about 1760, with his mother, a widow, was probably the son of William Coppernall, found in Schenectady in 1720. The children of William Coopernail, all dead now, only remembered that he came from Schoharie, or somewhere west of Albany. He married Sophia Keil, born in Neuremburg, Germany, 1746, who came to the country with other members of her family, and settled among the Elseffers, in Rhinebeck. They had children as follows : Anna and Elizabeth, twins, born October 26, 1778. Philip, baptized March 29, 1781 ; Henrich, baptized November 2, 1783 ; Catharine ; John, born 1789 ; Wiiliam, born 1792. Anna married Philip Smith ; Elizabeth, John Titemore ; Philip, Rebecca Shaefer ; William, Deborah Row ; John, Maria Feroe ; Catharine, Henry G. Livingston, Jr. William Coopernail, the father, was in the Revolutionary army, and visited home on a permit over Washington's own signature. This paper was in the possession of the family for many years, but is now lost. The twins, We have heard their mother say, were born in his absence in the army, and were able to walk about the house when he was at home on this visit. Anna died April 17, 1864, aged eighty-six years. The last words we ever heard her utter, were that she came into the world in the midst of a terrible war, and should go out of it in the midst of another. She lost two or three grandsons in the battles of the Union army. When in her last illness, a child was born whose grandmother and great-grandmother were both her own daughters.

She sent for the child in order that she might be able to say, before she left the world, that she had held in her arms a child in the fourth generation from herself—a great-great-grandchild. It was brought to her by the grandmother, and placed in her arms while reclining in her bed. When it had been taken from her, the grandmother—her daughter, a strong, healthy, loving woman—lifted her mother out of the bed, and, seating herself, held her in her own arms while another smoothed and softened her bed for her last sleep. Her thirteen children were all living and at her funeral, the youngest forty-one years old. She was a strong, pure and noble mother. The lamps of her intellect and love never grew dim while she lived, and are beaming brightly now in the memory of all who knew her. A colored woman, nearly as old as herself, who had been her slave, walked four miles to be at her funeral and weep at her grave.

CHRISTIAN SCHELL.

Christian Schell was baptized by Dominie Johann F. Ries, of the Rhinebeck Lutheran Church, on the 11th of August, 1779.

He married Elizabeth Hughes, of Hyde Park, widow of Captain Pope, by whom he had eight children, as follows: Emily, Richard, Julius, Robert, Augustus, Edward, Francis and Julia. In 1805 he kept a store on the post road where Ezra Van Vradenburgh now resides—a place known at this date as "Bear Market." In 1812 he bought the mill property at the junction of Landsman and Rhinebeck creeks, of Colonel Henry B. Livingston. In 1816 he was on the Flatts, and built the stone store and dwelling on Platt's corner, and conducted a prosperous mercantile business therein to the close of his life. He died on the 18th of March, 1825, aged forty-six years; his wife died July 16, 1866. His son, Augustus, was graduated at Union College, and bred to the law, commencing his studies with John Armstrong, in this village. He was collector of the port of New York, and is widely known as a lawyer, financier and politician. Robert is president of the Bank of the Metropolis, and Edward of the Manhattan Savings Bank. Richard, born May 29, 1810, died November 10, 1879. He was elected State senator in 1856, and representative in Congress from New York in 1875.

ABRAHAM VAN KEUREN.

Abraham Van Keuren was the son of Abraham, born September 20, 1711. He was born February 9, 1752, and died April 25, 1817. His wife was Eve Dumond, born October 17, 1755; died November 3, 1824. Their children were, Abraham, born April 4, 1774, married Christina Gedney; Garrett, born February 14, 1785, married Sarah Hagadorn; Catherine, married Nicholas B. Van Steenburgh; James married, 1st, Caroline Van Steenburgh; 2d, Margaret DeLamater.

Thomas Reed's farm, in the north of the village, comprises part of the land conveyed to Peter and William Ostrander, by the elder Henry Beekman, in 1714. At the death of William Ostrander, in 1733, his son had the land divided, and set over to Peter his share by deed. On the 18th of November, 1749, Peter sold his share to his son, Jacob. On the 6th of November, 1761, Jacob sold it to Johannes Valentin Casparus. On the 2d of March, 1771, Johannes Valentin Casparus sold it to

Everardus Bogardus, who sold it to Johannes Turck, of Kingston, in the same year. In 1775 this land was in possession of Peters Ten Broeck and his wife, Catharina Rutsen. and in the same year sold by them to William Schepmoes. On the 5th of May, 1783, Johannes Turck and his wife, and William Schepmoes and his wife, sold it to Abraham Van Keuren, of Kingston. Abraham Van Keuren thus came into Rhinebeck at the close of the Revolution.

ROBERT SCOTT.

Robert Scott was born at Fries, in the county of Norfolk, England, August 21, 1760. His wife, Elizabeth Kitching, was born at West Ashley, Lincolnshire, October 10, 1762. They were married December 7, 1784. Their children were: Elizabeth, born at Ganesborough, March 21, 1786; Ann, born at Derby, April 29, 1787, died at Nottingham, April 26, 1788: Allen, born at Horncastle, August 12, 1789; Ann, born at Lynn, in Norfolk, September 29, 1791; Robert, born at New York, February, 1796, and died at Rhinebeck in the same year; Mary, born at Rhinebeck Flatts, November 6, 1798; Jane, born at Rhinebeck Flatts, September 23, 1801. In a record made by himself, Robert Scott says he left England, sailing from London, August 21, 1794, and arrived at New York October 10th in the same year. "My reasons for leaving England," he says, "were, first, for the sake of religious liberty, not being able to take the oaths then required of those who dissented from the Episcopal Church; second, for the sake of civil liberty; third, because I saw from Scripture prophecy that the time was at hand when all the kingdoms which sprang from the Roman monarchy, and had been subject to papal jurisdiction, would undergo great calamities and changes by pouring out the vials; and that this country would probably prove an asylum during those troubles."

CHRISTIAN OTTO SCHULTZ.

Christian Otto Schultz was born January 22, 1712, in Germany, at Bredenfeld, in the dukedom of Mecklenburgh-Strelitz; died at Rhinebeck, November 5, 1785. His wife, Christina Margaret Sharpenstein, was born in April, 1713, in Germany, at

Sasenburgh, in the county of New Witt. Died at Rhinebeck, October 20, 1779, at the residence of her son, John Schultz. They had eleven children born in Rhinebeck, Dutchess County, N. Y., as follows:

1. Anna, born August 28, 1737; married H. Dencker, August 31, 1756. 2. Abraham, born December 4, 1738; married Deborah Killburn, March 17, 1765. 3. Isaac, born July 28, 1740; married Mary Killburn, March 17, 1765; died 1803. 4. Christopher, born January 12, O. S.; married Rebecca Churchill, January, 1768; died 1808. 5. Margaret, born March 6, 1745; married, first, Bastian Brown, February 22, 1767: second, Richard Schell; died 1818. 6. Christian, born October 27, 1746; married Hannah Gardner. 7. Frederick, born April 5, 1748; married Margaret Crapser December 3, 1771; died 1819. 8. Peter born May 26, 1750; married Anna Vanderhoff January 19, 1772; died 1837. 9. William, born July 23, 1752; married Anna Killburn September 19, 1799. 10. Jacob, twin brother to William, married Ursula Schryver August 17, 1799. 11. John born February 18, 1755; married Anna Van Steenburg; born January 8, 1767; died January 7, 1801.

John Shultz and Anna Van Steenburgh had ten children: Sarah, married John G. Ring; Christian Otto, William, Benjamin, born January 21, 1790; died April 4, 1793; Abraham, born September 28, 1791; married Mary Smith; (Jackson S. Schultz of New York, is their son.) Benjamin, born April 29, 1793; married Catharine Ackert (born September 13, 1794) June 13, 1813; died April 4, 1873; John William, born November 23, 1796; Christina Margaret, born November 28, 1799; married Henry H. Traver; Jane Ann, twin to Christina Margaret, married Frederick Schaffer; Mary, born September 24, 1801; married George Snyder.

THE SIPPERLY FAMILY.

This name is Zipperly in all the old records. The name is not found among the taxable people in the town in 1723; and yet Barent Zipperly obtained a lease in 1721, from the Beekman heirs, of the farm, out of which were reserved the four acres for the church and cemetery lot at Pink's corner. In 1724, the same farm was leased by the same parties with the same reservation to Hendrick Beam. In 1726, Barent Zipperly purchased from Hans Adams Frederick the lease of the farm which embraced the land which is now the church and cemetery lot of the " Rhinebeck Stone Church " (St. Peters Lutheran Church). In 1729, Barent Zipperly was one of the four Lutheran trustees who sold the Lutheran interest in the church and church lot at Pink's corner to the Reformers. In 1730, five acres were detached from his farm by Gilbert Livingston, and given to the Lutherans for a church and cemetery lot. A tombstone in this cemetery tells us he died, and was buried therein in 1734. We have no doubt all the Zipperlies who have had birth, have lived and died, and are now living in Rhinebeck, were descended from this man. His farm remained in the possession of his son, Michael, until 1768, when he sold the lease to the trustees of the church for a glebe.

Michael Zipperly married Regina Schever, and had two children baptized in the German Reformed Church, as follows : Johannes, May 21, 1739; Anna Barbara, May, 1741. We have not consulted the records of the Lutheran church for other children which he probably had. Frederick Zipperly, brother to Michael, married Maria Catharina Wegeli, the daughter of Hans Michael Wegeli, who was the original owner of the Zipperly farm, now the property of William I. Lown. Frederick Zipperly's will bears date, 1743; he probably died within this year. He probably had a daughter, Christina, married to Peter Brosius. He certainly had a son, George, married to Anna Maria Reichert ; a daughter Elizabeth, married to Johannes Schmidt ; and a son, Johannes, married to Rebecca Schaffer.

George Zipperly and Anna Maria Reichert had children as follows ; Frederick, married Elizabeth Neher ; David, married Lena Benner ; Elizabeth, married Jonas Simons ; Catharina, died unmarried.

Johannes Zipperly and Rebecca Schaffer had children as follows : Frederick, married Christina Fraleigh ; John, married Rachel Fraleigh ;. Henry, married Elizabeth Neher ; George, died unmarried ; Jacob, married Elizabeth Benner ; David, married Catharine Hoff ; Catharine, married George Traver ; Elizabeth, married John Lambert; Rebecca, married David Teal; Anna Maria, died unmarried.

THE COOKINGHAM FAMILY.

We trace the Cookinghams of Rhinebeck back to two an_ cestors; to Johan George, who was married to Anna Schmidt, by Dominie Van Hovenburgh, in 1755, the record stating that he was born in Germany; and to Daniel, who was married to Anna Maria Treber, daughter of Bastian Treber, December 9, 1756, by Dominie Johan Casper Rubel, of the German Re- formed Church.   These men were doubtless brothers, and relat- ed—probably brothers—to Barbara, the wife of Michael Boltz, who appears in our records for the first time in 1738.   The name was differently spelled by different ministers, and also by the same minister.   Dominie Mancius spelled it in one case Cuck- enhan, and in another, Kukenheiner.   Dominies Cock and Ru- bel spelled it Kuckenheim.   George Kuckenheim and Anna Schmidt had daughters, Maria Barbara and Annatjen, and a son, Petrus; and Daniel Kuckenheim and Anna Maria Treber had a son, Johan Michael, and a daughter, Margaretha, baptized in the German Reformed Church.   There were more children, which, for the want of family records, we are unable to trace. One branch of the family settled in the town of Milan, and be_ came Quakers.

THE BARRINGER FAMILY.

This name is Berringer in all the old church records.   Jo- hannes Berringer's name appears among the heads of families taxed in the North Ward in 1723.   He was possibly the com- mon ancestor of all the Barringers now in Dutchess and Colum- bia Counties.   The deed for the old Barringer farm, now the property of Thomas Reed, was given to Conradt Barringer by Henry Beekman in 1734.   He is doubtless the same person who was a trustee of the German Reformed Church in 1729, who was a freeholder in the precinct of Rhinebeck in 1740, and who appears in the old church records with Elizabeth Staal for a wife in 1741.

On the 14th of September, 1741, Jacob Berringer and Ger- trout Schneider had a son, Conrad, baptized, the sponsors being

Conrad Berringer and Lizabeth Staal. On the 16th of September, 1744, Frederick Berringer and Margaret Zufelt had a daughter, Elizabeth, baptized, the sponsors being again Conrad Berringer and Elizabeth Staal. On the 14th of October, 1744, Henrich Berringer and Elizabeth Best had a daughter, Elizabeth, baptized, the sponsors being Henrich Schever and Elizabeth Berringer. Now we assume that Conrad Berringer and Elizabeth Staal were the parents of Jacob, Frederick and Henrich Berringer, and that the wife of Conrad was a widow, and stood sponsor with Henrich Schever at the last baptism.

Jacob Berringer and Gertrout Schneider had children baptized in the Rhinebeck German Reformed Church, as follows : Conrad, September 14, 1741 ; Petrus, March 11, 1750; Wilhelm, November 20, 1753 ; Jacobus, July 4, 1756. Frederick Berringer and Margaret Zufeldt had children baptized in the same church, as follows : Elizabeth, September 16, 1744; Jacob, October 12, 1746; Philip, April 24, 1753 ; Anna Maria, December 7, 1755; Christina, August 27, 1758.

Henrich Berringer and Elizabeth Best had children as follows : Conrad, married January 23, 1763, Margaretha, daughter of Zacharias Schmidt ; Elizabeth, baptized October 14, 1744; married, April 4, 1763, Petrus, son of Zacharias Schmidt ; Henrich, baptized April 26, 1747, married 1st, January 19, 1772, Sarah Boehm ; 2d, Anna Gerges ; Hannah, married Conrad Finger; Catharina, baptized October 26, 1755, married Jacob Moul ; Helena, baptized September 24, 1758, married Abram J. Kip ; Jacob, baptized May 13, 1761 ; George, born March 19, 1763, married, 1st, December 14, 1787, Anna Maria Snyder ; 2d, July 3, 1808, Catharine Ackert ; Johannes married Elsjen Blass.

Henrich Berringer and Sarah Boehm had children as follows : Elizabeth, baptized February 14, 1773 ; Rebecca, baptized December 4, 1774 ; Jacob, baptized April 27, 1777 ; Catharina, baptized May 30, 1779 ; Annatjen, baptized July 8, 1781 ; Johannes, baptized March 6, 1785 ; married Maria Elsever; Sarah, baptized July 19, 1789, married Philip Kip ; Jeremias, baptized December 30, 1795. By his second wife Henrich Berringer had one child, Martin, baptized November 30, 1800.

George Berringer and Anna Maria Snyder had children, as

follows : Jeremias, baptized August 3, 1788 ; Elizabeth, baptized March 6, 1791 ; Catharina, baptized October 6, 1795 ;
married Daniel Cookingham ; John, born August 18, 1793, married Sallie Bennett (died leaving one child, a son, George) ; Elias,
baptized December 6, 1798, married Maria Shoemaker ; Maria.
By his second wife the children were, Ephraim and Julia.   Anna
Maria Snyder, first wife of George Barringer, died March 3, 1808 ;
Catharine Ackert, his second wife, died March 24, 1843 ; he died
August 28, 1849.

THE WELCH FAMILY.

This family came into Rhinebeck, probably from Kingston'
in about 1740.   Their first residence, we are told, was in a
house at the corner, now occupied by the residence of Guernsey
Crandall.   Jan Welsch and his wife, Margareta Maklean are
found on the records of the Reformed Dutch Church in 1742.'
The names might be those of people of Irish descent, and yet
they are known here only as people of Holland, or Low Dutch
extraction ; and they were connected from their first appearance
in the town with the Dutch Reformed Church.   They had a son,
Jermias, baptized in this church on November 7, 1742 ; Abraham, October 7, 1744 ; Cornelia, or Cornelius, June 13, 1747 ;
Benjamin, September 23, 1750.   After 1760 we find a number
of the name in our old church records.   Whether they were all
sons of Jan Welsch and Margareta Maklean, or whether some
were his brothers, we are not certain.   We find Jan Welsch, Jr.,
with Annatjen Van Vredenburgh for a wife, having a son John,
baptized November 29, 1761 ; and we have found that this
baby, in time, became the well known deacon and collector,
John Welch, whose wife was Annatjen Van Wagenen, and
whose children were as follows : John, baptized July 15, 1787 ;
Annatjen, born February 12, 1789 ; Benjamin, born October 2,
1793 ; James, born December 13, 1795 ; Barent, born June 1,
1800 ; Margaret, born March 1, 1803 ; Peter, born March 2, 1808 ;
Deacon John Welsch died December 8, 1753 ; his wife, born
February 27, 1768, died July 11, 1847 ; and his children are now
also all dead.

Besides the Deacon's father, we find that there was a William Welsch and a Samuel Welsch whose wives were Van Vre-

denburghs. They were probably three brothers with sisters for wives. There was an Abraham Welsch with Annatjen Westphal, and a Cornelius Welsch with Leah Westphal for a wife. They were probably also brothers with sisters for wives.

We think the Abraham had a former wife of the name of Elizabeth Teal; and the Cornelius, a second wife of the name Annatjen Schmidt. But they and their children have long since left the world, and there is nobody left able to correct us if we have made a mistake; and we will indulge in no further speculations.

THE SNYDER FAMILY.

This name is German, and Schneider in all the old church records. There were no taxable Schneiders in Rhinebeck in 1723. They were, therefore, not among the High Dutchers for whom the tract called Rhinebeck was laid out. In a census taken in 1740, there were two—Johannes P. and Christovel. The tradition among the descendants of George Schneider and Catharina Schmidt is, that he was a native German, and had attained to manhood when he came to Rhinebeck. He wrote a good hand, and left other evidence that he had received a better education than fell to the lot of his neighbors, who had had their birth and schooling in America. He joined the Rhinebeck German Reformed Church by letter, December 21, 1755, which shows that he had had a church membership in a former place of residence. There is no evidence that he had either father, mother or brother in this country; Anna Margretha Schneider, the wife of Wilhelm Peter Wallis, may have been his sister.

He married January 8, 1760, and, we are told, soon after settled on the farm which, in the memory of many people still living, was the property of his son, Doctor Peter Snyder, and is now the property of Edgar Haynes. His marriage record says he was the son of Johan Ernest Schneider, a name not found in any of our records. His descendants, in the first generation, will be found in the family record of Zacharias Schmidt. His son, Zacharias, begat John Z. Snyder, and John Z. Snyder begat Philip Snyder, the Agricultural Editor of the Philadelphia Press.

THE ACKERT FAMILY.

These people are Eckerts in all the old church records. They came into the town at a very early date, and pretty certainly with the Palatines who fonnded Rhinebeck. Adam Eckert's name is found among the people assessed in the North Ward in 1723. He was doubtless the first occupant of Abraham Brown's old stone house, built in 1719.

Johan George Eckert and Anna Catharine Eberts, his wife, had a daughter, Maria Barbara, baptized in the Rhinebeck German Reformed Church in 1731 ; a son, Johan Adam, May 22, 1739 ; a son, Johan Peter, September 14, 1741. At the first of these baptisms the sponsors were Johan David Eckert and Maria Barbara Eckert; at the second, Adam Eckert and Anna Eckert; at the third, Adam Dipple and Catharina Eckert, his wife. We have thus Eckert men and women on the old church records between 1731 and 1741. Whether they were all descendants from Adam, who built Abraham Brown's house, we are not prepared to say. Nicklaus Eckard was in Queensbury, one of the German camps in Columbia County, N. Y., in 1711, and may have been father or brother to Adam. Of Martinus Eckert, whose wife was Salome Escher, we are told his father lived somewhere near Henry Schryver's, and had seven sons and one daughter, the sons being Solomon, John, Jacob, George, Adam, Peter and Martinus. These were all men in the prime of life at the outbreak of the Revolutionary War, and two or three of these, loyal to the king, entered the British army. Martinus, who, with his worthy family, lived and died in Rhinebeck, was doubtless a patriot. We have his record as follows:

Martinus Eckert married Solome Escher, daughter of Johannes Escher and Sophia Seger, and had children as follows: Henry, moved to Ulster County ; John M., married Catharine Progue ; Peter M., married —— Wager ; Maria, married Martin G. Ackert ; Catherine, married, first, —— Progue ; second, Henry Norris; Jacob M., born April 29, 1783, married November 6, 1802 ; Margaret Prougue, born October 27, 1785,

Jacob M. Ackert and Margaret Progue had children as follows: Henry, born May 8, 1804, died 1806 ; Lydia Caroline, born December 23, 1808, died 1856; Jacob Henry, born February 7, 1809 ; Martin Adam, born December 16, 1811 ; Philip Andrew, born November 15, 1813, died 1856. The father of this family died May 19, 1875 ; the mother died July 21, 1860.

Jacob H. Ackert married Lydia Maria Moor, August 29, 1829. They had children as follows : Philip Jacob, born February 5, 1832 ; Regina Moor, born March 16, 1838 ; Hon. Alfred Theodore, of New York City, born April 15, 1840.

Jacob M. Ackert married at nineteen years of age. At the organization of the public schools in the State of New York, in 1805, he became a school teacher. In 1808 he was captain of Governor Morgan Lewis's sloop Julia, sailing from the governor's dock in Rhinebeck—called by him Wurtemberg, and others Wittenburg Landing—to New York. He was captain of the Julia until 1812, and we are told he sailed a sloop from the Rhinebeck State Dock in 1819. Wurtemberg Landing is now Kelly's Dock. It has not been a public landing place for freight or passengers in fifty years,

THE PULTZ FAMILY.

This name in the old records is differently spelled by different ministers. An old family record spells it Poltz, Dominie Mancius spells it Pols, and Dominie Cock, Boltz, Johann Michael, the first of the name, married Barbara Guckenheim, May 10, 1738. He was born July 12, 1711, and died July 12, 1796. She died January 23, 1785, after she had been his wife for forty-six years. We are not told when she was born. They were doubtless both of German birth. They had children as follows : Michael, born December 16, 1739, baptized by preacher Schalter (Spaller ?) in the Rhinebeck Lutheran Church, married Margaret Dederick ; George, born December 27, 1740, baptized in the Rhinebeck Reformed Church, married Maria Ring ; Bastian, born February 22, 1742, baptized in the Rhinebeck Reformed Church, married Margaret Escher ; Anna, born August 3, 1743, baptized in the Rhinebeck Lutheran Church, died June 17, 1766 ; Gertrude, born March 7, 1744, baptized in the Rhinebeck Reformed Church, married George Freleigh ; Christina, born December 1, 1745, baptized in the Rhinebeck Lutheran Church, married George Adam Schuck, and had children—Anna, Petrus,

George (father to Sheridan Shook, of New York), Jacob, Gert-jen, Johannes, Catharina—Christoffel, born August 6, 1747, baptized in the Rhinebeck Lutheran Church, died unmarried; Catharina, born November 7, 1749, baptized in the Rhine-beck Lutheran Church, died, unmarried, October 23, 1769; DeWitt, born February 10, 1771, baptized in the Rhinebeck Lutheran Church; Daniel, born January 22, 1754, baptized in the Rhinebeck Lutheran Church, married Maria Typpel; Johannes, born April 30, 1755, married Berbel Marquat, and had children as follows (Hannah, Peter, Anna, Catharina, David, William, George, Frederick, Jacob, Philip, John); Barbara, born 1756, baptized in Rhinebeck, in the Stadtsburgh Church, married Johannes Ring. The family record of these births names the signs of the Zodiac under which they were born, and the last brings to our knowledge two important historical facts—that there was a church at Staatsburgh, and that Staatsburgh was in Rhinebeck.

THE ASHER FAMILY.

This name is Escher in the old records. The family came into the town in 1739, and thus nearly, if not quite, simultane-ously with the Pultzes and Cookinghams. There is a tradition in the family that Johannes Escher, the son of George Adam Escher and his wife, Maria Angenise Betz, was born on ship-board, October 15, 1739, when his father and mother were on their way to America from Germany. His sister, Catherina, was born February 15, 1742, and baptized by Dominie Weiss in the Rhinebeck German Reformed Church, March 2, 1742. Johannes Escher married Sophia Seger, and they were doubt-less the parents of Margaretha Escher who married Bastian Poltz, of Maria Escher who married Johan Christoffel Diel, of Salome Escher who married Martinus Eckert, of Johannes and Adam Escher.

Adam, son of Johannes Escher and Sophia Seger, born April 12, 1773, married, June 28, 1796, Anna Fraleigh, born June 28, 1777. They had children as follows: George, born February 26, 1797, died June 15, 1815; Andrew, born August 11, 1799, died September 14, 1809; Jacob, born December 3,

1801 ; John Michael, born September 5, 1813 ; Anna Maria, born August 6, 1816 ; Gertrude, born July 16, 1820, died March 29, 1829. Adam Asher, the father of this family, died April 27, 1821 ; Anna Fraleigh, the mother, died May 2, 1827.

Jacob Asher, married, January 7, 1829, Ellen Ostrom ; born April 30, 1809. They had children as follows: Saradah Emily, born February 20, 1830, married George Van Steenburgh, died July 21, 1855 ; Lewis Alvara, born October 13, 1831, married Emeline Eckert January 22, 1857 ; John Rensselaer, born February 27, 1834, married Mary Wolcott July 31, 1862, died March 5, 1879 ; Jane Ann, born September 20, 1836, married Stephen Cramer January 2, 1860 ; Delia Frances, born July 23, 1838, married William H. Johnson, September 28, 1858, died July 16, 1870 ; J. Howard, born December 27, 1840, married May 21, 1872, Olivia Welch ; Augustus F., born November 11, 1851. *Father died April* 28, 1860; *mother, February* 18, 1879.

John Michael Asher married December 3, 1840, Delia Caroline Ostrom ; born January 4, 1820. They had children as follows: Catharine Emeline, born December 26, 1841 ; married March 26 1872, William H. Johnson. George Livingston, born September 24, 1843 ; married October 2, 1876, Catharine Sleight. Anna Maria, born October 17, 1845 ; married June 2, 1874, John C. Brown. Franklin Ostrom, born November 13, 1847. Mary Ellen, born November 3, 1849; married, May 23, 1871, Fenwick W. Slauson. Delia Caroline, born February 26, 1852 ; died December 4, 1868. Herman Augustus, born November 12, 1855. Emma Gertrude, born November 13, 1857. *Mother died May* 1, 1863; *father, October,* 21, 1866.

Anna Maria Asher married Frederick Uhl. This is all we know of her.

Gertrude Asher died March 29, 1829.

John Asher, brother of Adam, born December 30, 1769, married the daughter of Michal Pultz, and died we do not know when. His son, Peter, born December 14, 1793, married Rachel Dederick, sister to Jacob Dederick, who married Jane Scott.

THE STREIT FAMILY.

The tradition in this family is that the, first of the name came from Germany, and settled on a place called Kiskatami

Nisje, northwest of Catskill. Henry Beekman, the elder, bought this land of the Indians about the year 1700, and petitioned the government unsuccessfully for a patent several times before his death. In 1719 a patent therefor was obtained by Henry Beekman, the son, and his brother-in-law, Gilbert Livingston, the parcel containing 2,300 acres. Streit had a farm on this tract. We are not told at what date. He married a lady of the neighborhood named Moul. He sold this farm, and bought one at Rhinebeck.

Frederick Streit and his wife, Catherine Maul, had a daughter, Christina, baptized in the German Reformed Church by Dominie Mancius, October 1, 1739; a son, Frederick, March 2, 1742, and a son, Ludowick, April 7, 1745. This Frederick Streit either came into Rhinebeck with brothers and sisters, or children of marriageable age. Johannes Bender and his wife, Magdalena Streid, had their son, Hans Velde, baptized March 2, 1742, and Jury Streid and Elizabeth Trumbour were sponsors at a Maul baptism in the same year. The Frederick Streid, born March 2, 1742, and married, February 7, 1762, Catharina, the daughter of Henrich Bender and Catharina Boetzer, had a child baptized as follows: Frederick, June 19, 1765. After this date these parties disappear from the record. On October 9, 1768, we find Frederick Streit with Elizabeth Rauh for a wife. Was it the same man with a second wife? On November 2, 1785, Frederick, probably son of Frederick Streit and Catherine Bender, with his wife, Catherine Mohr, have a son, Philip, baptized; on April 24, 1785, a son, Ludwig; on June 7, 1789, a daughter, Anna.

When Frederick Streit and his wife. Catharina Maul, came into Rhinebeck, they either came in with a family of Mauls, or found them here. Johannes Maul, with Elizabeth Tromboor for a wife, and Johannes Tromboor, with Elizabeth Maul for a wife, were here in 1738.

THE CRAMER FAMILY.

Johan Nicholas Cramer was born January 2, 1743. He joined the German Reformed Church at Rhinebeck, April 28, 1761. On the 26th of December, 1769, he married Elizabeth Typpel, born 1752. They had children born as follows: Catha rine, October 16, 1770; Christina, 1772; Maria, July 2, 1774; Leah, January 19, 1776; Jacob, November 22, 1777; Jacob, October 26, 1778; John, September 11, 1780; Lany, August 29, 1782; Elizabeth, August 24, 1784; Peter, January 12, 1788; Adam, February 10, 1790; Anna, January 1, 1792. Johan Nicholas Cramer married, for a second wife, Anna Bonesteel, born January 27, 1752. He died October 18, 1806; his first wife, March 9, 1795; his second, May 30, 1840.

THE TETOR FAMILY.

This is one of the High Dutch families for whom Henry Beekman laid out the lands of Rhinebeck. Their lands bounded on those of Hans Michael Wegile, now the property of William Lown. Frederick Zipperly had married the daughter of Hans Michael Wegile, and this was the channel through which the lands of the latter came into the Zipperly family. The name Tetor is differently spelled by different ministers, and often by the same man; and we think in Rhinebeck it became Tator. We find Henrich Deder, with Catharina Bender for a wife, in 1742. They had children baptized in the Rhinebeck German Reformed Church as follows: Johannes, March 2, 1742; Zacharias, October 2, 1743; Elizabeth, April 25, 1747; Abraham, May 15, 1751; Henrich, April 21, 1753; Catharina, February 15, 1755; Wilhelmus, April 8, 1757; they had a daughter, Margaret, married to Jacob Thomas, whose baptism we miss.

THE FULTON FAMILY.

John Fulton, an Irishman, seems to have come to Rhinebeck about 1770, and he seems to have come alone. He married Elizabeth Tetor. They had children baptized as follows: Catharine, August 30, 1772; Isabella, May 12, 1774; Henry, February 5, 1776; John, March 29, 1778; Ephraim, June 1, 1783; David, whose record we miss.

Isabilla Fulton became the wife of John Martin, and thus the mother of the Hon. Michael S. Martin. Hon. Augustus Martin, Ed. Martin and Joseph Martin, Esqs., and others of Red Hook.

THE VAN ETTEN FAMILY.

A gentleman who has looked into the history of Ulster County, informs us that on page 117, it says of the Van Etten family: "The Knickerbocker ancestor of this family was drawn to New York and settled at Rhinebeck between 1630 and 1633; for family tradition assigns him a large tract of land in that locality."

The writer of this history of Ulster County, thus puts settlers in Rhinebeck sixteen years in advance of Peter A. Jay, and thus commits a still more egregious mistake. The Van Ettens were brought into Rhinebeck by Henry Beekman, the second, probably in 1721. In this year he sold to Jacobus Van Etten, cordwainer, of Hurly, Ulster County, nearly four hundred acres of land, "computed to be about four miles east of Hudson's river," for one hundred pounds, subject to an annual quit rent of three shillings a year. The land was bounded on one side by lands on Crum Elbow Creek, sold to William Traphagen by said Beekman in 1719. The tradition of the family here is that Beekman disposed of this land at a small price subject to a nominal rent, one hundred acres for each one of four sons, to tempt them back from the river, in the expectation that others would follow. This Jacobus Van Etten was probably the same person who bought number one of the Gerrit Artsen & Co.'s patent from Lawrence Osterhout in 1741. If he had four sons at the time of this purchase, he added to their number afterwards; and he had a daughter, Annatjen, who married Gysbert Westfall; a daughter, Margreta, who married Johannes Kip; a daughter, Catharina, who married Frans Kool; a danghter, Helegond, who married Jan Maris. He had a son, Jan, who married Rachel Westfall; a son, Jacobus, who married Margreta Kool; a son, Mathew, born 1722, who married Neeltje Van Wagenen; a son, Isaac, who, we think, never married; and we think there were other sons.

There is a Peter Van Etten in the list of tax-payers in the ward in 1723; and we find a Johannes de Hoges Van Etten on the records of the German Reformed Church in 1730, with Rebecca Ostrander for a wife. The former might have been a son of Jacobus; the latter could not. They may have been brothers, but whoever they were, there were no Van Etten freeholders in Rhinebeck in 1714. If any people of the name settled in this region in 1630, they were certainly so thoroughly in the wilderness of the New World and so far from the feeble garrisons at New York and Albany, that they were probably slain by the Indians and devoured by the bears and wolves seventy years before any other white people settled on the soil of Rhinebeck.

THE MOOR FAMILY.

Henrich Moor and his wife were among the Palatines who settled in the West Camp, in Ulster County, N. Y., in 1710. There were thus people of the name of Moor among the Palatines, and it is possible all the people of the name in Red Hook and Rhinebeck, and always regarded as people of German origin, were descended from this pair.

The oldest Moor homestead of which we have knowledge is the old stone house near the Montgomery Place gate, now the property of Mrs. Aspinwall. Phillippus Moor, with Christina Lambert for a wife, appears in the records of the Rhinebeck German Reformed Church under the date of April 5, 1730. We think these were the parents of Andrew Moor, whose wife was Barbel Ham; of Phillippus Henrich Moor, whose wife was Engel Dederick; of Wilhelm Moor, whose wife was Anna Barbara Dederick; of George Moor, whose wife was Phillipina Barnhardt; of Christian Moor, whose wife was Christina Silbernagel; and of Michael Moor, whose wife was Catharina - Klum.

A record placed in our hands by a Moor descendant says: " Frederick, Philip, Christopher, Jacob, John, Peter and probably others were the children of the first settlers of the name." We think they were the children of Phillippus Henrich Moor and Engel Dederick, and, therefore, not of the first settlers of the name by two generations.

Phillip Mohr (Dominie Cock's spelling) was married to Anna Bender October 10, 1774; and we think Johannes Mohr, whose wife was Elizabeth Dederick; Christian Mohr, whose wife was Regina Schop; Jacob Mohr, whose wife was Anna Shuck; and Peter Mohr, whose wife was Christina Bender, were his brothers.

Petrus Moor, baptized November 27, 1743, married, December 16, 1770, Christina Bender. They had children as follows: Catharine, baptized July 4, 1773, married Jacob Moor; Henry, baptized March 12, 1775, married Gertrude Shook; Peter, baptized May 11, 1777, married Anna Maria Weitman; William, baptized April 4, 1779, married —— Lewis; Philip P., born March 4, 1781, married, May 23, 1808, Anna Maria Ring, born may 1, 1785; Anna, baptized June 1, 1783, married Henry Benner; Zachariah, baptized August 4, 1785, married Anna Feller; Andrew, baptized September 23, 1787, married —— Bartholamew; Nicholas, baptized March 14, 1790, married Anna Pitcher; Garret, married Lena Row.

Philip P. Moor and Anna Maria Ring had children as follows: Julia Anna, born May 2, 1803, married Frederick Traver; Katy Louisa, born March 1, 1807, married Frederick Burger; Lydia Maria, born March 4, 1809, married August 29, 1829, Jacob H. Ackert; Gertrude Christina, born February 20, 1812, married, in 1829, Peter Snyder; Barbara Caroline, born November 22, 1814, married, first, Rowland Traver; second, John H. Rikert; Philip Henry, born March 21, 1817, married Sarah Traver; Lucinda, born May 17, 1819, married Ephraim W. Pultz; John William, born June 21, 1831, married Julia Pells; Alfred Lewis, born August 18, 1823, married Margaret Schultz.

Philip P. Moor died April 15, 1856; Anna Maria Ring, his wife, died March 19, 1857. They were thrifty people. Their children all had a good start in the world; all have kept a balance in their favor in their reckoning with the world; and all are thus among our most highly-respected and trusted people.

THE STAATS FAMILY.

Johannes Staats, with Catharina Pister for a wife, appeared in the records of the Rhinebeck German Reformed Church at an early date. We are not able to trace a relationship between him and the Joachim Staats who purchased from Major Schuyler one-fourth of his Magdalene Island patent; and yet we presume there was a relationship. He was probably the first owner of the Staats homestead in Red Hook. Their children were as follows:

Philip, baptized October 2, 1739, married, January 7, 1765, Anna Maria Bender, and settled in Germantown, Columbia County; Johannes, baptized March 14, 1742, married Lena, daughter of the Lutheran minister—Johan Frederick Ries; Catharina, baptized April 7, 1745; Henrich, baptized October 6, 1747; Elizabeth, baptized April 24, 1753; Petrus, baptized May 8, 1757; Anna Margreda, baptized August 4, 1759, probably married Nicholas Bonesteel, baptized May 26, 1754, and probably settled on the post-road, in the old house, near Red Hook, known as the Bonesteel Tavern.

Henry Staats, only son, we think, of Johannes Staats and Lena Ries, married Christina, daughter of Abraham Srtaat and Christina Schuck, born June 14, 1802. They had children as follows:

Abraham, born June 25, 1823; Lizee, born January 21, 1826; Egbert, born May 30, 1828; Almetia, born February 8, 1831; Almeria, born November 30, 1834.

Henry Staats was, during his life, the owner of a dozen or more large farms in Red Hook and other places, by purchase, and was a man of energy, influence and wealth; but a generous and confiding disposition toward his sons, who had not inherited his faculty for making and saving money, had reduced his estate at his death.

BASTIAN BROWN'S FAMILY.

Heerman Braun, with his wife (whose maiden name it is assumed was Magdalena Hofman), and three children—viz., Bastian, John and Peter—came to America from Holland between 1730 and 1737. The tradition of the family is that they were driven from England to Holland by religious persecution. Heerman Brown's first appearance in the records of Rhinebeck was as sponsor, with Maria Magdalena Hofman, at the baptism of Maria Magdalena, daughter of Henrich Meyer and his wife, Lisbeth Monk, in the Rhinebeck German Reformed Church, May 11, 1738. He leased a tract of land of Col. Henry Beekman in the precinct of Rhinebeck, which included the Quick meadow, now the property of Patrick Halley, on the Post road, one-fourth of a mile north of the 96th milestone. On this he built a log house—his first residence. In 1753 he built the west half of the present stone house ; in 1763 he added the east part and basement. In 1751 he was a widower, and married the Widow Catharine Kissaler. There is no record of issue from this marriage.

On the 21st of February, 1767, Bastian, son of Heerman Brown, married Margaret Schultz, daughter of Christian Otto Schultz, by whom he had three children—viz.: Helena, baptized December 13, 1767, died young ; Peter, born 1770, married Elenor, daughter of Major John Paulding ; John, born 1773, married Lydia, daughter of Conrad Lasher.

Peter Brown and Elenor Paulding had children as follows: Sebastian, John, Margaret, William, Edwin, Abigail. Peter Brown died 1841.

John Brown and Lydia Lasher had children as follows : Margaret, Maria, Caroline, Abraham, Julia, Howard, Emeline, Cerelia. John Brown died 1824.

Sebastian, oldest son of Peter Brown and Elenor Paulding, married Eliza, daughter of Anthony Bard, by whom he had children as follows: Peter, born October 18, 1820, married Kitty Green ; Helen, born September 11, 1822 ; Emily, born January 11, 1825 ; Eliza, born May 13, 1827 ; Lewis, born March 2, 1830 ; Edwin, born December 21, 1833 ; John C., born February 12, 1837 ; Henry Harrison, born January 26, 1840.

A RED HOOK WILSON FAMILY.

John, James, Daniel and Robert Wilson were four brothers who settled in the vicinity of Upper Red Hook before 1770. John married Elizabeth, and James married Anna Kuhn, sisters, daughters of Simon Kuhn and his wife, Catharine Linck. Dan_ iel married Mary Hamilton, and Robert married Catharine Wil_ sey. Ruth Wilson, wife of Guy Magill, 1768, was probably a sister. These Wilsons were Irish, or people of Irish descent.

John Wilson and Elizabeth Kuhn had children as follows : Catharine, baptized March 27, 1774, married Col. Philip Pitcher, of Upper Red Hook ; Martha, baptized October 17, 1776, mar; ried first, Abraham A. Kip, second, Spencer Whiting ; Elizabeth, baptized October 3, 1779, married Joseph Cox ; John, baptized

April 7, 1782, died unmarried; Hannah, born 1784, married, 1804, John Drury, of Rhinebeck Flats.

John Wilson died before 1797, and his widow, Elizabeth Kuhn, married John A. Kip. John Wilson, the son, gave his name to his nephew, Judge John Wilson Drury, of Chicago, Illinois.

Martha Wilson and Abraham A. Kip had children as follows: Ann Eliza, married Jacob B. Van Steenburgh, and had a number of children (of whom John Alfred Van Steenburgh, of Rhinebeck, is one); William, twin to Ann Eliza; Ralph; John G.; Hellen.

The history of the old "Tamany Hall" hotel stand finds John Wilson and his family in Rhinebeck immediately after the close of the Revolutionary War. In 1746, Henry Beekman gave a life-lease to Jacob Van Ostrander, linen weaver, for two acres of land bounded and described as follows: "Lying on the westerly side of a plain, easterly to the King's road that leads from the said Beekman's gristmill to Rynbeek; northerly to the lot of ground belonging to Peter Van Ette; westward to the land of Arent Traphage, deceased, by a line N. 21° 45' W.; and so southerly so far as to make this lot of ground to contain two acres, or thereabout." The rent reserved was "one couple of fat hens" per year, for five years; after that, twenty shillings per year. It was, therefore, evidently a lease for land in a prim_ itive state.

Jacob Ostrander sold the lease to Johan Christover Armburster, tanner, in 1753, for £21. Armburster sold it, as a tavern keeper, to William Gillant, tavern keeper, in 1762, for £135. It is probable, from the increase in price, the old stone house was built by Armburster, between 1753 and 1762. William Gillant sold the property, as a tavern keeper, to J. Jury Cremer, tailor, in 1763, for £145. J. Jury Cremer sold it, as a tavern keeper, to Henry Schopp, saddle maker, in 1767, for £200. Henry Schopp sold it, as a saddler, to Johannes Van Steenburgh, gunsmith, in 1769, for £200. Johannes Van Steenburgh sold it, as a gunsmith, to David Van Ness, merchant, in 1783, for £300. David Van Ness sold it to John Wilson, in 1784, for £325.

John Wilson thus came into Rhinebeck in 1784, the year in which his daughter, Hannah, the wife of John Dury, was born. The property, in 1798, was in the possession of John A. Kip, Mrs. John Wilson's second husband. In 1809, Janet Montgomery gave him a lease of it, to continue during the life of John G., the son of his brother, Abraham A. Kip, a lad eight years of age.

ABRAHAM R. KIP.

Abraham R. Kip was the grandson of Jacob Kip, the patentee, by his son, Roeloff. He was baptized October 22, 1738. He married Lena, the daughter of Hans Jury Tremper and his wife, Susanna Typpel. They had children as follows: Roelof, baptized August 31, 1761; Hans Jury, baptized April 15, 1764; Abraham, baptized July 13, 1766, married Martha Wilson; Lena, baptized August 14, 1768; Sarah, baptized October 28, 1773; Jacob, baptized October 29, 1775; Catharina, baptized October 28, 1781, married, January 11, 1807, Capt. John W. Pitcher, of Upper Red Hook. Abraham R. Kip died February 11, 1830, aged ninety-one years; his wife, Hellena Tremper, died March 24, 1827, aged eighty-six years.

THE TRAPHAGEN FAMILY.

William Traphagen bought a small tract of land from Henry Beekman, in 1706, a larger one in 1710, which included part of the Hager, and, we think, all of the Teller farm, and all the land south of the river road, west of the post road and south to Landsman's Kill; and a tract, in 1719, on Crum Elbow Creek, named in the deed to Jacobus Van Etten in 1721. The old stone house known as the "Old States Prison," on the Flats, was doubtless his residence, and probably built by him soon after 1810. He died in 1736, and left three children: Giesje, who married, October 3, 1731, Isaac Kool; Arent, who married August 26, 1739, Leah Van Etten; and William, who married we do not know whom. Arent died before 1746, and William served as precinct clerk from 1749 to 1754. The wives of Peter and Cornelius Radcliff were doubtless the daughters of one or both of these men.

THE RADCLIFF FAMILY.

The Radcliffs, like the Van Nesses, make their first appearance in the records of the Camp, or Germantown German Reformed Church. Joachem Radcliff's wife, Hellitje Hogeboom, was probably sister to William Van Ness's wife, Gertroy Hoge. boom. Joachem Radcliff and Hellitje Hogeboom were pretty certainly parents to all the following children:

Petrus, baptized May 19, 1741, married Catharina Traphagen; Johannes, married Neeltjen Schermerhorn; Elizabeth, baptized 1746; Joachem, baptized 1748; Hellitje, married Adam Bergh; Cornelius, married Rebecca Traphagen; Rachel, married Petrus De Witt; William, married Sarah Kip; Jannetjen, married Rev. Ego Tonkins Van Hovenburgh. William Radcliff and Sarah Kip had children baptized in the Rhinebeck German Reformed Church, as follows:

Jacob, April 29, 1764; Klaertjen, May 18, 1766; William, born January 9, 1768; John, baptized June 7, 1772; Peter, July 3, 1774. These are all in the record before us; there may have been more. William Radcliff was one of the most influential men in the town of Rhinebeck in his day.

THE RED HOOK VAN NESS FAMILY.

These Van Nesses make their first appearance in the records of the Camp German Reformed Church. We think William Van Ness and his wife, Gertroy Hogeboom, were the parents of John Van Ness, whose wife was Jannetje Bradt; of William Van Ness, Jr., whose wife was Elizabeth Contyne; and of David Van Ness, whose wife was Cornelia Heermance, the sister of General Martin Heermance, of Rhinebeck.

David Van Ness and Cornelia Heermance had children baptized as follows; Gertrui, June 30, 1771, married Harry Lyle; Jacob, baptized ·November 8, 1772; Catharine, July 31, 1774, married William Radcliff, Jr.; Jannetjen, June 21, 1778, married John Radcliff; Wilhelm, March 29, 1784; Cornelia, June 24, 1786, married· John J. Close; Annatjen, November 17, 1787; Maria, October 25, 1789; Catalyna, August 13, 1791; David, April 14, 1798.

David Van Ness built the Punderson House in Upper Red

Hook, before the Revolution, and kept a store in it until after 1790. In 1798 he was General Van Ness, and owned the house and farm which became the property of Tobias Teller, and now belong to the heirs of William Chamberlin.

THE WHITEMAN FAMILY.

We learn from a descendant of this family that " about the year 1722, three brothers, Martinus, Johannes, and Henrich Weidman, set out from the canton of Zurich, in Switzerland, and settled in Rhinebeck. The name came to be written here, Weydman, then Weitman, and subsequently Whiteman. It imports in the original that the ancestors of these brothers were shepherds and huntersmen ; and the shield brought to this country by Henrich Weidman, the youngest of the brothers, represented a hunter, full armed.

" They were all followers of the Reformer, Zwinglius, and belonged to the German Reformed Church.

" Henrich Weidman, the youngest brother, had received advantages of education in the free city of Zurich, and came to be employed for some years as an agent of some of the lands of Gilbert Livingston, and subsequently of Robert G. Livingston. About the year 1743 he married Claphena Kuch, at Esopus.

" On the 1st of May, 1751, Henrich Weydman, then of Rhinebeck precinct, took from Robert G. Livingston, merchant, of the city of New York, a lease of the farm situated about two and a half miles southeasterly from the present village of Red Hook, which continued in the possession and ownership of his descendants for a period of one hundred and twenty-five years thereafter. In 1876, the sons of John Elseffer and Catharine (Whiteman) Elseffer conveyed the same to Garret Moore."

The sons and daughters of Henrich Weydman and Claphena, his wife, who attained majority, were as follows : Margret, married, January 19, 1762, Henrich Schmidt ; Anna, baptized January 4, 1747, married Hans Felten Schafer, and moved to Kinderhook ; Elizabeth, baptized October 24, 1748 ; Hans Henrich, baptized August 24, 1750, married, December 14, 1773, Marytjen Hoff ; Jacob, born 1752, married, 1775, Catharine, daughter of Frederick Neher; Zacharias, baptized February 15,

1755, married, January 24, 1773, Anneken Ostrander; Alida, youngest child, baptized May 27, 1757, married Hans Felten Bender. (Felten is frequently written "Fallentyne" in the same church book. Dominie Cock wrote the same name "Felten" and "Valentyn" at different dates.)

Jacob Weidman and Catharine Neher had children as follows: Henry, baptized June 27, 1779, married Rebecca Sharp, third daughter of George Sharp and Rebecca Tedter; Anna Maria, baptized September 28, 1782, married Peter P. Moor.

Henry Whiteman and Rebecca Sharp had an only child, Catharine, baptized August 9, 1799, married, June 6, 1819, John Elseffer.

John Elseffer and Catharine Whiteman had three sons, Henry D., Jacob W. and William L., named in the Elseffer family.

Jacob Whiteman, we are told, "was regarded as a great rebel by the Tories of the Revolution, and, with Gottlob Martin, George Sharp, and others, held frequent private council to advance the cause of the Revolutionary army. In 1796 he purchased the fee of the homestead farm before alluded to.

THE ELSEFFER FAMILY.

We learn from a member of this family that the name in the old country was Elzevir; in this country, at first Elsever, then Elsefer, and finally Elseffer. He further informs us that about the year 1580, Louis Elzever, a German printer, emigrated to Holland, to escape religious agitations in his native place; and soon thereafter "books bearing the imprint of Elzevir appeared." The name in the original, he says, "had a special significance, *Elze*, meaning a province, or anything country; and *Vir* meaning *the man*; hence the name imports, *the man of the country*, or the representative man of the province." Louis Elzevir, he says, had seven sons, five following the business of the father, and becoming distinguished therein, the other two returning to the Highlands of Germany. A descendant of one of the latter, with his wife and son, Lodiwick, about four years of age, embarked for America in the year 1738, intending to seek a home in Rhinebeck, where from thirty to fifty High

Dutch families had settled twenty-four years previously. Both parents died on shipboard, and the ship, in a disabled condition, made the port of Philadelphia instead of New York, the port of its destination. The boy, Lodiwick, fell to the care of a half-brother, of the name of ·Shop, who placed him in school, and at a suitable age put him to the trade of saddle and harness-making. Having attained his majority, he left Philadelphia and settled down to his trade in the ancient village of Rhinebeck, in the first house north of the German Reformed Church, in the year 1756.

Lodiwick Elsever, born 1734, married March 21, 1758, Susanna, daughter of David Reichert, baptized September 14, 1741. They had children as follows: Elizabeth, born October 7, 1759, married George Treber; George, born June 24, 1771, married Anna Maria Neher, daughter of Joost Neher, and granddaughter of Carl Neher, a prominent man among the first settlers; Anna Maria, born February 3, 1763; Eva, born November 12, 1764, married Frederick Tedter (she dying, Frederick.Tedter married her sister, Anna Maria, for a second wife); David, born December 11, 1766, married Elizabeth, daughter of Johannes Eckert, of Staatsburgh; Catharine, born May 6, 1769; Susanna, born July 16, 1772, married David Neher; Rebecca, born March 28, 1774.

George Elsever and Anna Maria Neher had children as follows: Louis, married Katy Schultz, and moved into the southeasterly part of Dutchess County; Maria, married John Barringer, and moved to the city of New York;.Henry, married Lydia Cookingham, and remained on the old Elsever homestead, which is still in the possession of his widow and his only child, Eliza Ann, wife of John H. Cotting; Susanna, married John I. Teats, of Milan, and has an only child, the wife of William P. Stall; George, moved to Michigan in the early settlement of that State; Eliza, married Nicholas Ostrom, of Rhinebeck.

John Barringer and Maria Elseffer left a daughter, Emeline, who married John Savage, and resides at Elizabeth, N. J.; and a daughter, Sarah, who married John Martyne, and resides at Plainfield, N. J.

David Elsever and Elizabeth Eckert settled on the place

now the property of Lewis D. Elseffer, and had children as fol_
lows: Anna Maria, born August 24, 1788, married John N. Bonesteel; Susanna, born September 30, 1790, married John P. Mesick, of Claverack, Columbia County, N. Y.; Elizabeth, born
March 10, 1793, is unmarried, and living with her sister, Grace
Elseffer, in Red Hook; John, born August 24, 1798, married
Catherine Weitman, and became the owner of the old Weitman
homestead in the town of Red Hook; Lewis D., born December
16, 1802, married Cornelia Shook, and has an only son, John L.,
who resides with him, on the paternal homestead, the first house
south of the stone church (St. Peter's Lutheran), and thus one
of the farms laid out for the High Dutchers by Henry Beekman,
the patentee, in ancient Rein Beek, before 1714.

John N. Bonesteel and Anna Maria Elseffer had children
as follows: Margaret E. Atwell, of Burlington, Vt.; Catharine A. Faure, of New York City; and David N. Bonesteel,
deceased. Mrs. Mary B. Pier, of Staatsburg, is the only daughter of the latter.

John Elseffer and Catharine Weitman had children as fol_
lows: Henry D., deceased; Jacob W., counsellor at law at Red
Hook; and William L., civil engineer in the city of New York.
John Elseffer was a magistrate in the town of Red Hook for
twenty-four consecutive years, and elected a member of the
Legislature of New York of 1843.

THE SHARP FAMILY.

The six thousand acres of land (now Germantown, in
Columbia County, N. Y.), bought by Governor Hunter for the
Palatines, of Robert Livingston, in 1710, were conveyed by the
government to Jacob Sharp and others, in 1724, in trust for
themselves and all the other Palatines willing to remain thereon.
This Jacob Sharp had three children—viz.: Petrus, George and
Catharine.

Petrus Sharp married Eva Schneider, and remained on the
old Germantown homestead. They had seven children—viz.:
Peter, Abraham, Jacob, George P., Eva, Sarah and Maria.

George Sharp married Margaret Tedter, in 1771, and settled in that part of Rhinebeck which is now Red Hook. They

had eight children—viz. : Catharine ; Peter G., baptized May 28, 1775 ; Henry ; George ; John ; Isabella, baptized November 8, 1777 ; Rebecca, baptized February 6, 1780 ; Maria.

Catharine Sharp married Philip Rockerfeller, of German-town. Their daughter was the mother of the late Gen. Philip H. Lasher, of Tivoli, and Stephen Lasher, now of Elgin, Ill.

Peter, son of Peter Sharp and Eva Schneider, became a physician, and practiced his profession in Kingston, N. Y.

Abraham, son of Peter Sharp and Eva Schneider, married, first, Helen C., daughter of Capt. John W. Pitcher, of Upper Red Hook ; second, Helen C., daughter of John the Baptist, son of John the Baptist Kip, of Rhinebeck, and thus cousin to his first wife. By the first wife he had Catharine Eveline, who married Edwin Knickerbacker, of Madelin ; and Helen C., who married Abraham Pells, of Kingston. By the second wife he had Mary L., who married Thomas Little, of Brooklyn, N. Y. ; Sarah C., who married William Bayles ; and Col. Jacob, who married the daughter of Gen. Cook. He was a brave and gallant officer in the Union army during the Civil War, and is now Governor of the Soldier's Home at Milwaukee, Wis. Abraham Sharp commenced business as a merchant at the Old Red Hook landing, and finally settled as a merchant in Upper Red Hook Village, where he died.

Jacob, son of Peter Sharp and Eva Schneider, remained at the old homestead, in Germantown ; George P., his brother. moved to Kingston, in Ulster County, where he became a hardware merchant in the firm of Sharp & Sahler ; Eva, their sister, married Wessel Ten Broeck, of Kingston, and died without issue ; Sarah and Maria, the other sisters, settled in Kingston, and this is all we know of them.

1. Catharine, daughter of George Sharp and Margaret Tedter, married Mathias Chrysler ; Jacob M. Chrysler, of Lockport, N. Y., is a son of this marriage.

2. Peter G., son of George Sharp and Margaret Tedter, married Jane Kiersted, and settled in Kingston as a merchant, became a prominent business man, and a man of wealth and influence.

3. Isabella, daughter of George Sharp and Margaret Tedter

married Abraham Wood, settled first in Schoharie, then in Albany, and finally in New York City. Rebecca Broas, of Jersey City, is a daughter ; and Abraham W. Kennedy, of New York City ; Samuel Kennedy, of the Port Warden's office, New York City ; John Elseffer Kennedy, Deputy Marshal of the Southern District of New York ; Edward M. Kennedy, of Brooklyn ; and Henry Whiteman Kennedy, counsellor at law, in New York City, are grand-children.

4. Rebecca, daughter of George Sharp and Margaret Tedter married Henry Whiteman, of Rhinebeck. Their only daughter, Catharine, married John Elseffer, whose descendants are named in the Elseffer family record.

5. Henry, son of George Sharp and Margaret Tedter, married Helen Hasbrouck, settled in Kingston as a merchant, became a leading business man, and a man of wealth and influence. Gen. George H. Sharp, now for the second time Speaker of the State Assembly, is their only son.

6. George, son of George Sharp and Margaret Tedter, settled in New York City, and became the leading member of the firm of Sharp & Tuttle, in Pearl street. He was a member of the State Legislature in 1836.

7. John, son of George Sharp and Margaret Tedter, married and settled in Schoharie County, New York, where he left descendants.

8. Maria, daughter of George Sharp and Margaret Tedter, married Nicholas Bouck, cousin to Governor William C. Bouck ; settled and left descendants in Schoharie County, New York.

THE BONESTEEL FAMILY.

Nicholas Bonesteel and Anna Margretha Kuhns, his wife, with some of their children, were among the earliest settlers of what is now the town of Red Hook, possibly at a period as early as 1714. His name is among the people taxed in the North Ward in 1723, at which time it is believed he held, by life-lease, the farm bounded northerly by the road leading to Barrytown, easterly by the post road, southerly by the Benner farm, and westerly by the Hans Waldorph farm. A portion of the village of Red Hook is now on the easterly part of this farm.

We are indebted to a friend for the pedigree of this family which follows : The first settler, he informs us, had a large family of children. Barbel married Michael Simon ; Elizabeth, Balthaser Simon ; Jerusha, Andries Michel ; Nicholas, Jr., Anna Elizabeth Treber ; Anna Barbara, Jacob Meyer ; John Peter, Elizabeth Simon ; Philip, Elizabeth Hagadorn ; Frederick, Catharine Meyer. In the oldest book of the Rhinebeck Lutheran Church we have these records : David Bonesteel and Anna Maria, his wife ; Michael Bonesteel and Elizabeth, his wife ; Jacob Bonesteel and Elizabeth, his wife. The latter had a son, Michael, baptized November 22, 1772.

. It would be difficult, perhaps impossible, to obtain the names of all the descendants of this numerous family. Hence a few have been selected in whose cases the records seem clear. Nicholas Bonesteel, Jr., who married Anna Elizabeth Treber' is believed to have been the person who, in the year 1749, was road-master on the King's highway, from Cole's bridge to the Hog bridge. Records of their children remain as follows : Anna Margretha, baptized September 4, 1743 ; Catharina, baptized April 7, 1745 ; Elizabeth, born October 1, 1750 ; Nicholas, baptized May 26, 1754 ; Philip, baptized December 21, 1755 ; Henry, baptized May 8, 1761.

Nicholas Bonesteel, grandson of the first Nicholas, baptized May 26, 1754, married Eva ———. Their son, Philip, married Elizabeth Ray. The daughter of the latter, Mary Bonesteel, born in Florida, Montgomery County, New York, October 2, 1790, married Benjamin Wood. The daughter of the latter, Mary Ann Wood, born at DeReyter, New York, April 22, 1811, married the late Hon. Ezra Cornell, March 19, 1831. He was born in Westchester County, January 11, 1807. Their son, Alonzo B. Cornell, is the present Governor of the State of New York.

Philip Bonesteel, third son of the first Nicholas, whose wife was Elizabeth Hagedorn, took from Henry Beekman, October 27, 1774, a perpetual lease of the farm heretofore mentioned, excepting twelve acres along the post road. This lease was conveyed by the said Philip Bonesteel to his son-in-law, Nicholas J. Stickle, and his son, Peter Bonesteel, August

15, 1798, he dying soon after. They conveyed the same farm to Lemuel Haines, April 21, 1808.

Philip Bonesteel and Elizabeth Hagedorn, his wife, had children as follows: Philip, married and settled in Woodstock; Peter, married Elizabeth Tedter, and moved, in 1803, near to Bay Quinty, in Upper Canada; Anna, born January 16, 1752, married Zachariah, son of Carl Neher, prominent in the history of the Rhinebeck Lutheran Church; Nicholas, born November 21, 1753, married Margaret Staats, sister of " Hans Staats," and settled on the farm on the post road between the 102d and 103d mile stones, in the house known as the Bonesteel tavern, now owned by Samuel Ten Broeck; Henry, born February 20, 1762; Jeremiah, baptized May 20, 1767, moved to Stone Arabia, Montgomery County, N. Y.; Elizabeth, baptized October 2, 1769; Magdalena, baptized February 28, 1772; David, baptized December 20, 1775, moved to Rensselaer County, N. Y.

Zachariah Neher and Anna Bonesteel left a son, Jeremiah Neher, who resided many years midway between Red Hook village and Barrytown. Jeremiah Neher had three daughters, viz.: Polly, married Peter Lewis, and had one son, John N. Lewis, of Red Hook; Anna, married Charles L. Crooke, and had a daughter, Mary, wife of Hon. James Emott, and a daughter Cornelia, wife of LeGrand Dodge, Esq. The youngest daughter married Jacob Lewis, whose son, Charles C. Lewis, resides in the city of New York.

Nicholas Bonesteel and his wife, Margaret Staats, had children as follows: Philip N., married Alida Van Bramer, and had three children, viz.: Virgil D., Margaret, and Catharine Harmena: John N., married Maria Elseffer, and had three children, viz.: David N., Margaret, and Catharine. Jacob N. married Gertrude Ring, and had two children, viz., Margaret, wife of Marmont Edson, and John N., both of Brooklyn, N. Y. Henry N., married Helen Miller, and had five children, viz.: Philip H.; Peter; Delia Eliza, wife of Jacob W. Elseffer, Esq.; Catharine Augusta, widow of John Christian, of Minneapolis; and Helen Louisa, wife of Rensselaer Platner, M. D., of Clermont, N. Y.

Philip N. Bonesteel was a prominent merchant, a magistrate and post master in Red Hook for many years; was Colonel of a regiment of cavalry, and for some years a trustee of Hartwick Seminary. His son, Virgil D., graduated at Yale College, be-came a lawyer, resided at Pough'keepsie, and held the office of Surrogate of Dutchess County for four years. The Colonel re-purchased the old Bonesteel homestead, embracing 210 acres of land, on the 30th óf April, 1823. His children all died without issue.

THE FRALEIGH FAMILY.

Stephan Frolich, with a wife, two daughters over nine and one under eight years of age, was among the Palatines settled in the West Camp in Ulster County in 1710. Stephen Froelick was a freeholder, and the only one of the name in what is now the town of Rhinebeck, in 1723. He obtained a lease from Henry Beekman for the farm on the post road, now the proper-ty of Goertner Fraleigh, a descendant in the sixth generation, in 1719. We have no doubt he was the person found in the West Camp in 1710, and the ancestor of all the Frolichs and Fra-leighs who have lived and died and are now living in Dutchess County. He made his will in 1749, in which he released two children, without naming them, of all their obligations to his estate, and leaves his property to his wife, Barbara. We find in the old German Reformed Church records that Catharine Frolich was the wife of Johannes Weist in 1741 ; Ursula Frolich, of Marden Burger, in 1745 ; Martinus Frolich, the husband of Anna Maria Hagedorn in 1756 ; Petrus Frolich, of Margaretha Flegeler in 1766 ; Maria Frolech, the wife of Gerhard Dederick in 1766 ; Henry Frolich, the husband of Margaret Van Lowen in 1768, and George Frolich, the husband of Gertrude Pultz in 1770. There are, probably, Frolich records in the Rhinebeck Lutheran and Flatts Dutch Reformed Church, the books of which are not now before us. The Staatsburgh in which Do-minie Hartwick preached and baptized the children was near the Frolich homestead, and his records are in the Rhinebeck Lutheran book. Peter Fraleigh became the owner of the farm at the death of his father, and the graveyard known as Peter Frolich's took its name from him, and was on the opposite side of the road from his house. The Bergs, Burgers (Burckhards in the old records), Frolichs and Van Benschotens and Schryvers were buried in this ground, and generally without tombstones.

A family record before us says Peter Fraleigh was born August 15, 1720, died January 26, 1792. Margaret, his wife, born August 25, 1724, died June 2, 1805. This is not the beginning of the record. We have placed it first because the first in date. It is preceded by the record of Stephen which follows, and we are left in doubt whether Peter was father or elder brother to Stephen.

Stephen Fraleigh, born July 28, 1742, married, October 23, 1764, Maria Van Benschoten. They had issue as follows: Maria, born April 13, 1765; Margaret, born July 22, 1767; Solomon, born December 18, 1768; Peter, born November 10, 1770; Elsjen, born January 26, 1775; Lanne, born January 26, 1781, died March 28, 1794. The mother died August 11, 1812, aged sixty-six years; the father died April 11, 1820, aged seventy-seven years.

Solomon Fraleigh married Christina, daughter of Conrad Lasher, born March 28, 1770, married, September 5, 1789. They had issue as follows: Maria, born October 5, 1790; Conrad, born May 27, 1792; Peter, born April 25, 1794; Stephen, born November 12, 1796; Lydia, born April 12, 1799.

Petrus Frolich and his wife, Elizabeth Felder, appear in the records of the German Reformed Church for the first time on the 9th of July, 1780. On this day, their son, Johannes, was baptized by Dominie Cock, the sponsors being Johan Felder and Anna Maria Streit; on April 21, 1782, their daughter, Elizabeth, was baptized, the sponsors being Peter Eckert and Elizabeth Frolich; on September 3, 1784, their son, George, was baptized, the sponsors being Johannes Stickel and Elizabeth Behm; on December 3, 1786, their son, Phillippus, was baptized, the sponsors being Phillippus Felder and Anna Milthaler. Peter was another son, and Hannah another daughter of this family. She married John A. Stickle, died January 12, 1850, aged seventy-four years, and was thus born in 1776. This is the well-known Red Hook family of Fraleighs, whose ancestor was doubtless also Stephanus, the first settler of the name. Peter married Elizabeth Smith; Johannes married Catharine, daughter of Henry Tidter, Jr., and his wife, Anna Maria Proseus; Philip married Anna Tidter, sister to Catharine, the wife of his brother, for a first, and Anna Benner, daughter of Peter Benner, for a second wife; George married Catharine Mohr; Elizabeth, we think, married Henry Stall. These men became, and these sisters married men who became wealthy farmers, and highly-respected citizens of Red Hook.

THE SCHRYVER FAMILY.

Albtirtus Schriber was a freeholder, and the only person of the name, in what is now the town of Rhinebeck, in 1723. He was, probably, the ancestor of all the Schryvers who have lived and died and now are living in Dutchess and Ulster Counties, and possibly of all in the State. He was a German, and doubt-less, a Palatine. His wife was Eva Lauerman, and their children were probably, Christina, wife of Johon Jacob Sickener; Elizabeth, wife of Petrus Van Etten; Nicholas, husband of Anna Maria Dederick; Martinus, husband of Eva Burkhard; Johan Emerich, husband of Elzabeth Burkhard (now Burger); Petrus, of whose wife we are not certain. A tombstone in the cemetery of the Reformed Dutch Church says Mrs. Eva Schryver died July 28, 1817, aged 87 years; there is none to the memory of her husband.

Where the tent of the first Schryver was pitched, we have not learned. Nicholas Schryver bought of Henry Beekman the farm now owned by David H. Schryver, a descendant in the fifth generation, from Alburtus, the first, on the 1st of May, 1739. On the 10th of August, 1744, he sold it to his brother, Peter, for fifty pounds. On the 17th of November, 1770, Peter sold it to his two sons, Johannes and David for two hundred and forty pounds. We thus find two sons of Peter. If he had others, and daughters, we have not found them. Nicholas had a son, Christian, baptized September 30, 1744, and a daughter, Catharina, October 7, 1747; Martin, had a son, David, baptized September 7, 1766, and a son, Adam, January 28, 1769. These are in the German Reformed book. There may be others in the Reformed and Lutheran books which we have not con_sulted.

We find Johannes Schryver with Greetchie Tarpenning for

a wife, having a daughter, Eva, baptized March 4, 1764, and a daughter, Rachel, August 24, 1766. We find Johannes Schryver again, with Neeltjen Van Benschoten for a wife, having a daughter Elsjen, baptized August 15, 1773, and a daughter Maria, July 9, 1775. Whether we have here, two Johannes Schryvers, or the same man with a second wife, we are not informed; and whether, being the same, he was the son of Peter, and had other children, we are not informed. David, the son of Peter, married Rebecca Pawling, sister to Major John Pawling, and had children as follows: David, married Hellitje Radcliff, daughter of Peter Radcliff and Catharina Traphagen; Henry died unmarried; Barney married, first, Miss Pells; second, Miss Man; Peter lived and married in Sullivan County, New York; Catharine married Henry Van Aken; Elizabeth married Henry Uhl; Hannah married John Benner; Rebecca married Mathew Van Etten. David Schryver died May 7, 1813, aged 65 years; his wife died April 13, 1832, aged 92 years.

David D. Schryver and Hellitje Radcliff had children as follows: William, Allen L., James, Margaret and David H., the latter retaining the old homestead in a handsome new house, on the line between Hyde Park and Rhinebeck. Since the purchase by Nicholas Schryver in 1739, the place has never had any but Schryver owners. David D. Schryver died May 22, 1862, aged 82 years; his wife died February 13, 1848, aged 63 years.

John T. Scrhyver, for many years a prominent and successful business man in Rhinebeck, was a descendant from Alburtis Schryver, the Palatine, but through which one of the sons, we have no positive information. His father was Jacob Schryver, and his mother a lady of the name of Ten Broeck. He married Helen Conklin. Their children were Nicholas Van Vranken, Mathew Van Benschoten, George Washington and Rachel. Nicholas died unmarried, Mathew married, first, Margaret Teller, second, Miss Sleight;. George married Maria Fellows;* Rachel married Stephen A. DuBois. Mathew is childless; George

---

* The aneestors of Mrs. Maria Fellows Schryver on both her farher and mother's side were Palatines. Her maiden name of Fellows, in the old Church records, is sometimes Veller, generally Feller, and when written by Dominie Cock, always Felder. It is not long since it became Fellows.

died leaving four children, one son and three daughters ; Rachel and her husband are both dead, and have left an only child, Doctor John C. DuBois, of Hudson, N. Y.

THE TRAVER FAMILY.

The descendants of this old Palatine family are still numerous in the town and vicinity. Bastian Traver was the only one of the name in the list of tax-payers in what is now the town of Rhinebeck in 1723, and it is possible all of the name now here, or who have ever been here, were his descendants. His wife was Christina Uhl, who was also of Palatine descent, the name in the old records being Ohle. Traver, in the same records, is sometimes Dreber, but generally Trieber. We have found none of the name who were prepared to trace the line of their descent further back than their grandfathers, though they were in the sixth or seventh generation from the first settler of the name.

CHAPTER XXVIII.

RHINEBECK IN THE CIVIL WAR.

In the Civil War which broke out between the Free and Slave States, on the election of Abraham Lincoln to the presidency of the United States in 1860, Rhinebeck contributed the following soldiers to the Union Army:

EXPLANATION.—*Killed in battle ; † Wounded ; ‡ Saulsbury Prison ; § Died in hospital.

One Hundred and Twenty-eighth Regiment, Company C.—
Francis S. Keese, Captain ; Howard H. Morse, First Lieutenant ; Charles W. McKown, orderly Sergeant ; J. Howard Asher, † Second Sergeant ; John W. Keese, Fourth Sergeant ; George Tremper, Second Corporal ; Frank W. Rikert,‡ Third Corporal ; Derrick Brown, Fifth Corporal ; Clement R. Dean, Sixth Corporal ; David H. Hannaburgh, ‡ Eighth Corporal. Privates— James M. Braley, † John W. Kip, § Lemuel Marquart, George W. Hamilton,† John H. Van Etten, Charles Rynders, Martin V. B. Hawkins, William H. Hawkins, James A. Fraleigh, † John W. Myers, † William A. Noxon §, Calvin Rikert, John Gay, Edward F. Tater, Evert Traver, Charles W. Marquart, † Albert Ostrom, Robert P. Churchill,* Jasper DeWint§, Charles

Wooden,† Patrick Lyden, Robert H. Hayner §, Benjamin H. Brown, Peter Scally, John E. Cole, Nathan Day, Robert Riseley James L. H. Holdrige, James K. Brown, William B. Brown,‡ Joseph Brown. *

One Hundred and Fiftieth Regiment, Company F.—John L. Green, Captain ; Isaac F. Smith*, Corporal ; Elias A. Briggs, Corporal ; James M. Sheak, Corporal; William T. Francisco, Wagoner. Privates—Philip Bowman, Jefferson Champlin, William B. Doyle, Thomas M. Fraleigh, Joseph LaBonta, John E. Odell, Stephen H. Rynders, Samuel K. Rupely, John McKinny. *Company G.*—Renselaer Worden, Alexander Worden, § Philander Worden, § Walter R. Bush. *Company K.*—Wade H. Van Steenburgh, First Lieutenant ; Landon Ostrom, First Sergeant ; Enos B. Sylands, Third Sergeant ; Henry Lamp, Fourth Ser_ geant; Jacob Heeb, Fifth Sergeant; Benjamin J. Hevenor, Corporal. Privates—Charles M. Buckland, Leopold Oswold, George A. Clark, William H. Dederick, John Griner, Amos T. Lillie, Jacob Miller, DeWitt Shaffer, Charles Wynans, Law_ rence O'Brien, Frederick W. Pottenburgh, Stephen R. Tater, Harvy M. Traver, George A. Wager,§ Alfred Wooden, George W. Buckmaster. *Company B.*—William Holridge, Edward Tater, Elisha Holdridge, Adam Weishaupt.

Forty-fourth (People's Elsworth Regiment).—Privates—Jacob Z. Hegeman, Charles Luff,* Edward Luff, Peter Norris, Samuel Risely, John Raymond, Philip Sylands, Stephen Hamilton.

Twentieth Regiment, N. Y. State Militia.—Jacob Teal, † Andrew J. Kip, George Mann, Charles Asher, William Norris, William Rikert, George Traver, Douglass Marquardt, Thomas Price.*

Regiments Unknown to Us.—Albert Prosius, † Thomas O'Brian, Alfred Lewis,§ James W. Lewis,§ Avnor Proper, Samuel DeWint,§ John DeWint,§ Andrew Fraleigh,§ Ambrose Ostrom, Richard Sylands, David Wager, George Gay, Jacob Handschue, David McCarty.

We have given the names of all of whom we could get knowledge. We shall regret to learn that we have not found all for whom the town should have had credit.

OUR HOME GUARD.

To account for our " Home Guard " we find it necessary to account for the war, in doing which we shall add a page to our History that will interest those who were unborn or mere children when it broke out, or who shall be born hereafter.

The Republican party held for the main doctrine of its creed that the chattel slavery, retained by fifteen of the States of our Union, was a " relic of barbarism," and that, as such, it was the duty of Congress to prohibit it in the common territories. The slaveholder held that it was a " divine institution," and that, as such, he had a divine right to carry it into the common territories, and a constitutional right to have it protected therein by the general government. The Democratic party, embracing all the slaveholders and nearly all the voters in the Slave States, strong in the Free States, and casting a majority of the popular vote, held that, whether slavery was a " divine institution " or a " relic of barbarism " were questions of which the Constitution of the United States did not permit Congress to take cognizance ; that, to effect the union of the States, Congress had been bound to protect slavery to the full extent of its jurisdiction ; and that in the common territories, where it had supreme authority, it was as much bound to protect the property which a man had in his slave, as that which he had in his house or his horse. The Supreme Court of the United States had rendered a decision confirming this view, and the slave States, declaring the doctrines of the Republican party " revolutionary," resolved among themselves, and gave notice to the country, that they would not abide the election of a President of the United States who would owe his success to his endorsement of the doctrines of the Republican party. Notwithstanding this menace, the Republican party elected the President in November, 1860, and, true to their resolution, the Southern States voted themselves out of the Union, formed themselves into a confederacy for mutual defence and protection, and expelled the general government from their territories.

The constitution to which these States had assented made it the duty of the general government to collect the duty on

imports in all the States ; to maintain free commercial intercourse between them ; to cause the laws passed by one to be
respected in all the others ; and to carry the mail. The hearts
of the Southern people having been estranged from the general
government, it was no longer possible for the President to ex-
ecute the laws of Congress in their midst with their consent.
He had, therefore, either to abandon his trust, or to break the
power by which he was resisted. He resolved on the latter course,
and hence the war.

In Rhinebeck, as elsewhere, the people who remained at
home continued the debate at the street corners and in the
market places. The Democrats insisted that their Southern
fellow-countrymen had been insulted and outraged in the election, and, therefore, received great provocation for what they
had done. The Republicans, alarmed and exasperated by the
strength, persistence and prowess of the Southern armies, became intolerant of the speech of their Democratic neighbors,
pronounced it "traitorous," and organized the " Home Guard,"
fully "armed and equipped," to admonish them to keep a patri-
otic restraint on their tongues. They treated us to an occasion
al dress parade, but were never called to the performance of
serious or repressive duties. Some of its members are reposing
in our beautiful Union Cemetery, but their graves are not honored on Decoration Day, and we give them this page in our
History to keep them in grateful remembrance.

The Republican loved his cause, which was good, and the
Democrat loved his country, which was at stake ; and, to the
honor of both, the cause and the country, have both been saved
by their mutual efforts. The extinction of slavery was not the
object with which the Republican party entered the contest ;
and yet, if it had not become the fruit of the military success,
there would have been no return to the country for its outlay
of blood and treasure that might not have been had without
cost.

Though not foreseen by the statesman or philanthro-
pist, the time for the emancipation of the slave, and the baptism of the nation in blood for the washing away of the sin of
his bondage, had fully come. As the fruit of the war, the law

written in the hearts of men has been written into the Constitution of the nation with the point of the soldier's spear, by the
light of burning homes and harvests, in the blood of its sons.
It is now committed to the care and keeping of men who know
no law that has not been thus written on stones or visible
parchment, and we shall have peace and prosperity until the
waters, become poisoned by stagnation, are again "troubled by
the *angels*," and thus fitted for the healing of the people, crip-
pled and made sore by oppression.

APPENDIX.

OLD BUILDINGS.

THE houses of the settlers in the wilderness of the New World, we are told, were at first built after this fashion : " A square pit was dug in the ground, cellar fashion, six or seven feet deep, and as long and as broad as was deemed neeessary. This was cased all around with timber, which was lined with the bark of trees or something else to prevent the caving in of the earth. This cellar was floored with plank, and wainscoted overhead for a ceiling ; a roof of spars was reared clean up, and the spars covered with green sods or bark, so that they could live dry and warm in their houses with their entire families for two, three and four years, it being understood that partitions are run through these cellars, which are adapted to the size of the families." The Dutch secretary, Van Tienhoven, informs us that " the wealthy and principal men in New England, in the beginning of the colonies, commenced their first dwelling houses in this fashion for two reasons—first, in order not to waste time building, and not to want food the next season ; secondly, in order not to discourage poor, laboring people whom they brought over in large numbers from Fatherland."

Of the ninety-seven people in Rhinebeck in 1723, nearly all who built houses probably built them in this fashion. Of course, all trace of them disappeared in the next generation, and the houses built later, and of stone, are all that are now left us.

It is not certain that there was a single settler in the town of Rhinebeck anywhere before the year 1700. The Kip house, which became part of the Beekman house, and is now part of the Heermance house, was built in 1700. It is claimed that the old Bonesteel tavern, on the post road near Red Hook Village, was built in 1711, because a brick was found in it bearing this date. There was no Bonesteel found in this country in 1714. Nicholas Bonesteel was here in 1723, and probably the owner of the house at this date. The Van Steenburghs were here in 1740. The stone house which was the residence of

Nicholas B. Van Steenburgh, in the northern part of the village, and which was taken down by his son, William, a few years since, had a stone lintel inscribed as follows: RSB | TSB | BSB | MSB | ABIG | SNDP | April 15, 1731. These initials are in two rows.

Tunis Pier was here in 1723. The farm, now the property of George F. Cookingham, was sold to Christoffel Cramer by Henry Beekman, in 1739, bounded on the south by the creek and Tunis Pier. The old stone house being demolished on the south side of the creek, had a stone inscribed as follows: "W. T. P. 1764." This house, like the Kip houses at the river, and apparently all the stone houses built by the first settlers, had but one room on the ground floor, and received an additional room, either of stone or of wood, in after years. We think the date on the Cookingham house was on the addition, and the original room built at a much earlier date. The stone house now occupied by Jacob L. Tremper, has a stone inscribed, " Jan Pier, 1774." We think this house also received an addition to the original house, probably by Isaac Davis, who occupied it after 1796, and owned, and, we presume, built the mill in the immediate vicinity, still in the recollection of many of us. The stone house now owned by Ann O'Brian, on the post road in the south of the village, is on lands leased to Johannes Benner, in 1739, and may have been built by him about this date. The old house taken down by Lewis Asher, a short time since, was the miller's house, and doubtless came into being with the mill, before 1730. The lower mill was built after the upper. The old stone house near it was also the miller's house, and not older than the mill. The old parsonage of the Reformed Dutch Church was a stone building; but as the church had no pastor before 1740, and probably not until after 1750, this house was probably not built until after the latter date. The house in West Market street, known as the " Old State Prison," and re-cently taken down, was probably older than 1730, and built by William Traphagen, who had a deed from Henry Beekman, the father, for lands as far back as 1710, which probably covered the land occupied by this house.

The house known as " Old Tammany," further north, was

kept by a Kip in 1798, and the stone part of the house was probably built many years before this date. Therewas a stone house on the premises which became the property of Alfred Drury, and was taken down by him some years since, It was doubtless built at an early date, but we have not learned by whom. The stone house taken down by Charles I. Cramer was also old, but how old we have not learned. We think it was built on land sold by Henry Beekman, the father, to Jacob Kip, in 1714, and sold by him to Gerardus Lewis, his son-in-law, in 1720. Gerardus Lewis probably built the house. The old stone house at the " flat rock" was built in 1730, by Isaac Kip. John Kip, the son of Hendrick, had a house north of the old Roliff Kip house before 1715, Hendrick Kip having taken one third of his share of the Kip lands north, and the other two thirds south of Jacob's lands. John sold the north to his uncle, in 1716.

The house occupied by Abraham Brown, south of this vil. lage, we are told, was built in parts at different dates, the north part by Adam Eckert, in 1719, and the south part in 1763. The initials on the north part are as follows: A. N. E. Peter Brown's house, we are told, was built by Heerman Brown, the common ancestor of the Rhinebeck Browns, in 1753. The date on the knocker of the old Monfort Tavern is 1760. The Bergh house, formerly the residence of Major John Pawling, has a stone over the door inscribed " J. P. N. P., July 4, 1861." The stone house below Monroe's, now the property of Lewis Livingston, Esq., once Van Steenburgh's, and later Smith's Inn, is old, but there is no record to tell us how old.

TOWN AND PRECINCT SUPERVISORS.

Our town records do not tell us who were Justices of the Peace by appointment of the provincial or State authorities. We have found incidental references to Arnout Vele, Martin Hoffman, Gerrit Van Wagenen, John Van Deusen, and Gerrit Van Benthuysen as Justices of the Peace for the precinct of Rhinebeck before the Revolution. And we have found that in 1798 Isaac Kip, Jr., and Isaac Stoutenburgh, Jr., consented, as Justices of the Peace, to the manumission by Frederick Streit

of his slave, **Cuffee** Rock. And though we have no record
of their election, we have found that Jacob Heermance, John
Tappen, and James Montfort were Justices of the Peace for
the town of Rhinebeck between 1828 and 1833.

WARD SUPERVISORS.

Henry Beekman.............	from 1722 to 1724
Barent Van Wagenen	" 1724 to ——
Barent Van Benthuysen..................................	" 1732 to 1734

PRECINCT SUPERVISORS.

John Van Deuse..........	from 1749 to 1751
Gerrit Van Benthuysen............................	" 1752 to 1755
Petrus DeWitt......	" 1756 to 1757
Gerrit Van Benthuysen........................	" 1758 to 1760
Petrus DeWitt...	" 1761 to 1761
Peter Van Benthuysen...............................	" 1762 to 1762
Peter Ten Broeck....................................	" 1763 to 1766
John Van Ess.........	" 1767 to 1771
James Smith.........................	" 1772 to 1774
John Van Ess..	" 1775 to 1775
Peter DeWitt...	" 1776 to 1780
Anthony Hoffman.......................................	" 1781 to 1785

TOWN SUPERVISORS.
(Town organized March 7, 1788.)

Peter Contine	from 1786 to 1788
William Radcliff..	" 1789 to 1791
David Van Ness....................................	" 1792 to 1794
Peter Contine, Jr..	" 1795 to 1797
Isaac Stoutenburgh.......................................	" 1798 to 1800
Andrew Heermance......................................	" 1801 to 1803
Peter Contine. Jr......	" 1804 to 1805
David Van Ness	" 1806 to 1808
John Cox, Jr..................	" 1808 to 1812

(Red Hook taken off June 2. 1812.)

John Cox, Jr..	from 1813 to 1818
Coert DuBoise	" 1819 to 1820
Christian Schell.......................................	" 1821 to 1824
Garret Van Keuren	" 1825 to 1829
Isaac F. Russell.......................................	" 1830 to 1832
Frederick I. Pultz...	" 1833 to 1834
Henry S. Quitman	" 1835 to 1836
Conrad Ring..	" 1837 to 1839
John Armstrong, Jr......................................	" 1840 to 1840
James A. A. Cowles	" 1841 to 1843
Nicholas B. Van Steenburgh ....•....	" 1844 to 1844
Moses Ring	" 1845 to 1845
Tunis Wortman....................................... ...	" 1846 to 1847
James Monfort..	" 1848 to 1848
Isaac I. Platt	" 1849 to 1849
Jacob G. Lambert.....................................	" 1850 to 1850
Ambrose Wager	" 1851 to 1851

James C. McCarty	"	1852 to 1852
James Monfort	"	1853 to 1853
John N. Cramer	"	1854 to 1855
Richard B. Sylands	"	1856 to 1856
Theophilus Nelson	"	1857 to 1857
Richard J. Garrettson	"	1859 to 1859
James C. McCarty	"	1860 to 1861
Andrew J. Heermance	"	1862 to 1863
Ambrose Wager	"	1864 to 1865
Smith Quick	"	1866 to 1866
William M. Sayer	"	1867 to 1867
Robert L. Garrettson	"	1868 to 1868
Virgil C. Traver	"	1869 to 1872
John G. Ostrom	"	1873 to 1873
Joseph H. Baldwin	"	1874 to 1876
James H. Kip	"	1877 to 1878
William Bergh Kip	"	1879 to 1880

PRECINCT CLERKS.

Johannis A. Ostrander	from	1749 to 1756
Peter Ostrander	"	1757 to 1765
Abraham Glimph	"	1765 to 1765
William Beam	"	1766 to 1785
Ledowick Elsever	"	1786 to 1786

TOWN CLERKS.
(Town organized, March 7, 1788.)

David Elsever	from	1787 to 1790
William Radclift, Jr.	"	1791 to 1791
Henry Lyle	"	1792 to 1792
John Cox	"	1793 to 1793
Henry Shop	"	1794 to 1812

(Red Hook, taken off, June 2, 1812.)

Henry Shop	from	1813 to 1816
Henry F. Tallmage	"	1817 to 1819
Garret Van Keuren	"	1820 to 1820
John Fowks, Jr.	"	1821 to 1825
Jacob Heermance	"	1826 to 1826
William B. Platt	"	1827 to 1828
Henry De Lamater	"	1829 to 1830
Henry C. Hoag	"	1831 to 1831
Conrad Ring	"	1832 to 1834
Stephen A. DuBoise	"	1835 to 1835
Henry W. Mink	"	1836 to 1836
Tunis Wortman	"	1837 to 1843
George W. Schryver	"	1844 to 1844
Tunis Wortman	"	1845 to 1845
George W. Bard	"	1846 to 1847
John C. McCarty	"	1848 to 1849
Albert A. Rider	"	1850 to 1852
Tunis Wortman	"	1853 to 1853
Albert A. Rider	"	1854 to 1854
Tunis Wortman	"	1855 to 1855
Harvey M. Traver	"	1856 to 1856
Tunis Wortman	"	1857 to 1857
Calvin Jennings	"	1858 to 1858
Tunis Wortman	"	1859 to 1859
George H. Ackert	"	1860 to 1861

John D. Judson..........................	" 1862 to 1862
George W. Hogan.......	" 1863 to 1863
Simon Welch..............	" 1864 to 1864
James A. Monfort	" 1865 to 1865
Jacob H. Pottenburgh	" 1866 to 1866
Jacob Rynders........................	" 1867 to 1867
Edward Brooks........................	" 1868 to 1868
William H. Sipperly..................	" 1869 to 1870
Tunis Wortman.......................	" 1871 to 1872
Jacob Rynders........................	" 1873 to 1873
William H. Hevenor	" 1874 to 1876
Jacob H. Pottenburgh	" 1877 to 1880

JUSTICES OF THE PEACE.

Jacob Heermance................................from 1828 to 1832
John Tappen .... " 1829 to 1832
James Monfort .... " 1830 to 1834

ELECTIONS RECORDED.

Smith Dunning 1833
Edward E. Cowles, in place of Smith Dunning.......................1834
Abraham Van Keuren, for four years................................1834
Stephen McCarty, for four years 1835
Wm. J. Stewert, to take the place of E. E. Cowles.................1835
James Monfort 1836
William J. Stewert..1837
Abraham Van Keuren 1838
Stephen McCarty 1839
James Monfort 1840
Stephen McCarty...1840
John B. VanWagenen 1840
William J. Stewert 1841
Isaac F. Russell 1842
Moses Ring..1843
Tunis Wortman 1844
James Monfort 1845
Cornelius E. Wynkoop 1846
Moses Ring..1847
Tunis Wortman 1848
William Bates...1849
James Monfort, for full term 1850
John G. Ostrom, to fill vacancy...................................1850
John G. Ostrom..1851
Tunis Wortman 1852
Moses Ring..1853
Hazard Champlin 1854
Theophilus Gillender 1855
Tunis Wortman 1856
William Bates...1857
Moses Ring..1858
Theophilus Gillender 1859
Tunis Wortman, for fill term 1860
Isaac F. Russel, to fill vacancy 1860
John G. Ostrom, for full term.....................................1861
Jacob I. Van Wagenen, to fill vacancy.............................1861
Isaac F. Russell...1862
John N. Cramer 1863
Tunis Wortman 1864

William Van Wagenen...... 1865
Isaac F. Russel..1866
Jacob M. Hogan.. 1867
Henry W. Mink.. 1868
Tunis Wortman............................ 1873
Isaac F. Russell...1870
Theophilus Gillender, full term........ 1871
William B. Vibert, short term 1871
Conrad Marquardt.... 1872
Tunis Wortman...................... 1873
Isaac F. Russell, full term........... 1874
Virgil C. Traver, short term...1874
Theophilus Gillender 1875
James A. Monfort......... 1876
William Cross.............. ....: 1877
Robert B. Emerson.. 1878
Theophilus Gillender...................................... 1879
James A. Monfort............................... 1880

In the sixty-three years which intervened between the commencement of our records, in 1749, and the separation of Red Hook from Rhinebeck, in 1812, the office of Supervisor was held by fourteen different persons, eight of whom were from Red Hook, five from Rhinebeck, and one of uncertain residence. The eight Red Hook men held the office for forty-two years; the five Rhinebeck men for eighteen years; and John Van Dense, of uncertain residence, for two years.

UNITED STATES SENATOR FROM RHINEBECK.

John Armstrong, by appointment of the Governor, in 1803; by election in 1804. Appointed Minister to France in 1804, and resigned the office of Senator.

REPRESENTATIVES IN CONGRESS.

Egbert Benson, - - 1st and 2d Congresses.
Isaac Bloom, - - - - - 8th Congress.
Philip J. Schuyler, - - - - 15th Congress.

In 1812 the towns of Rhinebeck and Clinton, in Dutchess County, voted with Columbia County in the election of a member of Congress.

STATE SENATORS.

Anthony Hoffman, - - - - 1788–9–90.
Thomas Tillotson, - - - - 1791 to 1799.
Robert Sands, - - - - 1797 to 1800.
Peter Contine, Jr., - - - - 1798 to 1801.
Morgan Lewis, - - - - 1811 to 1814.
Peter R. Livingston, - - - 1820–22; 1826–29.
William Kelly, - - - - 1856 to 1858.

MEMBERS OF ASSEMBLY FROM RHINEBECK.

Anthony Hoffman,	- 1778-9; 1784. Red Hook.
Peter Contine, Jr.,	- - - 1788. Red Hook.
Thomas Tillotson,	- - - - 1788-9-90.
David Van Ness,	- - - 1891. Red Hook.
William Radcliff,	- - - - - 1792-3.
Philip J. Schuyler,	- - - - - 1798.
Abraham Adriance,	- - - - 1800-2.
Koert DuBois,	- - - 1810-11; 1820-21.
John W. Wheeler,	- - 1818-20. Red Hook.
David Tomlinson,	- - - - . 1819.
John Cox,	- - - - - - - 1822.
Peter R. Livingston,	- - - - 1823.
John Armstrong, Jr.,	- - - - - 1825.
Cornelius C. Elmendorf,	- - 1827. Red Hook.
Francis A. Livingston,	- - - - 1828.
George Lambert,	- - - - - 1833.
Freeborn Garrettson,	- - - - 1835; 1845.
Edmund Elmendorf,	- - - 1841. Tivoli.
William H. Feller,	- - 1851. Red Hook.
Augustus Martin,	- - 1852-3. Red Hook.
Ambrose Wager,	- - - - - 1855-58.
Richard J. Garretson,	- - - 1860.
Edmund Green,	- - - 1862. Red Hook,
John N. Cramer,	- - - - - 1864.
Alfred T. Ackert,	- - - - - 1868.

STAATSBURGH.

The author of the History of Rhinebeck is indebted to Mr. Edward Braman, of New York, for the following appropriate and interesting communication:

As Staatsburgh, or Pawling's purchase, was for so long a period a part of Rhinebeck Precinct, it would not be inappropriate to give a short sketch of its early history, and some of its earliest settlers. The results of an attempt to do so, with such material and notes as are at hand, is embodied in this communication. Time will not admit of more.

Henry Pawling, of Marbletown, died about 1695. His will, proved 25th of March, that year, was made in 1691. He left all his property to his wife, born Neeltje Roosa, for her life-time, or until she should marry, with remainder to his children. Those surviving him were Jane, Wyntie, John, Albert, Ann, Henry and Mary. On the 26th of May, 1701, Neiltie Pawling, widow of Henry Pawling, gentleman, Jane Pawling, maiden, Richard Brodhead and Wyntie, his wife, and John Pawling, sold to Samuel Staats, of the city of New York, esquire, and Dirck Van den burgh, of the same place, gentleman, all their rights in the tract, in Dutchess County, called Pawling's Purchase, for £130. But, as Albert Ann, Henry and Mary, children of the said Henry Pawling, were "infants under the age of one and twenty," their rights were not conveyed. Dirck Van den burgh probably soon conveyed his interest to Dr. Staats. It may be that the name of Staats-burgh was suggested by the names of these two proprietors.

Of the Pawling heirs, Albert Pawling, born 1685, married Catharine Beekman, widow of Capt. John Rutsen, but had no children. He died in 1745, leaving a large estate. After providing liberally for his wife and mother (who was still living in 1745), he left the residue of his estate to Levi Pawling, third son of his brother Henry, with remainder to John, the brother of Levi.

Ann Pawling married Tjerck De Witt, of Kingston, and had five children. To one of these, Petrus, his father, Tjerck (will proved 1762), left all his land in Pawling's Purchase, "the same as conveyed to me in sundry conveyances."

Henry Pawling lived at Marbletown. His son, Col. Levi Pawling, was a prominent man in Ulster County, delegate to the Provincial Convention in 1775, and commissioned Colonel of one of the four regiments of the Ulster militia, in the same year. Another son was Major John Pawling, mentioned hereafter.

Mary Pawling, born 1692, married Thomas Van Keuren, of Marbletown; but who, in a deed to John Pawling in 1767, styles himself of Staatsburgh.

Dr. Samuel Staats was the son of Major Abram Staats, of Albany, and Catrina, his wife, daughter of Jochem Wessels. He learned his profession in Holland, and resided there many years, returning to New York about 1688. He was twice married. His first wife, Johanna Rynders, was the mother of all

his children.   His second wife, whom he married in 1709, was
Catharina Howarden, probably widow of Thomas and mother
of Margaret Howarden, who married Robert Livingston.   He
had nine children living in 1703, but in his will, dated September 21, and proved November 14, 1715, he names only six.
These were Certrude, widow of Peter Neagle, but who married
in 1716, Andries Coeymans; Sarah, married, in 1704, Isaac
Governeur; Catalina, married, in 1713, Stephen Van Cortlandt;
Anna Elizabeth, married, 1713, Philip Schuyler; Johanna born
1694.*

Sometime subsequent to the death of Dr. Staats, a survey
of the purchase was made by Charles Clinton.   It was divided
into two ranges of lots, the first nine on the river called "water
lots," and nine in the rear called " wood lots," extending to
Crumelbow Creek.   A division was made between the heirs of
Pawling and Staats, by which lots 1, 10, 3, 13, 9 and 18 fell to
the former.   These, by virtue of sundry conveyances, came
finally into the hands of Major John Pawling and Captain Petrus
De Witt, who were, as has been seen, first cousins.

Major John Pawling had married his cousin, Neeltje Van
Keuren, and in 1761 he built the stone house on the post road,
now owned by the heirs of Edwin Bergh.   It bears the inscription
" J. P., N. P., July 4, 1761."   He was a leading man in his day.
He took an active part in the Revolution, and was personally
acquainted with Washington, and many of the prominent men
of that day.   Late in life he suffered severe reverses of fortune.
He died December 30, 1819, aged eighty-seven, and was buried
in the Reformed Dutch Churchyard at Rhinebeck.   By his
first wife he had four children.   His second wife was Maria Van
Duser, of Claverack, by whom he had ten children.   She sur-
vived him, and died in 1832, aged eighty-four.

Captain Petrus De Witt owned the south half of lot No. 3
(the same as afterwards owned by William C. Emmet, where he
had his residence, which he called " Wittmount "), and also a
landing, storehouse, etc., to which there was a public road; and
there a considerable business was carried on in the days of sloop

*Anthony White and Johanna Staats were married in New York,   January 26
1717 ; probably this lady.

navigation. About 1782, he sold Wittmount to Brockholst Livingston, who had just returned from Spain, where he had been Secretary of Legation, under his brother-in-law, John Jay. Captain De Witt owned lots 9 and 18, at the south end of the purchase. On this was a log house to which he removed, and made preparations to build a handsome brick mansion. He had the brick made on the place, but the Quartermaster of the Continental Army encamped at Fishkill and Newburgh, needing bricks for ovens, heard of these at Staatsburgh, seized and carried them away to Fishkill. It is said they were never paid for, and Captain De Witt, fearing a repetition of the exploit built a frame house, which he filled in with sun-dried bricks, though the immense chimneys were of the usual red bricks.

Captain Petrus De Witt married Rachel Radcliff, sister of Jannetje, wife of Dominie Van Hoevenburgh, and doubtless daughter of Jochem Radcliff and Hilletje Hoogeboom. He died January 3, 1790, aged 67, and she, July 20, 1794, aged 70. They were buried at Rhinebeck. He left one son and two daughters—Colonel John De Witt, of De Witt's (since Le Roy's) Mills, who married Catharine, daughter of Dirck Van Vliet, of the present town of Clinton ; Hilletje, who died unmarried, and Ann, who married Philip Dubois Bevier, " of Rochester in the county of Ulster, esquire." The daughters inherited Rocksdale, which they sold, in 1809, to their cousin, Henry Van Hoevenburgh. After some changes, a large part of this estate, including the mansion, became the property of Cornelius Van Vliet, nephew of the wife of Colonel John De Witt. Mr. Van Vliet was father of the late Dr. Isaac F. Van Vliet, of Rhinebeck. In 1869, the other part was purchased by Alfred De Witt, a grandson of Colonel John De Witt, who makes it his occasional residence.

Lots 2 and 12 were sold to Teunis Van Benschoten, 13th of May, 1758, by Lewis Morris, Jr., of Morrisania, who inherited from his mother, Catharina Staats. Perhaps Van Benschoten never settled on these lands, but he and Elsie, his wife, sold them, 15th of October, 1773, to Christian Bergh. Lots 6 and 15 were sold by Gertrude Coeymans, of the province of New Jersey, widow, 22d of May, 1761, to Christian Bergh, of Dutchess County, yeoman, for £1,000. Ten years later, Mr. Bergh built a stone house, which remained until 1854. Upon its east wall, facing the road, was carved, on two hearts joined, " C. B., A. M. B.,—A. B., H. B.,—Je. 21, 1771 " (June 21, 1771, probably), the initials being his own, his wife's, his son Adam's and those of the latter's wife. After the death of Christian Bergh, this property was owned by his son, John, who, with Elizabeth, his wife, released it to Charles Shaw and others, of the city of New York, 7th of March, 1789. In the following year they sold the southerly half to Captain Jesse Eames, of Framingham, Mass., and the northerly half to Captain Isaac Russel, of Sherburne, in the same State. In these two deeds, the lands are said to be part of a tract " commonly called Malmesbury, or Pauling's purchase." This preserves the memory of a fortunately unsuccessful attempt to change the name of Staatsburgh. These purchasers had been in the army, in the War of the Revolution, and, passing through Staatsburgh in charge of some prisoners, after Burgoyne's surrender, were so charmed with the country that they decided to remove to it after the war. Captain Eames died in 1829, aged ninety, and Captain Russell, in 1821, aged seventy. Isaac F. Russell, of Rhinecliff, is the youngest son of Captain Russell.

Anna Elizabeth Schuyler conveyed lots 4 and 11 to Isaac Feller, 27th of March, 1764. The latter, 17th of December, 1767, sold to Timothy Doughty and John Cornell (both, probably, from Long Island), and they, 9th of May, 1775, sold, for £1,025, all of lot 2 and part of lot 11, to Margaret Uhl, of Beekman Precinct. She was the second wife of Daniel Uhl, of " the Clove," and was now a widow with a family of sons and daughters. Her sons, John and Captain Frederick, succeeded to the property, one of the finest in Staatsburgh, and it was the homestead of the family about half a century. Captain Frederick Uhl married Huldah, daughter of Captain David Mulford.

Catalina (Staats) Van Cortlandt owned lots 7 and 16. Her heirs sold these 9th of May, 1775, to Captain David Mulford, of Easthampton, Long Island. He died of small pox, January 31, 1778, aged 55, and was succeeded by his son, Job Mulford. The latter, who married Hannah, daughter of Mrs. Margaret Uhl, was father of the late David Mulford. Most of this prop-

erty has remained in the family to this day. They held their
" centennial" in 1875. The village of Staatsburgh is mostly
built on lot No. 7.

Lots 5 and 14 fell to the share of Sarah Gouverneur, and
descended to her daughter, Sarah, second wife of Lewis Morris,
who sold to Peter Prosius and George Stover, about 1774. November 22d, that year, these two divided the lots, Prosius taking
the northerly, and Stover the southerly halves of each, excepting that previous to this time 125 acres off the east end of lot
14 had been sold to Jacob and Adam Shaver, and 25 acres to
Everardus Bogardus. All these are Rhinebeck names. Prosius
sold his part to Jacob Lewis the next year, for the latter mort-
gaged it to Mrs. Morris, 16th of June, 1775. Stover had mort-
gaged his part to her also. These mortgages were foreclosed
by Samuel Ogden, executor (and son-in-law) of Mrs. Morris,
and sold to Morgan Lewis, of the city of New York, May
4, 1792. General Lewis obtained re-leases from all the parties
interested, shortly after. Jacob Lewis was then deceased, leaving a widow, Rebecca, one son, Leonard, and four daughters,
all married but the youngest. Stover was living at Claverack.
Christiana, wife of Prosius, re-leased dower. Her maiden name
was Zipperly. The house built by Jacob Lewis is still standing.

About 1776 Captain Christopher Hughes came to Staatsburgh from New Haven, where he had been in partnership with
Benedict Arnold in the West India Trade. He was a man of
means and enterprise, and invested largely in land, both in
Staatsburgh, and in the Patent of Hyde Park. His residence
was at the forks of the road at the top of the " Clay Hills," on
the northerly half of lot 3. He married, as his second wife,
Abigail, daughter of the first David Mulford, and they had, besides sons, two daughters; Elizabeth, who married Christian
Schell, and Abigail, who married Elijah Baker, and inherited
the homestead. Mr Baker built the large white mansion north
of the old Hughes house. Christopher Hughes, a son of Captain Christopher by his first wife, married Rachel, daughter of
Major John Pawling, and was ancestor of the present Hughes
family of Staatsburgh. Captain Hughes died May 22, 1805,
aged 60.years.

There were doubtless other residents than those named in Staatsburgh, before the Revolution, but on the post road the properties were large, and the proprietors owned many slaves. Among the largest slave owners were the DeWitts and the Uhls. The negroes had their own burying ground, still known to the residents. There were often two or more dwellings on the same property, besides the negro houses, some of which were occupied by persons engaged in mercantile or mechanical pursuits, both at the landing and on the post road, at an early day. Job Mulford is described as of " Rhinebeck Precinct," merchant, in 1778.

Several of the inhabitants of Staatsburgh signed the " Revolutionary Pledge," at Rhinebeek, in 1775, as John Pawling, Petrus DeWitt, David and Lemuel Mulford, and others, as will be seen on reference to the list.

EDWARD BRAMAN.

New York, January 20, 1881.

AN OLD SETTLEMENT.

Jacomintie's Vly was deeded to Gerrit Artsen, Jan Elting and Arie Roosa by the Indians, on the 8th of June, 1686, but not covered by the royal patent to these people from Governor Dongan in 1688. It was included in the patent to Henry Beekman for his Rhinebeck lands in 1697, and on the 2d of January, 1705–6 he sold it to the heirs of Jan Elting for sixteen pounds, subject to a rent of two shillings per annum, Jacomintie being the name of Jan Elting's widow. Passing from one owner to another, the Vly, in 1757, was the property of Barent Van Wagenen, Gose Van Wagenen and Mathis Sleight. At this date the quit rent was all in arrears, and paid by these parties in a settlement set forth in the following old document in possession of Captain William Van Wagenen. The remarkable thing about this settlement is that Henry Beekman, the son, charged the rent, not from the date of his father's patent, but from that of Artsen & Co., which was ten years older, and which did not include the Vly.

"The quit rent of Jacomintiess Vly, at 2s. per annum. Bar ent Van Wagenar for one half thereof, must pay 3 parts from 5 parts, for the other half thereof he must pay 5 parts from 9 parts, so he must pay 14d. a year for his part.

"Gose Van Wagenar, for one half thereof he must pay 2 parts from 5 parts, for the other half thereof he must pay 2 parts from 9 parts, so he must pay $7\frac{1}{4}d$ $\frac{1}{2}$ a year for his part.

Mathis Slaught, for one half thereof he must pay 2 parts from 9 parts, so he must pay $2\frac{1}{2}d$ $\frac{1}{2}$ a year for his part.

Barent Van Wagenar Pays £0. 1s. 2d. a year.
Gose Van Wagenar Pays 0. 0. $7\frac{1}{4}$. $\frac{1}{2}$ year.
Mathis Slaght Pays 0. 0. $2\frac{1}{2}$. $\frac{1}{2}$ year.

£0. 2s. 0d.

1757, being 69 years to pay for these three.
Barent V. Wagenar Pays £4. 0s. 6d.
Gose Van Wagenar Pays 2. 2. 5.
Mathis Slaght Pays 0. 15. 1.

£6. 18s. 0d.

RINEBECK, 26 Oct., 1757.'

"Then Received from Johannes Van Wagenar Six pound Eighteen Shillings, it being in full for quit rent due on a ma_ dow called Jacomintie's Vley to the year of one thousand sev_ en Hundred fifty & eight, & on January the Twenty Seventh to that time, it being paid to me.

HEN. BEEKMAN."

Made in the USA
Las Vegas, NV
27 May 2021